£8.45

11·A·85

KU-713-268

Children's Conversation

Michael McTear

Basil Blackwell

© Michael F. McTear 1985

First published 1985

Basil Blackwell Publisher Ltd
108 Cowley Road, Oxford OX4 1JF, UK

Basil Blackwell Inc.
432 Park Avenue South, Suite 1505,
New York, NY 10016, USA

All rights reserved. Except for the quotation of short passages for the purposes of criticism and review, no part of this publication may be reproduced, stored in a retrieval system, or transmitted, in any form or by any means, electronic, mechanical, photocopying, recording or otherwise, without the prior permission of the publisher.

Except in the United States of America, this book is sold subject to the condition that it shall not, by way of trade or otherwise, be lent, re-sold, hired out, or otherwise circulated without the publisher's prior consent in any form of binding or cover other than that in which it is published and without a similar condition including this condition being imposed on the subsequent purchaser.

British Library Cataloguing in Publication Data

McTear, Michael
   Children's conversation
   1. Interpersonal communication in children
   2. Oral communication
   I. Title
   155.4'13   BF723.C57

   ISBN 0–631–13984–2
       0–631–14249–5 Pbk

Library of Congress Cataloging in Publication Data

McTear, Michael.
   Children's conversation.

   Bibliography: p. 275
   Includes index.
   1. Language acquisition.   2. Conversation.
   I. Title.
   P118.M394 1985   401'.9   84–21638
   ISBN 0–631–13984–2
       0–631–14249–5 Pbk

Typeset by Freeman Graphic, Tonbridge, Kent
Printed in Great Britain

ho 228591 -4

LEEDS POLYTECHNIC

476947

SV

75, 79

29.5.86

410.31

Contents

Preface

Conversation is such a common human activity that we are in danger of taking it for granted. We are aware of the complex processes involved in the acquisition of language by children in terms of how they learn to pronounce words, combine them into sentences and express meanings. One of my main aims in this book is to show that the acquisition of the ability to initiate and sustain conversation is just as complex. The development of conversation is traced from early infancy through the preschool years to early adolescence, with the central part of the book presenting a detailed analysis of the conversations over a period of two years between two preschool children.

A second aim of the book is to present a framework for the analysis of conversational development. In this I have drawn on the rapidly developing literature in discourse and conversation analysis as well as on studies of pragmatic and discourse disability. It is my hope that the presentation and discussion of many theoretical, methodological and practical issues will be of benefit to teachers and speech therapists as well as students of child language.

In writing this book I have drawn on the work of many scholars. My debt to them is acknowledged in the references, but I would like to mention especially Susan Ervin-Tripp, Catherine Garvey and Elinor Ochs, whose pioneering studies of children's discourse inspired my own research. I have also benefited immensely from the comments of many colleagues and I would like to mention in particular Martin Atkinson, Brendan Gunn, Margaret MacLure, Lesley Milroy, Michael Stubbs and John Wilson. I would also like to record my appreciation of the assistance given by David Crystal, who encouraged me to write the book and provided many helpful comments and guidance on earlier drafts. Grateful thanks are also due to Geraldine Dick who typed the greater part of the manuscript.

Needless to say, this work would not have been possible without the support and encouragement of my wife Sandra, who showed patience and understanding during the many hours when I withdrew myself from family life to write the book.

Finally, I would like to thank my daughter Siobhan and her friend Heather, whose friendship and conversations are documented throughout this book. The tedious hours of transcription and analysis were often lightened by the many gems produced by these two lively young children. In recognition of what we as adults can learn from observing children, I dedicate this book to the two children who have taught me so much about conversation – Siobhan and Heather.

Michael McTear

Conventions and layout of transcribed examples

Speech is set out vertically, each new turn beginning on a new line. New utterances within turns also begin on a new line.

Contextual information and non-verbal behaviour are specified where necessary and enclosed in round brackets ( ).

Utterances, or part of utterances, about which there is doubt are enclosed in angular brackets < >. Where two interpretations are possible, they are both given, separated by an oblique stroke /.

The speech is transcribed in standard English orthography, although occasionally a child's idiosyncratic pronunciation is represented ortho-graphically (for examples, *I nam* for *I am*). Where necessary, pronunciation is transcribed phonetically using IPA (International Phonetic Association) symbols and square brackets [ ].

The following is a list of additional symbols used. Stops and commas are not used as in normal punctuation.

?   Used at the end of an utterance where an interrogative meaning is considered to have been intended. Also used for codings about which there is some doubt.

capitals Used where part of an utterance receives unusually heavy stress.

*   Used to indicate unintelligibility. One asterisk represents one syllable.

. . .   Stops represent pauses, one stop corresponding roughly to one beat.

(0.8)   Otherwise, pauses are measured in seconds (to nearest 0.1 second) by stopwatch and enclosed in round brackets where they occur, either between or within utterances.

_____ Underlining. Where utterances overlap because more than one speaker talks at the same time, the overlapped portions are underlined and located adjacent to each other, where possible.

- Hyphen indicates a hiatus, either because an utterance has been interrupted by another speaker, or because the speaker makes a fresh start.

= Equals sign indicates that an utterance has been latched on to an immediately preceding utterance, with no perceptible gap.

Discourse coding scheme

The following coding conventions were used in the transcriptions.

Exchanges

I Initiation – an utterance which breaks continuity with the preceding discourse and predicts a response.

R Response – an utterance which is predicted by and responds to a preceding utterance.

R/I Response/initiation – an utterance which is predicted by and responds to a preceding utterance, and which simultaneously predicts a further response.

R/(I) Response/(initiation) – an utterance which is predicted by and responds to a preceding utterance, and which simultaneously provides for the possibility of a further response.

cont Continuation – an utterance which continues or adds to a previous utterance within a turn.

cont (I) Continuation/(initiation) – an utterance which continues or adds to a previous utterance in a turn, and which provides for the possibility of a further response.

I$_r$ Reinitiation – an utterance which attempts to elicit a response following null or unsatisfactory responses.

Symbols

[Exchange.

[Series of linked exchanges.
[

} Links between utterances within a turn.

) Thematic links between non-adjacent utterances.

Conventions within the text

Within the text the following conventions are used. An asterisk * marks either a string which is ill formed in isolation, or a string which makes a discourse sequence ill formed and is therefore inappropriate in context. Linguistic forms are indicated either by italics if they occur in running text, or by being placed on separate numbered lines. Single quotes are used to mark glosses, meanings or propositions, and for cited material. Italics are used for technical terms introduced in the text.

1

Studying conversational development: aims, scope and methods

It might come as a surprise to many that one of the most expanding areas of interest within child language research during the past decade or so has been the development of children's conversational skills. Academics have invested considerable time and effort in collecting, transcribing and analysing samples of conversations involving young children, and the results of these studies are beginning to appear in journals and collections of readings. What, we might ask, could be the purpose of these investigations? What possible use might they have? Most would see the value of investigating other more traditionally researched aspects of child language development, such as their acquisition of a system of sounds, the development of inflections and word order combinations, and the development of word and sentence meanings (that is, the areas known as phonology, syntax and semantics). We might even stretch our research interests a little further and include the study of how children learn to use words and sentences appropriately in particular situations or contexts, the area which is known as pragmatics. Beyond this, it is generally assumed that there is no problem. Children learn how to pronounce words, how to combine them and so on, and presumably make use of these abilities when participating in conversation. In other words, conversation is often assumed to be so natural that it does not merit or require serious investigation. Certainly anyone, such as a parent or teacher, who is frequently in the presence of young children could be forgiven for failing to see any problem. Young children seem to ask incessant questions, to make persistent demands for attention and to produce endless comments and observations. The problem is often getting them to stop talking. Indeed, such children seem to have little difficulty in starting up and maintaining conversations.

The belief that conversation is natural is one of the major barriers to serious research into the development of conversational ability and, as a consequence, into the nature of conversational disability. Of course, this problem confronts much research into behaviour, whether social, linguistic or cognitive. One way which linguists have adopted as a means of highlighting an area of unsuspected complexity, or of bringing to attention unnoticed regularities, is to examine deviant cases – that is, instances which 'break the rules'. So, for example, judgements of what is grammatical can be supported by an examination of cases of ungrammaticality. In this way, the rules of grammar can become apparent and can be delimited. Applying this procedure to conversation, we could look at cases where conversational 'rules' are broken. We can imagine examples where people do not say the right thing at the right time, where questions are not answered appropriately, where people speak out of turn, do not make clear what they are referring to, and so on. In these cases, the fact that we notice some 'deviance' suggests that there is some regularity to conversation, that the way in which conversationalists behave can be described as governed by rules. An alternative approach, and one which is illustrated in this book, is to trace the development of conversational ability in children. We can contrast the early 'communication' of the neonate with the conversational behaviour of, for example, four-year-olds. A detailed analysis of the differences would give us some insight into what young children have to acquire in order to become mature conversationalists. One of the main purposes of this book will be to examine the development of conversational ability in young children, asking what is involved in learning to participate in conversation and illustrating the answer to this question with some empirical research data. This will then lead us to consider some aspects of conversational disability in children.

Before doing this, however, we need to outline the scope of our enquiry. There are certain questions which we need to consider, which include the following:

1 What do we mean by conversation?
2 Is conversational development related to language development in general, in terms of the acquisition of traditional areas of enquiry such as phonology, syntax and semantics?
3 What is involved methodologically in the study of conversation?
4 How is an account of conversational development relevant to those involved professionally with young children's language, such as speech therapists and teachers?

We will begin by defining the subject area which we have been calling conversation. Following this, we will look at the relationship between conversational development and language development in general. We will then discuss some of the possible applications and implications of the study of conversational development. The chapter will conclude with a discussion of methodological issues in the study of conversation and will introduce the data which forms the basis of the empirical research to be reported in the course of the book.

Conversation: towards a definition

So far, we have been using the term *conversation* rather loosely. We will now propose a more precise definition and attempt to distinguish conversation from other terms used widely in the literature within roughly the same frame of reference, such as *communication* and *interaction*. One dictionary definition of conversation is as follows:

> The speaking together of two or more persons: informal exchange of ideas, information etc.
> (Funk and Wagnell's *Standard Dictionary of the English Language*, 1967)

Several points can be made about this definition. The first is that conversation involves *talk* between two or more persons. However, although we will be looking primarily at the talk which occurs in conversation, we must also stress the importance of the non-verbal behaviour which accompanies conversational talk, as we will see shortly.

A second point concerns the description of conversational talk as informal. To a certain extent this description is useful if it excludes talk which has been rehearsed, as in the performance of a play, or talk which takes place under highly formalized conventions, such as a debate. Media discussions, which are often prepared in advance, would seem to fall into the border areas of our definition because the talk is not spontaneous, although its actual performance may share many features of spontaneous conversation such as turn-taking and the use of gestures and other non-verbal behaviour. However, the term 'informal' excludes many types of talk between two or more persons which we will wish to include in conversation. For example, we will wish to look at a whole range of speech events such as job interviews and classroom talk between teachers and pupils, on the grounds that these events are on a continuum between the most informal end of the scale, which would include casual conversation, and the most formal end. We will not wish to deny that formality has an effect on the nature of talk. Recent work in sociolinguistics (for example, Labov 1972a) has shown how contextual factors, such as the degree of formality of the situation, can be correlated with the selection of phonological and syntactic variables by speakers. We will also see how the degree of formality has a bearing on conversational features such as exchange structure and turn-taking. However, the emphasis on formality distinguishes between types of talk which are similar in many ways. So, rather than insisting on informality as a necessary aspect of conversation, we will propose instead the term *naturally occurring*. This will still exclude talk which is not spontaneous, while at the same time allowing us to look at a wider range of speech events involving talk between two or more persons.

The final part of our dictionary definition – 'exchange of ideas, information etc.' – also requires some comment. This definition is unfortunate, as it puts the emphasis on the transmission of information in talk between persons – on the referential function of talk to the exclusion of its social and interpersonal functions. Yet many recent accounts of conversation restrict themselves to this dimension. We can cite two representative examples. The first is from a recent book on discourse analysis where, in a chapter on exchange structure, the authors argue that the exchange is 'the unit concerned with the negotiation of the transmission of information' (Coulthard and Brazil 1981:101). Ironically, many of the examples which they cite to illustrate descriptive problems in the analysis of spoken discourse do not fall easily within this definition or indeed within their proposals of exchange structure. We will return to a more detailed consideration of such descriptive problems in chapter 2. The second example which is worth citing comes from a recent book on the acquisition of language in a conversational context (Howe 1981:6). Here the author similarly requires that 'successive remarks must request or provide information if they are to be regarded as conversational'. The following is cited as an example in which the mother and child 'take turns to address each other without conversing in the ordinary sense of the word':

(1)   (Mother watches Barry building blocks)
       Mother: build it high
       Barry: no

We might ask why such a sequence is regarded as non-conversational. The first turn involves a common conversational act, a *directive* (or *request for action*), while the second turn is systematically related as one of the possible responses to a directive (in this case, a *refusal*). Indeed, as we will see in our discussion of request sequences in chapter 5, the choice of request forms and responses and the negotiation of request sequences require a complex use of talk which it is difficult not to see as conversational, in the sense in which we have been describing – that is, naturally occurring talk between two or more persons. Indeed, a conception of conversation which is too narrow excludes much which, as we will see in chapters 2 and 3, is of developmental significance. To take one further example from Howe (1981:96): some sequences are cited in which the mother appears to have misunderstood the communicative function of her child's preceding utterance. Such exchanges were excluded from the analysis, as exchanges were regarded as conversational only 'where there were grounds for believing that the mothers' responses were appropriate'. Disregarding the methodological issue of determining appropriacy in conversational data, one of the important aspects of early parent–child conversations, as we will see in chapter 3, is the way in which parents try to make sense of their children's utterances, treating them as conversational contributions and thus providing for their children a model of how conversation works. The restriction of conversation to the exchange of or transmission of ideas and information implies a qualitative analysis which excludes much of what is actually involved in the management of conversational interaction.

One further related point can be mentioned briefly. There is a popular misconception that the analysis of conversation involves an account of the *content* of utterances, of the motives people have for saying what they say and, in developmental, instructional and therapeutic contexts, is concerned with telling people what they ought to say. Our concern in this book, however, is primarily with the abstract principles which underlie participation in conversations, that is, with the ways in which conversations are managed rather than with what is actually said. Having said this, we will find that, in the end, content and structure are interdependent. This point will become clearer when we look at the main issues to be discussed in this book. These include the following: how participants initiate and close conversational exchanges, how they take and assign turns at speaking, how they know what sort of response is appropriate in relation to preceding utterances, what possibilities are open to participants at any given moment in a conversation and how these are constrained by factors such as politeness and the participants' interactional aims and strategies. These points will be exemplified and developed further in chapter 2.

So far, we have defined conversation as naturally occurring talk involving two or more participants and we have emphasized the importance of social and interpersonal aspects of conversation in addition to its function as a means of transmitting information. We can now look at some other terms which are often treated as being roughly synonymous with conversation as we have defined it. We have already made use of the term *interaction* in our definition of conversation and the ensuing discussion. Another term which is widely used is *interpersonal communication*. Although there is a fair degree of overlap between these terms, it might be worthwhile attempting to distinguish between them. Conversation implies interaction, if we understand interaction as referring to reciprocal behaviour in which participants act on and react to each other's behaviour. However, interaction does not imply conversation, as interaction need not involve any speech at all. Consider, for example, an exchange of waving as a greeting or the range of messages which can be communicated by an exchange of glances. The term *conversational interaction* would be appropriate for our present purposes, although for convenience we will generally use the more manageable term *conversation*.

As with interaction, interpersonal communication includes more than speech and need not involve speech at all. Communication has often been distinguished from interaction on the grounds that, whereas communication involves an exchange of meanings, interaction can occur without the participants sharing the same meanings (Bullowa 1979:3). This distinction is, in fact, central to an account of the comparison between interactions involving infants and caretakers, where the infant's behaviour is non-intentional and so not considered as communicative, and later stages where meanings are shared and the child's behaviour can reasonably be described as intentional (see further discussion in chapter 3). In sum then, when we refer to conversation in this book, we will be implying interaction, with the emphasis primarily on naturally occurring verbal interaction. The extent to which this interaction is communicative is one of the issues underlying most of the discussion throughout.

We have been careful to mention that conversation involves more than talk between two or more persons. Although our focus will be mainly on verbal aspects of conversation, it is important to emphasize the role of non-verbal behaviour. Non-verbal behaviour includes gesture, gaze, body orientation and aspects of speech production such as hesitations. We can distinguish between those non-verbal behaviours which convey information unintentionally and those which function primarily as a means of communication. Clear cases of the former would include dress and gait, which often indicates a person's affiliations and attitudes, though not necessarily intentionally. Pointing as a means of bringing something to the other's attention, and nodding as a means of conveying assent, would be clear cases of intentional non-verbal behaviour which can be considered as non-verbal surrogates of speech. In many cases it is difficult to draw this distinction, as the fine-grained analyses of Scheflen (1965), Argyle (1975) and others have shown. Consider, for example, hesitations, gestures and patterns of eye movement which accompany speech but which occur largely below the level of consciousness and would thus be considered non-intentional. These non-verbal behaviours can, however, as we shall see throughout, play an interactional role. For example, gestures and eye contact are an important non-verbal means of regulating the smooth transition of turns in face-to-face interaction (Duncan 1974). Hesitations can occur when speakers recycle their utterance during the course of its production and redesign it in order to take greater account of the listener's needs, which in turn are also communicated non-verbally during the course of the current speaker's turn (Goodwin 1981). Hesitation can also be used intentionally – for example, as a means of mitigating certain types of utterance such as a refusal of a request (Wootton 1981). In sum, then, although we will deal primarily with verbal aspects of conversational interaction, we will refer to non-verbal behaviour when it is relevant to the analysis.

Language development and the analysis of conversation

We turn now to the question of the relation between studies of conversational development and the more widely researched and familiar areas of the acquisition of syntax, semantics and phonology. As we noted at the beginning of this chapter, it is only recently that attention has been directed towards conversational data in child language research. Indeed, the study of child language development within the past 20 years or so has moved through a series of phases, determined to a large extent by shifts of emphasis within linguistic theory. We can trace these developments briefly, in order to show how researchers have come to show a greater interest in conversational data.

Child language research in the sixties was characterized by studies of grammatical development, which took the form of attempts to write 'grammars' specifying the rules underlying children's utterances. In keeping with early transformational-generative linguistics, these rules were not concerned with the meanings or functions of the children's utterances. This approach gave way to the 'rich interpretations' of the early seventies, in which attention was focused on the semantic relations believed to be expressed in children's utterances. often the context of the utterance, in the sense of both the ongoing situation and the preceding discourse, was inspected as a means of supporting these interpretations. This was one way in which conversational data became relevant for child language researchers. However, as MacLure (1981) points out, the interest was not in the interactional aspects of conversational data as such, but more in the data as an analyst's resource – that is, as a means of interpreting more reliably children's utterances. Gradually, by the later seventies, investigators began to feel the need to attend to the social and interpersonal aspects of children's language. Hymes (1972) claimed that *linguistic competence*, in the narrow sense of a knowledge of the syntactic and semantic rules of a language, could not account for the ability to use language appropriately in real, everyday situations – that is, for what he called *communicative competence*.

This new concern coincided with the emergence of pragmatics and discourse analysis. Pragmatics can be described as the study of language in context. It is not an additional level of language, to be added on to syntax, semantics and phonology. Rather, pragmatics pervades language use at all levels. For example, we can explain a speaker's choice of phonological variants pragmatically by reference to contextual features such as the degree of formality of the situation or the social roles and purposes of the participants (Labov 1972a; Trudgill 1974). To take an example from Belfast vernacular: situational variables play a part in determining whether intervocalic [th], as in *mother, brother*, is deleted or not. Deletion is more likely to occur in casual speech than in more careful speech (Milroy 1980).

Similarly, syntactic choices can be explained pragmatically. For example, the choice between definite and indefinite articles reflects the speaker's assumptions about the hearer's ability to identify the objects and persons being referred to (Hawkins 1978). Likewise, the choice between different request forms reflects social variables such as the roles and status of the participants, the nature of the requested action, and so on (Ervin-Tripp 1976) (see further discussion in chapter 5).

Discourse analysis looks, among other things, at language above the level of the sentence and at connections between sentences. In written texts, discourse analysis can be concerned with the structure of paragraphs, with the cohesion of texts and with the distribution of information within texts. In conversation, discourse analysis can involve relating the functions of utterances to their forms, examining the structure of conversational sequences or looking at the allocation and distribution of conversational turns. The convergence of these interests has led to a new phase in child language research, in which attention is now being focused on the development of the ability to use language and on the interactive contexts in which language is learned. We will explore several aspects of this interest in conversational data in the remainder of this section.

The interactive context of language learning

One of the major insights to be derived from modern research in child language development is that children are actively engaged in the process of language acquisition; that they are, as it were, continually searching for the abstract rules and principles which underlie the production and comprehension of grammatical sentences. Children have been described as testing hypotheses about language: conversely, language has been seen as a 'formal problem space' for children (Karmiloff-Smith 1979; Maratsos and Chalkley 1980). This approach tends, however, to see the child as actively working out the rules of language in isolation. A complementary approach is to examine the interactive context of language learning, on the basis that children acquire language during the course of interaction with other human beings. One consequence of this approach has been to direct attention to a detailed analysis of interactional situations involving children. This has been done in various ways over the last decade or so and for a variety of purposes. One approach has been to examine the nature of the language addressed to the child. Studies of language 'input' have investigated the effects of the caregiver's speech on language development, by correlating variables in the caregiver's speech such as MLU (mean length of utterance), syntactic complexity, and the use of particular grammatical forms with measures of the child's rate of language development (see, for example, the papers in Snow and Ferguson 1977). Many of these input features have been found to be interactionally occasioned. For example, a high use of questions — one of the most widely cited characteristics of 'motherese' — has been explained in terms of the caregiver's attempts to involve the child in interaction. Questions are an attention-getting device which can focus the child's attention on a specific object or issue. In addition, they have the social function of requiring a response and so are a useful means of eliciting talk from the child. Repetitions are often occasioned by the child's failure in the earlier stages of development to acknowledge the other's utterances (Berko-Gleason 1977), while parental expansions can be explained not so much as attempts to teach and correct the child's syntax, but rather as a means of making sense of the child's utterances by treating them as meaningful conversational contributions (MacLure 1981). We will return to this aspect of caregiver–child conversation in more detail in chapter 3.

A second approach to conversational data has looked at the question of interactional styles, suggesting that certain styles might be more facilitating for development than others. An early attempt along these lines made the distinction between the caregiver's acceptance or rejection of the child's communicative acts, although this work was formulated at a theoretical level with little attention to the dynamics of conversational interaction (Nelson 1973). Wells (1980) has made a detailed comparison between the interactive styles of two mothers. Similarly, Howe (1981) distinguished three different maternal interactive styles. We can illustrate the nature of this type of investigation by summarizing briefly some of the findings from the study by Wells. One major distinction between the two mothers discussed by Wells was that the first mother was 'supportive'; that is, she tended to use utterances which acknowledged and incorporated the content of the child's utterances and also elicited further talk from the child. The second mother's interactive style, on the other hand, was described as 'tutorial'. This mother tended to ask the child test questions to which she herself knew the answer, while her responses to her child's utterances mainly took the form of corrections. Wells does not make qualitative judgements about these distinct styles, and indeed, given our present state of knowledge of the processes of language development within an interactional context, such a descriptive analysis is as much as we can optimistically expect. Moreover, as Wells is careful to point out, the effect of interactive styles is not unidirectional. Some children might themselves be more facilitating by occasioning a wider range of conversational acts from their caretakers. The first child in Wells's study, for example, displayed a wider range of conversational acts and so elicited speech which was qualitatively more sophisticated. The second child, on the other hand, produced utterances which were often functionally ambiguous and generally contributed less content to the conversation. In other words, any account of interaction needs to treat the behaviour of each participant as reciprocal and as interdependent, rather than to separate out each participant's behaviours and measure the effects of one on the other (see also Lieven 1978).

Another way in which conversational data has been used has been in the explanation of the emergence of linguistic structure. Bruner (1975) presents a strong version of this approach, by attempting to trace the ontogenesis of case relations and topic-comment structures back to features of early caretaker–child interaction such as the means whereby joint attention is established. Bates and MacWhinney (1979) have made similar proposals, although as Maratsos and Chalkley (1980) and others have pointed out, the acquisition of syntactic knowledge cannot be explained sufficiently in terms of such functional or interactional hypotheses. Ervin-Tripp (1977a) illustrates a somewhat different approach which involves a detailed examination of the conversational context in which new structures are first used. She discusses the following example:

(2)   Mother: oh, what did you draw?
      E: nana nana
      Mother: did you draw a banana?
      E: yeah, I draw a banana in a garden
      Mother: a banana in a garden
      E: in a garden
                a banana in a garden

In addition to making the obvious observation that the child's production of *banana* rather than her first attempt at *nana* might be the result of parental feedback, Ervin-Tripp notes that this child had not previously produced structures in which locatives were combined with other sentence constituents, that is, of the type illustrated in the child's second utterance: subject–verb–object–prepositional phrase. Ervin-Tripp describes such new structures as a 'syntactic burst of performance' and suggests that their emergence can be explained here in terms of the 'boasting' context in which the child is participating and which the mother has elicited and encouraged. She hypothesizes that such a syntactic burst would be less likely to occur in contexts of rejection or refusal. Similarly, contexts in which the child is pushed towards greater referential explicitness could provide the motivation for the development of relative clauses and syntactic distinctions between articles, tenses and so on. We will pursue this point further when we consider children's reinitiations in chapter 4. For the moment we can note that, although much of this work is exploratory, it is based on a detailed account of conversational interaction, taking into consideration preceding discourse, the nature of the interaction and background information about the child – aspects which were previously disregarded in earlier accounts of syntactic development.

We can further illustrated the relevance of discourse context by looking briefly at a study carried out by Scollon (1979). Scollon makes a detailed examination of the relation between a child's utterance and other adjacent utterances, either those of the child or of its interlocutor. He shows how children can express a proposition sequentially across several utterances rather than within one utterance. The following are some examples from Brenda, the child he studied:

(3) (Brenda lifts her foot and holds it over the tape recorder, pretending to step on it)
Brenda: tape
         step

(4) Brenda: [mama . mama . mama . mam]
             [ʃ . ʃi . ʃ . ʃiʃ . ʃu´ . ʃuʃ]
    Suzanne: shoes

(5) Brenda: hiding
    Ron: hiding
             what's hiding?
    Brenda: balloon

(6) (Brenda is looking straight into an electric fan with her hair blowing back)
    Brenda: [fẽĩ]
             [fœ̃]
    Mother: hm?
    Brenda: [fœ̃]
    Mother: bathroom?
    Brenda: [fanĩ]
             [faĩ]
    Mother: fan, yeah
    Brenda: [kʰu]
    Mother: cool, yeah. Fan makes you cool

Several points can be noted about these examples. The first is that Brenda's words, although occurring as single words each with their own intonation contour, were often interpretable as being semantically related. For example, in (6) she may have been describing the fan as cool. Scollon describes the expression of semantic relations across several utterances as *vertical constructions*, and he sees this developmentally as a precursor of a later stage in which the child uses horizontal constructions, or expresses the relations syntactically within one utterance. For example he noted that, when Brenda was producing two-word utterances, she would often combine words within one intonation contour which had previously only been related vertically. Vertical constructions continued to be used, however. For example, Brenda produced the two-word utterance *see that*. However, an examination of the sequential context showed that this utterance was related vertically to a preceding utterance, as follows:

(7)   Brenda: Brenda
                 see that

Scollon sees this combination of vertical and horizontal constructions as a precursor of later syntactic structure, in this case, a subject–verb–object structure.

A further point is that many of the sequences were constructed interactively; that is, they involved both the child and a parent. In the case of (5) and (6), it seemed that Brenda was expecting some acknowledgement from her conversational partner before continuing. Example (4) can also be explained within an interactional perspective. In addition to indicating phonetic instability, this example can be seen as an attempt to ensure successful communication by modifying the utterance until it received acknowledgement. More generally, children's self-repairs, as we will see in chapter 7, are a useful guide to the state of the child's linguistic development. Rather than ignoring self-repetitions and self-repairs, as is often the case in child language studies, we will find it informative to focus attention on such sequential aspects of talk. In this way, we will see that a detailed account of the interactive context of language development may illuminate some aspects of the processes whereby children acquire language.

Conversational data has also been used as a basis for the investigation of the development of conversational skills, and this will be the main concern of the book. However, we will also be considering the other approaches which we have outlined, since conversational development and the development of linguistic structure are to some extent interdependent, as we have already seen. However, we will be more concerned with what children have to learn in order to initiate and sustain conversations.

There are two main research traditions on which we might draw when examining the development of conversation in children. The first sees conversational ability as evidence of cognitive development in aspects of intellectual growth such as egocentrism and decentration. This tradition focuses on the development of referential communicative skills, usually investigated under experimental conditions. We will consider this work only briefly, as it has been well documented elsewhere (see, for example, Lloyd and Beveridge 1981). We will mainly be concerned to show how this work differs from our present approach.

The second research tradition, which will be the focus of the book, analyses the development of children's use of language, using naturally occurring talk as data. We will outline the main aspects of this tradition.

First, however, we will look briefly at the notion of child egocentrism and studies of referential communication.

Egocentrism and the development of referential communication

Much of current work on children's communicative development, particularly in studies carried out by psychologists, has been influenced by Piaget's theory of child egocentrism (1959; first published in French in 1926). Piaget's findings are based both on studies of children's conversations in a nursery school in Geneva and also on experiments designed to test children's ability to communicate information effectively. Piaget concluded that children's early communication is deficient and he explained this deficiency in terms of a theory of *child egocentrism*.

What do we mean by egocentrism? Many definitions have been proposed and Piaget himself is inconsistent in his own accounts. We are not concerned, however, with the everyday notion of being 'self-centred'. One crucial aspect is a failure to take the listener's perspective into account in the transmission of information. Piaget first noted this deficiency in observational studies of children's naturally occurring conversations, by measuring the extent to which they responded to each other's turns. However, as these early attempts to characterize conversational ability suffer from a failure to take into account many important indicators of children's conversational skills, and since many subsequent studies, based on more adequate models of conversation, have indicated much less egocentrism than Piaget originally estimated (see, for example, Mueller 1972; Garvey and Hogan 1973; Keenan 1974), we shall not consider this early work further but shall look rather at experimental studies of referential communication.

Two main aspects have been investigated in experimental studies of referential communication:

1 The ability to describe referents accurately so that they can be discriminated from non-referents.
2 The ability to take the listener's perspective and to adapt the information according to the listener's state of knowledge and the demands of the communicative situation.

The first aspect is generally investigated using a task in which speaker and listener are separated by a screen and the speaker is required to describe certain objects and shapes from an array in front of him so that the listener is able to select similar objects and shapes from a similar array in front of himself. This type of task has commonly been referred to as the 'Glucksberg and Krauss' paradigm, as it has been widely used in experiments by these two investigators (see, for example, Glucksberg and Krauss 1967; Krauss and Glucksberg 1969). Inability to provide sufficient and accurate information would result in the listener being unable to select the appropriate referent. For example, among instructions to select from a series of toy farm animals, *take the cow* would be insufficient if there were more than one cow in the listener's array. (See Maratsos 1976; Warden 1976; Karmiloff-Smith 1979 on the development of the use of the definite and indefinite articles in children.) Thus the speaker has to determine which attributes of a referent are discriminating and which are redundant or unnecessary.

The second aspect of referential communication is often referred to as *role-taking ability*. This involves the ability to be aware of the listener's perspective and to take it into account when structuring the content of the message. An additional requirement is the ability to take account of feedback from the listener and to redesign the message in the light of this feedback. (Some experimental designs do not, however, permit listener feedback.) A typical example is a task in which a subject is shown non-verbally how to play a board game and then is asked to explain this game to a sighted and an unsighted listener. The task explores the hypothesis that children's information will be more appropriate as a function of age owing to an increasing sensitivity to the different input requirements involved in the two listener conditions. For example, explanations accompanied by pointing or in which referents were inadequately described would not be suitable for an unsighted listener (see Flavell et al. 1968 for a full account of such experiments). Detailed reviews of the literature on the development of referential communication skills can be found in Glucksberg et al. (1975), Asher (1978), Dickson (1981) and Lloyd and Beveridge (1981).

There are several problems with these experimental studies of the development of referential communication. One problem concerns the experimental setting, which is often unnatural in comparison with the more spontaneous situations in which children engage in conversation, and which often involves tasks at a level of difficulty that is too complex or too abstract for the child. Experiments in which more child-oriented tasks were used tended to produce results which indicated that children's role-taking abilities were not as deficient as Piaget had suggested. This was particularly the case when the children were adequately instructed in the nature of the task and knew what was required of them, and when the task involved basic human purposes and interactions which would be familiar to the child rather than the more abstract problem-solving required by Piaget's experiments (Hughes 1975; Donaldson 1978). The level of difficulty of a task is an important factor. An inability to describe a referent accurately to an unsighted listener may result from problems in describing its distinctive features rather than from general role-taking abilities. Maratsos (1973), for example, found that children aged three to five years were able to take into account important aspects of the listener's perspective provided the experimental task was simple enough, but that they were less successful on more difficult tasks. This suggests that the encoding required by the task was too difficult, not that the children's role playing was egocentric. Performance in such tasks is affected by the workload involved and can be downgraded as a function of increasing processing demands (Shatz 1978a). Similar processes occur with adults. Consider, for example, the familiar task of asking someone to describe a spiral staircase without using their hands or to describe how a new piece of equipment works to someone who is blindfolded.

Studies of referential communication, which suggest that young children are unable to take their listener's perspective into account, conflict with evidence from experiments carried out in more naturalistic settings and from observational studies of children's conversations. Several studies have measured the ability of children to adapt their talk to younger listeners (Shatz and Gelman 1973; Andersen and Johnson 1973; Berko-Gleason 1973; Sachs and Devin 1976; Gelman and Shatz 1977). We can illustrate from the study by Shatz and Gelman. In this study, children aged four and one-half were given a toy to play with and were then asked to explain its workings to a two-year-old, an adult and a peer. Differences between the messages were analysed using a variety of measures such as MLU, complexity of grammatical structure and the use of attention-getting devices. It was found that more complex structures such as subordinate and co-ordinate clauses, *that*-complementizers and WH-complementizers (what, where etc.) were used more frequently in speech to adults than to two-year-olds. Conversely, attention-getters were used more frequently to two-year-olds. In addition, the children often commented on their younger listener's cognitive and linguistic immaturity, for example, *she won't be able to get them out*. This suggests an ability to perceive the listener's perspective which was not evidenced by children of the same age in the more abstract experimental tasks described earlier. A similar conflict has been found in studies of the extent to which young children can utilize listener feedback. A study by Peterson et al. (1972) suggests that young children are unable to take account of listener indications of misunderstanding. This conflicts with findings from observational studies which show that young children are able to deal with requests for clarification by their listeners (see chapter 7).

The final point which we shall consider concerns the characterization of conversation as the transmission of information. This narrow focus overlooks other important aspects of what is involved in the participation in conversational interaction, as we saw in our discussion earlier in this chapter. As these aspects of conversation will form the focus of most of the remainder of the book, we will not elaborate further on them at this point. What does seem to emerge, however, from the literature on the development of referential communication is that, as far as the study of conversational development is concerned, we need an adequate model of what skills and abilities are involved in conversational interaction. We will take this point up in some detail in chapter 2. In the meantime, we will consider some general aspects of conversational development which have emerged in observational studies of children's talk.

Naturalistic studies of conversational development

There have been several different types of approach to the analysis of conversational data involving children. Ethnographic studies have shown how children have acquired at an early age the ability to engage in various speech events such as narrating (Kernan 1977), talk of trades (Mishler 1979), ritual insults (Labov 1972b), disputes (Brenneis and Lein 1977), and 'trick or treat' routines (Berko-Gleason and Weintraub 1976). Other studies have looked at the range of speech acts used by children (Dore 1977a) or the pragmatics of a particular speech act such as requests for action (Ervin-Tripp 1977b). Some studies have looked at interaction between children and adults while others have looked at peer interaction.

This book will focus on two main ways of characterizing conversational development. The first concerns the development of the ability to initiate and sustain contingent discourse. This approach involves an examination of the structure of conversation, the ways in which children produce relevant responses and handle embedded structures such as requests for clarification (see chapter 7). Also involved are the devices which children use to initiate talk (see chapter 4). We will be able to trace development from the earliest stages of interaction, where mothers and other caretakers impute intention to the infant's behaviours (chapter 3), to the stage where behaviours are intentional, reciprocal and socially adapted. Thus we will be able to show how children develop from an initial inability to initiate and sustain dialogue to a stage where they can produce extended sequences of contingent talk. We will see, however, that this development cannot be measured purely quantitively; that is, we will not be able to apply simple measures of length of sequence as an indication of the child's stage of development. There are two reasons for this. One is that conversational sequences are interactive units which are jointly constructed by the participants. For this reason it is impossible to separate out the contribution of any one of the participants independently of the other's contribution. Secondly, the length of a sequence depends on many external factors such as the nature of the topic being discussed, the children's level of interest, and whether they are tired. In some cases, short sequences indicate a more mature conversationalist who is able to avoid unnecessary repetitiveness or, in the case of disputes, is able to terminate a sequence and thus forestall further argument. A parallel in syntax is the use of MLU as a measure of syntactic development. This fails to take account of more elaborate syntactic processes such as ellipsis, which have the effect of shortening utterance length (Crystal 1974).

The second aspect of development which we will be considering concerns the choice of utterance at any given point in the conversation. Here we will see how children add to their repertoire of speech acts. In addition, we will see how particular speech acts, such as requests, become more differentiated. So, for example, a child might first use simple refusals (using *no*) as a means of turning down a request for action. Later the child might add further distinctions, for example between refusals which are accompanied by a justification and those which are not. Further development might concern the types of justification which the child uses to put off a request (see chapter 5).

Applications and implications of the study of conversational development

So far we have been treating the study of the development of conversational ability in children as a subject which is of interest in its own right. And indeed, given our present inadequate state of knowledge about this area, there is still a great need for further detailed empirical research. This book is intended as a substantive contribution to this need. It is also important, however, to consider the potential relevance of this research for practitioners such as speech therapists and language teachers. In this section we will attempt only to alert practitioners to some of the more important issues which will be the major focus of this book. We will return to a more detailed discussion of their practical implications and applications in chapters 9 and 10.

The term *ability* implies that it might also be possible to consider its converse – lack of ability, or disability. We mentioned at the beginning of this chapter that one of the means of studying the regularities which underlie normal behaviour involves looking at cases where the 'rules' have been broken or have failed to apply. As far as the development of conversation is concerned, we would wish to look at the question of whether there is such a thing as conversational disability. That is, we would be attempting to pinpoint a specific disability which can be described in terms of conversational rather than phonological, syntactic or semantic rules. Research in this area is still very much at the pioneering stage and is marred by considerable terminological confusion as well as by misconceptions as to the nature of conversation (see earlier). We will briefly outline some of the concerns of current research in this area and will return to a more detailed account of conversational disability in chapter 9.

The first point which we need to consider is whether conversational disability is something which is separate from other more specific language disabilities. For example, are there cases of children whose syntactic, phonological and semantic development is 'normal' but who have problems in engaging in conversation – that is, in putting their linguistic abilities to use in real situations? Conversely, are there children whose abilities in syntax, phonology or semantics are underdeveloped but who are nevertheless competent conversationalists? It might be the case that children with delayed or deviant syntax present problems in sustaining conversation precisely because of their syntactic disability. On the other hand, children's syntactic performance might be constrained by their inability to engage in conversation or even by the nature of the interactive situations which they typically encounter. In the latter two cases, syntactic and conversational disabilities would seem to be interdependent.

On looking at the current literature, we can certainly find cases of patients with language disorders who also exhibit delay in conversational development. Rom and Bliss (1981) studied the range of speech acts used by normal-speaking and language-delayed children and found that the language-delayed children were able to use a variety of speech acts but were delayed in their pragmatic development in relation to their normal-speaking peers. Similarly, in a study of children's responses, van Kleeck and Frankel (1981) found that the language-disordered children in their sample followed a similar developmental trend to normal-speaking children but that they were slower to develop more elaborate devices for responding. In these cases, language delay seemed to entail conversational delay. However, these results might have been an artefact of the experimental design which assigned children to groups of normal speaking and language delayed on an a priori basis. We can also note that conversational disability in these cases involved delay and not any deviant developmental pattern.

What might be more interesting would be cases where language delay and conversational disability are independent. There are certainly cases of patients with limited language skills who are active and effective communicators. Infants in the prelinguistic stage before the onset of speech are a case in point (see chapter 3). Blank et al. (1979) provide a case study of the other side of the picture. They describe a three-year-old child whose language was syntactically and semantically well developed but who lacked the ability to communicate. That is, as far as language ability was concerned, the child produced well-formed and age-appropriate utterances. On examining his use of language, however, Blank et al. found that, although he was able to initiate conversational exchanges, his responses were often inappropriate or absent altogether. The following is a typical example (Blank et al. 1979:346):

(8)   (Father and child are looking at a book)

Father	John
that's Pat's house. What's everyone doing at Pat's house?	
	knock, knock, knock (knocking on door in book)
come in	
	nobody's home
nobody's home? Well, isn't Pat home? (Pat is evident in the picture)	
	come back later
OK, let's go to Pat's new house	
	Pat's old house

As we can see from this example, there is little communication between John and his father. The father tries to initiate conversation by asking questions and he also tries to sustain the conversation by responding to John's utterances despite their apparent lack of relevance. John's utterances are not appropriate as responses, however, and indeed, as Blank et al. point out, any conversational exchanges which did arise could be attributed to the parents' degree of responsiveness to whatever John said rather than to any skill on John's part in initiating or sustaining the conversation. We will return to a detailed account of the development of these abilities in chapters 4 and 6.

Another aspect, which is of relevance to speech therapists, concerns the extent to which patients can generalize the language practised in the clinical situation to the everyday situations outside the clinic which they encounter. It is often the case that patients perform satisfactorily under the controlled guidance of the speech therapist but are unable to apply their newly acquired language skills elsewhere. Geller and Wollner (1976) describe a striking example of a child who was taught WH-questions and was able to produce them on demand in the clinic, but who used them inappropriately in spontaneous interaction, for example, with no apparent addressee and unrelated to any discernible context. Obviously language needs to be related to the contexts in which it is typically used. The teaching of language in isolation from its use does not provide a suitable basis for a patient's subsequent ability to use language effectively. In other words, some account has to be taken of pragmatic and discourse aspects of language in the clinic as well as the levels of form. What these pragmatic and discourse factors are will be outlined in chapter 2, while much of the remainder of this book will be devoted to a detailed empirical account of their development in children.

A related point concerns the nature of therapist–patient interaction. It is often the case that the need to elicit samples of language from the patient results in a type of interaction which is qualitatively different from the patient's normal use of language. Typically, therapists elicit language samples by asking *what's that* or *what's he doing* questions, which demand minimal elliptical responses. Patients also need to develop the skills of initiating conversation as well as responding. This involves, among other things, attention-getting skills as well as the ability to assess the listener's state of knowledge so that the content of the initiation can be presented appropriately (see chapter 4 for further discussion). It also involves choosing the appropriate form of the speech act in relation to the context and other pragmatic factors such as the interpersonal relationship between the participants (see chapter 5). Such issues are rarely considered in the clinic, precisely because the patient is usually cast in the role of responding to elicitations by the therapist which tightly constrain the range of language which can be used in the response. Thus more emphasis would need to be put on interactive situations which the patient encounters in everyday life. This could involve going beyond the clinical setting to an investigation of patients in more natural communicative settings and in more symmetrical interactional situations, for example, with their peers. Within the clinical setting, therapists also need to consider more closely the relation between their elicitations and the types of response they expect to elicit from the patient. Many elicitations require minimal responses in which one or more sentence elements are ellipted, as we mentioned earlier. Such practices are obviously unsatisfactory if the therapist's aim is to obtain an adequate sample of the patient's full range of syntactic structures, including full major sentences. A related point is that therapist–patient interaction is often artificial, with therapists asking questions to which they already know the answers as a means of exerting more control over the patient's responses. Thus, even within the clinical setting, there is a need for more 'natural' conversation. In order to appreciate what is meant by the term 'natural conversation', however, we will need to look in some detail at the structure and processes of conversation and to consider how conversation develops normally in children. These points will be our main focus in the chapters to follow. In chapter 9 we will return to a more detailed consideration of conversational disability, and we will look at some practical implications in chapter 10.

Conversational development and the school

There is a considerable literature on the question of the relationship between language and educational disadvantage. One aspect, which has been investigated more recently, concerns the nature of teacher–pupil interaction in schools. It has been shown that teacher–pupil talk differs from the type of conversational interaction to which children are accustomed at home and in play with peers. In classrooms the talk is controlled by one participant – the teacher. The teacher controls the distribution of turns and the topics for discussion. Teachers also have the right to comment on their pupils' contributions (and indeed this use of *feedback* is usually considered an essential part of pedagogic and therapeutic discourse), but pupils do not have a similar right to comment on the teacher's talk. There are also differences in the use of questions in the classroom. Many teacher questions do not have the function of requesting information unknown to the teacher; rather they serve to test the pupils' knowledge. These questions have often been referred to as *test questions*, *display questions* or *pseudo-questions*.

The finding that there are such differences between the language of the school and the language of the home has led some investigators to propose a theory of *discontinuity* to account for the lack of educational achievement of some children. According to this theory, some children have little or no experience of the interactional demands of the school because of the type of conversational interaction which they have experienced at home, and so they are less able to cope with classroom talk. It has to be stressed, however, that this theory is extremely controversial. Firstly, there have been few detailed analyses of the linguistic interaction of the home and school which could provide empirical support for such a theory. Secondly, those studies which do exist, such as the Bristol language development study (Wells 1981a), have not shown the clear-cut discontinuities which have been proposed. This issue will be discussed in greater detail in chapter 8.

It has also been proposed that some children have difficulties in the use of language to express more complex functions such as reasoning, predicting and imagining, and intervention programmes have been developed to meet this problem (see, for example, Tough 1981). Here the emphasis is on a qualitative (and often impressionistic) analysis of the content of the children's talk rather than on the conversational devices and strategies which are used to initiate and sustain the talk. As the main focus of this book is on these conversational devices and strategies, the discussion of content will be outside our scope, although naturally it will not be possible to separate form entirely from content and ultimately it will be important to achieve some integration between the two in a fuller analysis of discourse. We will look briefly at how young children achieve such an integration during their first year at school in chapter 8, and will discuss the implications of programmes designed to advance children's discourse skills in chapter 10.

Discourse analysis has also been used widely in the study of second- and foreign-language teaching in schools. We will consider two aspects of this research: the analysis of teaching content, including syllabus design and course materials, and the study of teaching and learning processes in second-language classrooms.

As far as teaching content in second- and foreign-language teaching is concerned, recent attempts to devise notional, functional and communicative syllabuses and teaching materials indicate an increasing interest in communicative and conversational competence (Wilkins 1976; Munby 1978; Johnson and Porter 1982). Several considerations follow this new emphasis. Firstly, it is necessary to specify the skills which the learners are to acquire. Various lists of communicative skills for second-language learners have been drawn up (see, for example, van Ek 1976, and discussion in Canale and Swain 1980). Such lists include the range of speech events typically encountered by native speakers of the target language as well as culturally determined interactional patterns and norms. A second issue concerns the teaching of the appropriate use of language, involving, for example, the use of politeness markers and modes of indirectness. Although some research has indicated that certain pragmatic aspects of language may be universal (Fraser et al. 1980), there are also many ways in which language usage differs across cultures. The work of Gumperz (1977) suggests that failure to appreciate such differences can result in communicative breakdown as well as give rise to or reinforce mistrust and prejudice among interethnic groups. Related to this is the need to develop strategic competence in second-language learners. This refers to those verbal and non-verbal communicative devices which can be used in cases of communicative breakdown or as a means of compensating for a lack of linguistic or communicative competence (Canale and Swain 1980). Stern (1978) suggests that such strategies are more likely to be acquired through experience in real-life communicative situations than in classrooms where there is little meaningful communication. Emphasis on role play and other communicative activities in the classroom might facilitate the development of these aspects of communicative competence (see Littlewood 1981 for a recent account of communicative language teaching).

A final point related to teaching content concerns the nature of the language which pupils encounter in the classroom. This is rather similar to the issue discussed earlier of the language of the speech therapy clinic. The types of dialogue used to teach conversational skills are a highly idealized version of real conversation. This does not necessarily imply that such dialogues are inappropriate. We need, however, to consider the degree of idealization which is desirable so that we are able to present learners with a model of conversation which they can practise and apply but which does not distort real conversational interaction to the point of artificiality. Learners often experience considerable difficulties when they encounter language in real situations, where speakers do not speak in the idealized style of specially prepared teaching materials. Recordings of naturally occurring conversations, such as those in Crystal and Davy (1975), are a useful means of acquainting learners with the style of conversation. Teaching could also focus more on the use of conversational devices such as hesitation markers and other such fillers, based on research into their usage in the target language.

The second area which we will mention briefly concerns the processes of teaching and learning in the second- and foreign-language classroom. Despite a long history of research in classroom interaction, it is only relatively recently that second- and foreign-language teaching and learning have been investigated. Allwright (1980), for example, has looked at patterns of participation in second-language classrooms. Such research is a means of describing the dynamics of teacher–pupil interaction as well as focusing on the learning experience of individual students. The roles played by teachers and learners in classrooms are usually rigidly defined so that teachers typically initiate conversational exchanges while the learners respond. As in the clinic, the learners' talk is constrained by the possibilities afforded by the teacher's elicitations. This can reduce the learners' contributions to a minimum. It also means that learners are unlikely to gain practice in initiating conversation and in the use of eliciting speech acts such as questions. We will return to a more detailed consideration of these issues in the light of our account of conversational development. In chapter 9 we will consider some aspects of the development of conversation by second-language learners. This will be followed in chapter 10 by a more detailed look at the practical applications and implications of the research reported in this study to the areas of second-language teaching and learning.

Studying conversational development: some methodological considerations

We turn finally to the question of the methods used to study conversational development. We will not attempt a full account of methodological issues in the collection of data, its transcription and analysis, as these have been well documented elsewhere (see, for example, Ochs 1979a; Wells 1979). Neither will we enter into a debate concerning the relative merits of experimental and observational approaches. Rather we will look at some issues arising from the empirical research to be reported in this book and will introduce the data on which the analysis is based.

Let us look first at data collection. Ideally we would hope for a method which yields reliable and representative samples of children's conversations. Two questions are relevant here. The first concerns the size of the sample and the extent to which it provides a representative picture of children's conversational abilities generally. The second, which is related, is concerned with the ways in which the data is collected and the extent to which this might affect the naturalness and spontaneity of the behaviours under observation.

The data for the present study consisted of a series of video recorded conversations between two young girls, my daughter Siobhan and her friend Heather. Siobhan was 3;8 (three years eight months old) at the time of the first recording and Heather was 4;0. Recordings were taken at regular intervals until the children were aged 5;5 and 5;9 respectively. The total amount of recorded interaction was roughly six hours. The ages of the children in relation to the recording sessions are given in figure 1.

	I	II	III	IV	V	VI
Siobhan	3;8	4;3	4;6	4;9	5;1	5;5
Heather	4;0	4;7	4;10	5;1	5;5	5;9

Figure 1 Ages of the children in relation to the recording sessions

It might be felt that such a small sample is hardly representative. Against this, it can be argued that, in our present state of knowledge about the nature and development of conversation, a detailed analysis of a relatively small sample is preferable to a more superficial analysis of a much larger sample, where many of the more interesting aspects of conversation might easily be overlooked. However, in order to make the findings of this research more general, I have incorporated into each of the chapters which analyse the data a review of other related research.

The second question concerns the extent to which the data can be considered as natural and spontaneous. We are familiar with the problem of what Labov (1972a) has described as the 'observer's paradox'. This is the problem that the study of natural talk requires careful observation, yet the presence of an observer can distort the extent to which the interaction is natural. This is particularly a problem when more obtrusive observational devices such as video recording equipment are employed. As far as the present data is concerned, recordings were carried out at the home of one of the children (some audio recordings were also made while travelling by car) and the children were mainly engrossed in spontaneous play, such as building with Lego blocks or using a doll's house, or negotiating roles for various pretend games such as mother–baby or nurse–patient. Generally these situations provided abundant talk from the children, though it is impossible to determine whether this particular dyad was more interactive than others. Comparisons with data from other studies of peer interaction would suggest that the children in the present study were not atypical (see, for example, studies by Garvey 1975; Ervin-Tripp 1979; Iwamura 1980).

The children did not appear to be unduly affected by the presence of the video camera. From time to time they asked to be allowed to look through it, but otherwise they ignored it and got on with their play. Their play did not appear to differ substantially from other occasions when they played together spontaneously without the presence of the camera.

It is perhaps necessary to say a few words about the reasons for the use of video recordings in this study. Video recordings were used mainly because of the importance of recording non-verbal as well as verbal behaviour. We have already noted the importance of non-verbal behaviour in conversational interaction. With young children, however, non-verbal behaviour is not just an accompaniment of talk but often rather an alternative to talk, particularly in the early stages (Bates et al. 1979; Ochs 1979a). As we will see in chapter 4, for example, many of the children's attention-getting and attention-drawing devices were non-verbal. These included the use of gaze to establish eye contact, touching and pointing. These devices were often used together with and sometimes instead of verbal devices. To omit them would be to overlook important aspects of the children's conversational abilities.

Turning now to transcription, we can look at the question of the level of detail of the transcription and of what is to be included and omitted. In the present data the transcription was orthographic, except for a few cases of 'deviant' pronunciation which gave rise to repairs (see chapter 7). In these cases a broad phonetic transcription was used. Otherwise phonetic transcription was not used as it was not considered relevant to the analysis. Major prosodic features were transcribed where they contributed to the analysis, as, for example, in the use of higher pitch as an attention-getting device or other features such as vowel lengthening, more careful articulation and voice quality features which had some bearing on the interpretation of the data. The same applies to non-verbal behaviours such as changes of gaze direction, postural shifts and pointing. Close attention was paid in the transcription to the length of pauses within and between turns as well as to points of overlap between turns and points of self-interruption and self-repetition. This level of detail was considered essential for the analysis of the children's self-repairs, their orientation to the precision timing involved in turn-taking and their awareness of syntactic units such as clauses as displayed in their self-corrections (see chapter 7).

Organisation of the book

In this chapter we have considered the aims, scope and methods involved in the study of conversational development. We have looked at some of the reasons why conversation should be studied as well as other aspects of language. The remainder of this book will be taken up with a more detailed account of the nature and development of conversation in children and with its relevance to speech therapists and teachers. The chapters are organized as follows.

In chapter 2 we will look at the structure and processes of conversation. As we have seen, conversational interaction is still poorly understood and inadequately documented. For this reason, we will discuss some of the central issues in the analysis of conversation, with particular emphasis on those aspects which are to be investigated in subsequent chapters.

Chapter 3 looks at early conversational development. Social and cognitive prerequisites for the development of conversation are discussed. Early parent–infant interaction is then examined as a possible source of conversational development and a comparison is made between interaction with parents and other adult caregivers and interaction with peers.

Chapters 4 to 7 report the empirical research described earlier. Chapter 4 is concerned with the initiation of conversational exchanges. Initiations were considered particularly important as they are an indication of children's ability to get and direct their listener's attention. They fall within the theoretical perspective of egocentric speech and are thus an important indicator of communicative development. They are also important from the point of view of a model of conversation as they provide evidence of the intimate relationship between verbal and non-verbal behaviour.

Chapter 5 looks at requests as one aspect of the development of speech acts and of pragmatic competence. Requests indicate the extent to which children are sensitive to social features such as the status of the addressee of the request, the nature of the requested action and its relation to the preceding discourse and the participants' interactional strategies. Chapter 6 looks at the devices children use to sustain coherent dialogue, while chapter 7 is concerned with processes of conversation such as turn-taking and the use of repair mechanisms to remedy conversational breakdown. Later conversational development is the subject of chapter 8, in which we look at the development of children's repertoires of different speech events and their understanding of situational and cultural variability, as well as the nature of interaction in the classroom. Chapter 9 looks at the question of conversational disability, while chapter 10 discusses clinical and educational applications.

2
The structure and processes of conversation

The analysis of conversation has been the concern of several disciplines. These include linguistics, psychology, sociology, anthropology, psychotherapy and the ethnography of speaking. One of the most exciting aspects of recent work in the analysis of conversation is in fact its multidisciplinary nature. As the view of conversation to be presented here is not restricted to any one discipline, it might be helpful first to introduce some basic terminology and to give a brief account of the particular theoretical perspectives which have been most influential. This will enable the reader to locate the present approach in the literature.

It might be assumed that linguistics would be the most likely discipline to be concerned with conversation. Paradoxically, this has not been the case. Instead, until recently linguists have generally been more concerned with the analysis of sentences in isolation from their contexts of use. Some linguists have made an important contribution to the analysis of stylistic features of conversation (see, for example, Crystal and Davy 1969, 1975; Ochs 1979b). The most influential approach to a *structural analysis* of conversation within a linguistic framework was developed by Sinclair and Coulthard (1975), using classroom talk between teachers and pupils as data. Subsequently, analysis was made of the discourse structure of other interactive situations such as doctor–patient interviews, media discussions and informal committee talk. An account of this work as well as several papers presenting recent developments within this framework can be found in Coulthard and Montgomery (1981). (See also Stubbs 1983 for a more extensive attempt to incorporate discourse analysis within an explicitly linguistic framework.) For our purposes, the most useful aspect of this work concerns the structure of conversational exchanges (see later).

A second approach on which we will be drawing is referred to as *conversational analysis* or more recently, by some of its proponents, as *conversation analysis*. This approach to conversation originates in ethnomethodology, which itself developed out of a dissatisfaction with the analytic methods of traditional sociology. Conversational analysis has been developed mainly in the United States by Sacks, Schegloff and Jefferson and also in Britain by Wootton, Drew, Heritage and others. One of its main strengths lies in its careful attention to minute aspects of conversational data such as points of overlap and simultaneous talk. The conversational analysts have made an important contribution to our understanding of the processes of conversational interaction, particularly regarding the 'work' which participants in conversations accomplish, as, for example, in the management of turn-taking. We will be looking in particular in this chapter at the research on adjacency pairs, turn-taking and repairs.

Speech act theory, which developed out of the work of philosophers of language such as Austin, Searle and Grice, has also made an important contribution to the analysis of conversation. Speech act theory is concerned with defining the properties of speech acts such as requests, promises, threats, warnings and so on, by proposing a set of conditions which underlie the appropriate performance of these acts and which enable us to distinguish one speech act from another. Thus, for example, when we make a promise we assume that we are referring to a future act which is of benefit to the hearer and which we sincerely intend to carry out. A threat would be distinguished from a promise in that it would not be of benefit to the hearer. In addition, speech act theorists have been concerned with the indirect relationship between the forms of utterances and the speech acts which they can convey. For example, the utterance *it's cold in here* could be a statement, but it could also convey an indirect speech act such as a request (to shut the door, turn on the heating and so on) or a variety of other speech acts. For our purposes, we will be looking in particular at the work of speech act theorists on requests and general principles of conversation.

The work of Labov and Fanshel (1977) should also be mentioned at this stage. Labov and Fanshel developed a model of discourse which they applied to a therapeutic interview. One aspect of their work involved further refinement of speech act theory – in particular, a more detailed account of indirect requests. In addition, Labov and Fanshel showed how utterances can convey several speech acts simultaneously. This multifunctional approach to the analysis of utterances will be important for our own analysis, as we will see shortly.

Finally, we can mention briefly the work of psychologists on conversation. Psychologists have been mainly concerned with features of conversation which are readily quantifiable such as hesitation markers, gaze direction and gestures. The frequency and location of such features is noted and used as a means of explaining speech planning and production processes (see, for example, papers in Butterworth 1981). We will draw on some of this work in our account of self-repairs.

These remarks are intended not to be exhaustive but merely to introduce and locate the main approaches to conversation on which this account is to be based. In the remainder of this chapter we will look in greater detail at particular aspects of conversational interaction which can be described developmentally. Before we do this, however, it might be helpful to give a brief outline of these aspects and show how they relate to one another and to traditional levels of linguistic description such as phonology, syntax and semantics. In figure 2 we can see the main aspects of conversation which will concern us in this book.

Conversation	Traditional levels of linguistic description
Turn-taking	Phonology
Exchanges	Syntax
Discourse content	Semantics
Appropriacy	
Repairs	

Figure 2 Components of conversation

Let us examine each of these aspects in turn and show how they relate to the three levels of linguistic description. We have already seen that *turn-taking* is an essential ingredient of conversation. Indeed, turn-taking might be taken to be a defining characteristic, as without turns conversation does not take place. However, turn-taking alone is not sufficient as a means of defining conversation, and indeed we will find that even young infants master the rudiments of conversational turn-taking before they are able to talk (see chapter 3). In other words, there can be turn-taking without any linguistic content.

So a second aspect of conversation concerns the nature and content of turns. We can look at how turns are related to each other interactionally. As we will see shortly, some turns set up expectations for a response while other turns respond to the expectations set up by preceding turns. This is one aspect of the *structure* of conversation – that is, the ways in which conversational turns combine into larger units as well as the permissible orders of occurrence of turns.

At the level of *discourse content* we can look at the ways in which speakers relate their turns topically and show links between and within turns. The most obvious aspect of this linkage can be see in the use of cohesive devices such as anaphoric pronouns and connectives. But at a deeper level there are links within a speaker's organization of his discourse content which reflect his perception of the temporal, logical and other types of sequencing events. This has often been described as *background know-ledge*, on which speakers rely in communication with other human beings. One of our concerns will be to investigate the extent to which children can assess the amount of shared knowledge in conversation with others and

whether they can make appropriate adjustments to their messages in order
to account for their listener's lack of knowledge in any given domain.

Related to content is the *appropriacy* of an utterance. There are usually
several ways of expressing a given message and, although each of these may
be grammatically acceptable, they may differ in terms of their appropriacy.
For example, some request forms are considered more polite than others,
and the appropriate use of a given request form depends on the speaker's
ability to match the form with the attributes of the listener (such as his
relative status) as well as to consider the nature of the action which is being
requested. We will see that appropriacy involves knowing when and how to
be polite as well as knowing how to exploit the resources afforded by
language for indirectness according to the demands of the given situation. It
will also become clear that appropriacy is context dependent and is achieved

collaboratively by the participants on each occasion. That is, what a speaker
deems to be appropriate has to be endorsed (either explicitly or implicitly)
by the hearer, or alternatively rejected (M. MacLure, personal communication).

The fifth component which we will be considering cuts across the
distinctions we have been making and concerns the ways in which conver-

sation can break down and the types of *repair* which can be applied. In turn-
taking, both speakers might speak simultaneously and so, for the conversation to proceed in an orderly fashion, some sort of remedial device is
required. In exchanges, a first turn might fail to elicit an expected response
and so the speaker has to repeat or adjust his utterance in order to make a
response more likely. Repairs to content are frequent. One common case is
where a speaker makes a wrong assumption about his listener's knowledge
and treats objects and persons to which he is referring as familiar, when they
are not. This often leads to a *request for clarification*, which in turn leads to
a repair of the original utterance. Finally, speakers can make inappropriate
judgements in their use of speech acts such as requests, in which case they
often repair by rephrasing or using a different, more appropriate form.

The relationships between these components of conversation and traditional levels of linguistic analysis will be brought out in our more detailed
discussion throughout the book. It might, however, be helpful to illustrate
with a few examples at this stage. Firstly, efficient turn-taking, in which
speakers avoid speaking at the same time and leaving lengthy gaps between
turns, depends on precise timing, for which a listener has to be able to
monitor the course of an ongoing turn and judge when it has reached a
point of possible completion. In order to do this, he will bring to bear his
knowledge of syntactic structure, which helps to determine whether an
utterance is complete or not, and of prosodic cues, which can indicate
whether the current speaker wishes to continue or to yield the floor. The
organization of the content of a turn also presupposes specific linguistic

abilities. For example, the specification of a person or object not present in the immediate environment can be achieved by the use of a relative clause and may also depend on tense marking in the verb phrase. Similarly, the highlighting of the main informational content of a message can depend on a speaker's ability to distinguish between old and new information, which requires an accurate usage of definite and indefinite articles as well as intonation, as in the placement of the nuclear tone. As a final example, we can take the use of appropriate request forms, where the ability to use a more polite form might depend on the prior acquisition of modal verb forms such as *could* and *would* as well as more complex grammatical structures such as *would you mind* + *verb* + *-ing*.

Our examples have suggested that conversational ability depends on the prior acquisition of specific linguistic abilities. However, as we shall see, the reverse is often the case and we will find that the acquisition of particular linguistic forms is often motivated by a requirement to communicate more effectively. To take one example, we saw that relative clauses are a means of identifying non-present discourse referents. It might be that the need to perform this communicative function motivates the acquisition of this particular syntactic structure by the child. The relationship between conversational and linguistic abilities will be a continuing underlying theme throughout this book, and we will return to it more specifically in chapter 9 when we discuss the nature of various types of conversational disability in children. But first we will look in greater detail at the various components of conversation which we have outlined.

The structure of conversation

It should be fairly obvious that utterances in conversation do not occur in isolation. Questions are usually followed by answers, complaints by apologies, excuses or counter-complaints, and so on. When we say something, we expect that what our conversational partner says next will be in some way related to what we have just said. In turn we will fit our utterances to those of our conversational partner. If this were not the case – if we never answered questions and if we never took account of the other's previous talk when making an utterance – then conversation would sound very strange indeed. People would be talking past one another, they would be unable to make sense of each other's talk, and they might suspect that the other was being rude or was drunk or insane. In other words, utterances in conversations are related to each other in such a way that the absence of an appropriate response is noticeable. Utterances do not then occur in isolation, but in some sort of sequence or structure – a situation which is in some ways analogous to the syntactic structure of sentences. In sentences, words do not occur in isolation but are related to each other in a regular and predictable way. By examining sentences, we can observe the distribution of words and morphemes, note what combinations are possible and impossible, see how they group into larger units such as noun phrases, verb phrases, and so on. In similar fashion, some analysts feel that conversation is structured and that analytic concepts such as distribution, co-occurence constraints and hierarchical units can be found in conversation just as in sentences. We will not attempt a rigorous structural analysis of conversation in this chapter but will look at some aspects of structure which are relevant to the analysis of the development of conversational ability in children.

Two types of structural unit have been proposed for conversation. The conversational analysts use in the term 'adjacency pair', while the Birmingham discourse analysts refer to the 'exchange'. Let us look at some examples of each of these.

The *adjacency pair* captures the notion that utterances often come in pairs. Thus we find examples of the following pairs of utterances in conversations:

Greeting–greeting
(1)   A: hello
      B: hello
Question–answer
(2)   A: where's John?
      B: in the pub
Statement–acknowledgement
(3)   A: Bill didn't remember my birthday
      B: oh dear

In some cases, more than one response is possible:

Request–compliance/non-compliance
(4)   A: would you mind posting this letter for me?
      B: sure/I'm too busy
Offer–acceptance/refusal
(5)   A: let me help you
      B: thanks/I can manage myself
Compliment–accept/downgrade
(6)   A: you did a fine job on those curtains
      B: thanks/oh it was nothing

We will not attempt to define the terms used here to illustrate adjacency pairs or, for the present, consider some finer points of detail concerning alternative types of response. The examples are cited merely to illustrate the ways in which pairs of related utterances can be recognized in stretches of conversation.

Adjacency pairs are not, however, sufficient as a descriptive unit. We can, for example, note that items can be inserted or embedded between a question and its answer, as in the following:

(7) A: have you seen Mary?
     B: Mary who?
     A: Mary Webster
     B: oh her, no I haven't

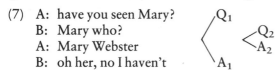

Here a second question–answer pair has been inserted between the first question (Q_1) and its answer (A_1). Such insertion or embedding would seem to be analogous to the embedding which occurs in sentences. Similarly, some utterances can be described as having a preparatory function in relation to a subsequent pair. For example, an utterance can prepare the way for a request or an invitation, as in the following examples:

(8) A: are you busy?
     B: no
     A: well then, would you mind posting a letter for me?

(9) A: are you doing anything tonight?
     B: no
     A: well then, would you like to go out for a drink?

If we identify the third turns in (8) and (9) as a request and an invitation respectively, then we might wish to analyse the first adjacency pairs not as independent question–answer pairs but as presequences – that is, as a prerequest and a preinvitation sequence.

We will not concern ourselves with the analytic problems that arise out of the notions of inserted sequences and presequences, or with the intricate interactional work that such units can be seen to accomplish (see, for example, Schegloff and Sacks 1973). We can note that, as far as structure is concerned, the adjacency pair is an unsatisfactory descriptive unit on at least two counts. In the first place, it does not account for relations between all the utterances in a conversation, even allowing for embedding and presequences. And secondly, within the descriptive apparatus of the conversational analysts, the units are not defined explicitly enough for us to be able to delimit the range of possible second pair parts and thus distinguish possible from impossible responses.

Like the adjacency pair, the *exchange* is the minimal unit of interaction, consisting of at least one move by one speaker which initiates the exchange, and a second move by another speaker which responds to this initiation. *Initiations* are prospective; that is, they set up predictions about what type of response is possible. Thus the first lines of the adjacency pairs (1)–(6) are initiating moves. *Responses* are retrospective; they fulfil the predictions set up by a preceding initiating move. The second lines in (1)–(6) are thus responses. A third type of move, *follow-up*, differs from initiations and responses in that it is neither prospective nor retrospective. That is, it does not predict a further response, nor is it a response to a preceding move.[1] The clearest cases of follow-up moves are to be found in classroom discourse, where the teacher elicits a response from a pupil and then follows this response with a move which accepts or evaluates the responses. The following is an example (Sinclair and Coulthard 1975:68):

(10)	1	Teacher:	what makes a road slippery?	Initiation
	2	Pupil:	you might have rain or snow on it	Response
	3	Teacher:	yes, snow, ice	Follow-up
	4		anything else make a road slippery?	Initiation
	5	Pupil:	erm oil	Response
	6	Teacher	oil makes a road slippery when it's mixed with water doesn't it?	Follow-up

In this example there are two exchanges, each with the structure initiation–response–feedback (IRF). The same structure also occurs in speech therapy in therapist–patient talk (Crystal 1979). In addition, we can note that the teacher's turn at lines 3 and 4 consists of two moves, one which is F in the first exchange and the other which is I in the second exchange. Thus the basic unit in interaction is not the turn but the move, as speakers can accomplish more than one move within any turn.

In classroom discourse, as in speech therapy, follow-up moves are frequent in exchanges in which the initiating move was an elicitation. Follow-up moves can, however, also occur in other eliciting exchanges, although they are not necessarily obligatory. The following is an example from doctor–patient discourse, cited in Coulthard and Brazil (1981:90):

(11)	Doctor:	and what's been the matter recently?	Initiation
	Patient:	well I've had pains around the heart	Response
	Doctor:	pains in your chest then	Follow-up
	Patient:	yes	Follow-up

We might wonder about the classification of the doctor's second move as follow-up, as it seems that the patient's second move is a response to this. If this is so, then the doctor's move might be seen as having predicted it; in other words, the doctor's move would be an initiation. Such problems of classification arise frequently, as a close inspection of examples discussed by Coulthard and colleagues will reveal. In some cases, however, intonation can help in the classification of moves. Speakers constrain the next type of move by the pitch on which they terminate their move. A high termination seeks confirmation, whereas a low termination marks the end of prospective constraints and usually occurs at exchange boundaries where the next speaker is not constrained to make a further response or follow-up, although he may do so if he wishes (Coulthard and Brazil 1981). So, in (11), if the doctor's second move had high termination, it would be classified as an initiation. With low termination, it would not set up prospective constraints and would, in this case, be a follow-up.

The Birmingham discourse analysts propose a fourth move, which is both prospective and retrospective. This move is coded R/I; it is simultaneously a response and an initiation. The following is an example:

(12)	A: where's the typewriter?	I
	B: is it in the cupboard?	R/I
	A: no	R

Coulthard and colleagues restrict R/I moves to polar interrogatives. The framework which we will present in the following will also include R/I moves, but will allow a larger class of elements to occur at this place in structure.

‑ Bringing together the discussion so far, we have seen that utterances in conversation form structures, which we can call exchanges. Utterances can be prospective, in which case they set up predictions or constraints on a next utterance. They can be retrospective, in which case they fulfil the predictions of a preceding utterance. In addition, utterances can be simultaneously prospective and retrospective or they can be neither prospective nor retrospective. We can illustrate these types as follows:

	Prospective	Retrospective
I	+	−
R	−	+
R/I	+	+
F	−	−

We have now introduced the types of move which occur in exchanges. The next point concerns their privileges of occurrence, that is, the orders in which they can occur and the combinations which are possible. Coulthard and Brazil propose that the largest exchange consists of five moves, in the following structure:

I	R/I	R	F	F

An expanded version of (12) illustrates this structure (Coulthard and Brazil 1981:103):

(13)	A: where's the typewriter?	I
	B: is it in the cupboard?	R/I
	A: no	R
	B: oh dear	F
	A: yeah	F

Alternative proposals for exchange structure within the same general framework can be found in Berry (1981), Burton (1981) and Stubbs (1981).

The problem that we now have to face is that much of conversational data, including the child data to be analysed in the following, does not fit neatly into the exchange structures proposed by the Birmingham discourse analysts. One of the problems is that speakers do not have to be compliant, polite or collaborative in everyday conversation. In the terms we have been using, they do not have to meet the predictions set up by a preceding utterance. Take, for example, the following set of possible responses to the initiating utterance *where's John?*:

(14) (a) at home
     (b) John who?
     (c) how should I know?
     (d) why do you want to know?
     (e) I'm not telling you

Only response (a) fulfils the predictions of the initiation in the narrow sense in which Coulthard and colleagues intend the term 'prediction' to be understood. Of the other responses, (b) asks for clarification, (c) suggests that the initiation has been inappropriately addressed to the wrong person, (d) queries the reason for the initiation and (e) refuses to provide the response. Yet these responses are certainly more appropriate than the following:

(15) (f) ten o'clock
     (g) green
     (h) two pints of beer

It would be difficult to see any relevance between the utterances (f)–(h) and the question *where's John?*

One way of tackling this problem is to distinguish between those utterances which support the discourse expectations of a preceding initiation and those which do not. Burton (1981) makes the distinction between supports and challenges. In (14), (a) supports the discourse expectations of *where's John?* Responses (b)–(e) challenge its discourse expectations in a variety of predictable ways, either by taking issue with some aspect of the content (as in (b)), or by querying the conditions underlying the speech act being performed in the initiating utterance. So, in the case of *where's John?*, we have an utterance which can be described as a request for information. Among the conditions underlying the appropriate performance of requests for information are the following: that the request is sensible, that the speaker of the request does not know the answer, that the speaker has the right to ask, that the addressee might know the answer, that the addressee is obliged to give an answer, and so on. The challenging responses (b)–(e) (and, of course, many other possible responses), can thus be systematically related to these conditions which underlie the requesting of information. In these cases, the addressee recognizes that a request for information has been made and demonstrates this in the response without actually supplying the information. This set of responses, which Burton calls 'challenges', are to be distinguished from irrelevant or deviant responses, as in (15), where the speaker either does not recognize that a request for information has been made, or misunderstands its content, or is being rude or intentionally irrelevant, and so on.

The question now arises of how challenging utterances are to be handled within the framework which we have been developing. We have already been referring to these utterances as responses. On the other hand, some of them can also be considered as initiations, as they set up expectations for further responses. This is particularly the case with requests for clarification and other challenges realized by interrogative syntax, but can include many other types of utterance. Burton treats challenges as initiations for this reason. However, the problem is that this fails to recognize that they are also functioning as responses. A small sample of child data will illustrate the problem:

(16) 1 Heather: do you like his big brother?
     2 Siobhan: no his br- that is his friend and he lives in a different
               house see?
     3 Heather: he lives in the same house
     4   that wee boy lives in the same house and the big boy
               lives in the same house
     5 Siobhan: no
     6   see the one with the sort of curly hair and black hair
               well he lives in a different house
     7 Heather: he doesn't

Looking at this extract informally, we can see that line 1 initiates by eliciting a verbal response in line 2. Yet line 2 does more than respond – it challenges the content of line 1. Moving on, we find that line 3 also challenges line 2 by rejecting its content. The same applies to line 5 in relation to line 4, and line 7 in relation to line 6. In other words, we have a series of initiations but no responses. This seems counter-intuitive. We can see how each utterance relates to its predecessor. We can also see how each utterance predicts a further response. In other words, it seems that a more satisfactory analysis would view the utterances in this sample as responding as well as initiating. Thus we might compare the following candidate analyses of the data of (16):

			A	B
(16) 1	Heather:	do you like his big brother?	I	I
2	Siobhan:	no his br- that is his friend and he lives in a different house see?	I	R/I
3	Heather:	he lives in the same house	I	R/I
4		that wee boy lives in the same house and the big boy lives in the same house		
5	Siobhan:	no	I	R/I
6		see the one with the sort of curly hair and black hair well he lives in a different house		
7	Heather:	he doesn't	I	R/I

We can see how analysis A fails to show that the children in this example are taking account of each other's utterances by responding to them and at the same time setting up expectations for further talk. Analysis B meets this requirement. However, analysis B seems to suggest that, once an exchange has been initiated, utterances simply follow one another until the topic is exhausted. In other words, the notion of structure is sacrificed, as utterances cannot be clearly assigned to one structural position. This would be analogous to a syntactic analysis which was unable to assign items clearly, for example, by allowing an item to be simultaneously part of a noun phrase as well as part of a verb phrase.

These problems can be met in various ways. Firstly, we can point out that conversational structure does not necessarily have to fit into the same patterns as syntactic structure. Where analogies can be found, these are useful as a means of demonstrating that conversation does have a structure. There is no profit, however, in rigidly applying a framework which does not fit.

A second point is that conversation is a joint production, which is created locally on a turn-by-turn (or move-by-move) basis. We need to distinguish between structures which can be imposed *post hoc* by the analysts and structures which the conversationalists are creating for themselves as they talk. In informal terms, conversationalists recognize that they are being asked for information, are the recipients of a complaint, compliment, excuse and so on. They usually say something relevant to what their partner has just said and, in so doing, usually expect their partner to say something in return. In some cases, nothing further needs to be said and a new topic can be initiated. Whatever happens, conversationalists can recognize whether their questions have been answered or their complaints met, and can distinguish these from *nonsequiturs*, misunderstandings and failures to respond. In other words, conversationalists create structure jointly as their talk proceeds. An analysis should reflect this process.

This leads to a third point – the need to define our terms more explicitly.[2] We have defined initiations as utterances which predict a response. We can also note that initiations can be marked in various ways: syntactically by mood, lack of ellipsis, lack of anaphoric reference and definiteness, prosodically by high pitch relative to the preceding utterance, and additionally by the use of response–eliciting devices such as vocatives and tags. Responses have been defined as being predicted by a preceding utterance. They are also marked in various ways: syntactically they permit ellipsis, anaphoric reference and definiteness, while prosodically they are realized by a step down in pitch relative to the pitch of the preceding utterance. Response/initiations share features of both. So, for example, in (16) Siobhan's line 2 contains anaphoric pronouns (*his, he*), marking this utterance as a response, but also the response–eliciting *see*, which marks it as an initiation. Obviously these definitions are fairly exploratory and by no means watertight. They are intended to reflect the means whereby conversationalists recognize the status of utterances as they occur at any given point in a conversation. The fact that they are not watertight may reflect the indeterminate nature of conversation, for, in many cases, conversationalists can disagree as to whether a given utterance requires a further response or not.

Before concluding this section, we should note that utterances vary in the extent to which they are prospective. Some utterances are highly prospective; if no response were to occur, then its absence would be noticeable. Requests for information and clarification are highly prospective; utterances which provide information are less so. Some utterances provide for further talk without actually predicting a further response. These utterances provide material for the other speaker to use as a means of continuing the conversation, if he so wishes. For example, in (16) Heather's *he doesn't* (as well as some of the preceding utterances) provides for but does not predict further responses. We will indicate such utterances as R/(I), meaning that a further response is optional. As yet, there is no explicit means of recognizing these utterances in data, beyond the rather unsatisfactory process of noting them on the basis of whatever response they actually receive. This has the benefit, however, of reflecting the way in which conversationalists can exploit the latent prospectiveness of an utterance by responding to it and thus constituting it retroactively as an initiation. We shall see that this process is crucial to our developmental account of conversation (see, in particular, chapters 3 and 6).

Accomplishing initiations

We have defined initiations as utterances which predict a response. Initiations open conversational exchanges. However, we have not looked at the interactional 'work' which is involved in the successful initiation of an exchange. That is the purpose of this section.

Among the various prerequisites for a successful initiation of conversation, we would assumed on a common-sense basis that the speaker must be able to gain and maintain the listener's attention and take account of the listener's knowledge in the construction of the initiating utterance. In addition, he should be able to take various remedial steps to reinitiate if the original initiation is unsuccessful. This shaping of an utterance to the needs of a listener has been referred to as 'recipient design' (Sacks and Schegloff 1979). In chapter 4 we will be exploring the extent to which children's initiations exhibit recipient design.

Before looking at the devices which can be used to accomplish initiations, we can introduce the problem informally by looking at an example of an unsuccessful initiation. The following utterance was addressed by Siobhan (aged 3;8) to Simon (aged 3;6), a previously unfamiliar child:

(17) Siobhan: but Heather's four now

Just before this utterance, the children had been discussing their ages. Siobhan then referred to Heather, who was unknown to Simon. She did not take account of the fact that Simon did not know Heather, by saying, for example, *my friend Heather.* Simon in turn did not request clarification, by asking, for example, *who's Heather?* So the children's communication was unsuccessful on two counts: firstly because Siobhan did not adequately identify the referents of her talk for her listener, and secondly because Simon did not take this up and seek clarification. (Other explanations are, of course, possible. For example, Simon may not have been interested enough to pursue the matter further.)

Looking at an unsuccessful initiation as in (17) helps to draw our attention to what is involved in the initiation of conversational topics. We can now turn to a more explicit attempt to specify the interactional work involved in initiations. Let us look at one proposal by Keenan and Schieffelin (1976) in which the following steps were identified:

1 The speaker must secure the attention of the listener.
2 The speaker must articulate his utterance clearly.
3 The speaker must provide sufficient information for the listener to identify objects and persons included in the discourse topic.
4 The speaker must provide sufficient information for the listener to reconstruct the semantic relations obtaining between referents in the discourse topic.

Initiations can break down at any one of these stages. We will focus in particular on steps 1 and 3, which we will refer to respectively as *attention-getting* and *attention-directing.* The devices used to accomplish these steps are both verbal and non-verbal. Devices which can be used to get the listener's attention are set out in figure 3.

Non-verbal	Verbal
Strategy 1	
1 Pointing	1 Name
2 Looking at object	2 Deictic pronoun or adverb
	3 Expressive particle
	4 Greeting term
Strategy 2	
1 Touching hearer:	1 Vocative
(a) Pulling	2 Locating directives, e.g.
(b) Tugging	*look at X, see X*
(c) Tapping	3 Interrogatives
2 Showing X to hearer,	4 Prosodic devices:
holding up X	(a) Whining
3 Giving X to hearer	(b) Screaming
4 Initiating eye contact	(c) Increasing pitch or amplitude
5 Movement towards hearer	(d) Whispering

Figure 3 Attention-getting strategies and means for expressing them

These devices, some of which we will illustrating in more detail in chapter 4, are multifunctional. Those listed under strategy 1 are also used by a speaker as a means of indicating that he has noticed an object. They can be repeated as a means of getting the listener's attention. Those listed under strategy 2 are primarily attention-getting but can also be used to direct attention to an object referred to in the utterance.

Attention-directing describes the devices used to identify for the listener the objects, persons and events referred to in the utterance. To take an example discussed by Atkinson (1979): if a speaker is to say *the car is broken*, he must, if he wishes the addressee to understand, ensure that the addressee can identify the referent of *the car*. The use of the noun phrase would not normally be sufficient unless the speaker could rely on one or more situational factors which would enable the addressee's identification, such as whether the car had been previously discussed in the conversation. The devices used depend on whether the referents are physically identifiable or not. For example, pointing would suffice in this example if the car being referred to was physically present. Referents which are not physically present require verbal attention-directing devices such as *you know X?, you remember X?*; or relative clauses, for example, *you know the car I bought last week?*

It might be argued that the work involved in accomplishing initiations is self-evident and therefore unproblematic. The developmental literature would persuade us otherwise. Both linguistic and cognitive knowledge is involved. For example, the appropriate usage of the definite article *the* involves, among other things, the ability to assess the extent of the listener's knowledge in order to know whether a reference should be marked as specific or non-specific. Children as old as nine years may have problems with the appropriate usage of the articles (Karmiloff-Smith 1979). One aspect of this difficulty is cognitive and involves the ability to assess the other's state of knowledge. The other aspect is linguistic; this involves the ability to relate articles to the complex system of determiners of which they are a part. Similarly, the ability to specify referents appropriately can depend on the prior acquisition of relative clause structures, tense and aspect, as can be seen from some of the examples we have cited.

It is often the case, however, that initiations are unsuccessful. Sometimes no response is forthcoming where one would have been expected. In other cases, the response is deemed unsatisfactory by the speaker who initiated the exchange. *Reinitiations* can occur in both cases, where the speaker tries again to secure a satisfactory response. Reinitiations are important developmentally as they give us some insight into children's ability to pinpoint the possible reasons why their utterances have failed to secure a response and the means they adopt to remedy this. Some examples will help to illustrate this point. If lack of attention is diagnosed as the source of the problem, the speaker can use an attention-getting device in the reinitiation. For example:

(18) Heather: (turns to face author)
                I want a drink and a biscuit
     Siobhan: I wanta get a drink and a biscuit (turns to face author)
     Heather: I want a drink and a biscuit
     Siobhan: I want a drink and a biscuit
     Heather: hey
                I want a drink and a biscuit
     Author: OK

Here, in addition to repeating the initiation, the children turn to face their addressee and then Heather uses *hey* as an additional attention-getting device. Combinations of verbal and non-verbal devices can be used in reinitiations. In the following example, Siobhan fails to respond to Heather's request for information. After a pause of 5 seconds, Heather tries again with a vocative. She repeats this strategy after a further 1 second. This time she increases volume and leans over towards Siobhan. Siobhan responds, but Heather rejects the response and reinitiates this rejection after a further 7 seconds, rephrasing her utterance and adding Siobhan's name:

(19) Heather: then why do you not look for them?
                (5.0)
                Siobhan
                (1.0)
                Siobhan (increases volume, leans over to face Siobhan)
     Siobhan: I'm too busy to talk

Heather: you are not
         (7.0)
         you aren't, Siobhan
Siobhan: yes I am

In addition to repeating initiations, speakers can rephrase the original utterance in various ways. Rephrasings are interesting developmentally, as they show children's ability to modify their utterances to take account of unsuccessful initiations, for example by isolating, reducing, expanding or reordering sentence constituents. Rephrased reinitiations will be illustrated in greater detail in chapter 4.

In sum, then, initiating an exchange involves both attention-getting and attention-directing. Both verbal and non-verbal devices can be used. Re-initiations can be accomplished either by whole or partial repetition of the original initiation with or without the various devices such as gaze, pointing, volume increase, vocatives and so on, or by a rephrasing of the initiation with or without the initiating devices.

Requests for action

We turn now to one of the most common initiating speech acts – requests for action. Requests for action (or *directives*) are attempts to get the hearer to perform an action. They can be realized by a wide range of grammatical forms. Consider, for example, the following forms which might be used by a parent asking a child to pick up a coat which has been left on the floor:

(20) pick up your coat
(21) would you pick up your coat?
(22) is that your coat on the floor?
(23) isn't that your coat on the floor?
(24) what's that on the floor?
(25) how many times have I told you not to leave your coat on the floor?
(26) you've left your coat on the floor
(27) you're a lazy so-and-so
(28) oh not again!
(29) do you think I've got all the time in the world to run around after you?

This is only a small selection of the possible forms which could be used to convey this request. As we can see, various syntactic forms can be used. For example, a request may be realized by an imperative, an interrogative, a declarative, an exclamative or a moodless form. In all the examples except (20) the request is not conveyed through the literal meaning of the utterance alone. Some of the forms are more indirect than others. For example, in (20) and (21) the required action is specified, but not in the other examples, while in (24), (27), (28) and (29) the object of the requested action is not mentioned either. The examples also vary in terms of politeness. We might accept (21), (22) and (23) as being reasonably polite, although other factors such as intonation could modify this. We would probably find (27), (28) and (29) particularly impolite. Finally, we might note that the selection of a particular form is closely related to the situation. For example, in this case politeness is not required, as a parent is requesting from a child an action which ought to have been done and which was the child's responsibility. So the nature of the relationship between the participants and of the requested action have a further bearing on the choice of request form.

Requests for action are interesting, then, as the selection of request forms is determined by social features of the speech situation such as the status of the participants, the degree of politeness to be conveyed, and so on. In a developmental study they indicate the extent to which children are aware of these pragmatic factors. Speech act theory is concerned with explaining the pragmatics of requests and relating their forms to their functions. For our purposes, we can apply the request form categories developed by Ervin-Tripp (1976) on the basis of transcripts of adult speech and used subsequently in an extensive analysis of children's requests (Ervin-Tripp 1977b):

Personal need or desire statements
I need a match (directed downwards to subordinates primarily)
Imperatives
gimme a match (directed to subordinates or familiar equals)
Embedded imperatives
could you give me a match? (directed most often to unfamiliar people, or those differing in rank)
Permission directives
may I have a match? (possibly addressed upward more often than downward in rank)
Question directives
have you gotta match? (non-compliance possible)
Hints
the matches are all gone (non-compliance possible, can be used in cases of familiarity or routine roles).

These categories indicate various degrees of indirectness and politeness, as in examples (20)–(29). However, although some of the forms are indirect in the sense that their request function involves more than their literal meaning, many of the forms have become conventionalized and are hardly likely to be interpreted according to their literal meaning. For example, *is Sybil there?* (telephone), *are there any vacancies?* (hotel desk), *you're in the way* (to child in doorway). These forms are usually interpreted as requests without any great difficulty, and indeed it sometimes requires special circumstances for them to be used to convey their literal meanings alone.

We can note, however, that the potential ambiguity of some of these forms is of strategic significance. Question directives and hints are frequently used as strategic devices when potential non-compliance is anticipated, as the hearer has the option of disregarding their directive function and responding to their literal meaning. Generally speaking, it seems that the greater the 'costs' involved in the request from the point of view of its recipient as well as the greater the risk of refusal, the more indirect the request is likely to be (Brown and Levinson 1978).

Another way of looking at requests concerns the conditions underlying their appropriate performance and the beliefs, expectations and attitudes of the participants in respect of these conditions. Thus Searle (1969), for example, includes in his conditions for requests the speaker's assumption that the hearer is able to perform the requested action, the sincerity condition that the speaker wants the hearer to perform the action, and the assumption by both the speaker and the hearer that the hearer will not do the act in the normal course of events of his own accord (otherwise the request would be redundant). These conditions have also been used to explain indirect request forms and non-complaint responses to requests. As this aspect of requests will be important for our subsequent analysis, we will examine some examples, drawing on the work of Labov and Fanshel (1977).

The conditions which Labov and Fanshel propose for requests are: that there is a need for the action, that there is a need for the request, that the hearer is able to perform the action, is willing or obliged to perform the action, and that the speaker has the right to make the request. If a speaker makes an assertion or request for information about these conditions, then he can be heard as making a request for action. In addition, the speaker can also refer to the existential state of the action (whether it has been performed or not), the consequences of performing it and the time when it might be performed. We can illustrate with Labov and Fanshel's examples:

Existential status
have you dusted yet?
you don't seem to have dusted this room yet
Consequences
how would it look if you were to dust this room?
this room would look a lot better if you dusted it
Time referents
when do you plan to dust?
I imagine you will be dusting this evening
Need for the action
don't you think the dust is pretty thick?
this place is really dusty

Need for the request
are you planning to dust this room?
I don't have to remind you to dust this room
Ability
can you grab a dust rag and just dust around?
you have time enough to dust before you go
Willingness
would you mind picking up a dust rag?
I'm sure you wouldn't mind picking up a dust rag and just dusting around
Obligation
isn't it your turn to dust?
you ought to do your part in keeping this place clean
Rights
didn't you ask me to remind you to dust this place?
I'm supposed to look after this place, but not do all the work

A few examples will suffice to illustrate how these conditions can also be used in putting off a request:

Existential status
isn't it dusted already?
I did dust it
Time
is it 3.00?
it's not the time I usually clean house
Need for action
it looks clean to me
doesn't it look clean to you?
Obligation
is it my turn to dust the room?
it's not my job

As we will see in chapter 5, there is some evidence that children are aware of the social implications of requests and of the conditions underlying requests and their responses.

It is important, however, to realize that speech acts such as requests occur not as isolated events but in interactive sequences. Treating requests in isolation disregards several important sequential considerations. For example, it is important in the case of reinitiated requests to show how the repeated or rephrased form relates to the original initiation. The same applies to the means used to express non-compliance. Even more important are the interactional relations between the utterances of the different speakers – for example, the ways in which a form chosen to reinitiate a request relates to the form used to express non-compliance. In this way we can come closer to capturing the nature of the interaction if we treat requests and their responses as ongoing, negotiated events produced at particular points in the interaction by the participants, each with his own aims, interests and strategies.

Let us look at the way request sequences can develop. For a working definition, we shall view a request sequence as consisting of any material relating to the request or, following Garvey (1975:49), as 'the scope of discourse within which the attention of the speaker and addressee is directed to the accomplishment of the request'.

In request sequences a request for action can be followed by either a compliant or a non-complaint response. Various embeddings such as clarification requests or delaying responses are also possible. Following compliance, the options available to the requester are limited – either to acknowledge the action implicity or explicitly and so terminate the sequence, or to reject the action if it turns out to be unsatisfactory. Following non-compliance, the requester can either accept explicitly or implicitly, or else reinitiate the request in some way. This can be achieved by various means which include repeating or rephrasing the request, providing justification or support for the request, or rejecting some aspect of the non-compliant response. The requestee can then either comply or continue to express non-compliance by providing additional justifications, rejecting the requester's justifications, rejecting the requester's rejections of the requestee's previous justifications, and so on. Some of these possibilities are set out in figure 4.

Speaker A	Speaker B	Speaker A	Speaker B
request action	action (+ acknowledge)	(acknowledge action)	
request action	refuse	withdraw: change topic	
request action	refuse + justification	accept justification	
request action	refuse + justification	reject justification	reject rejection of justification
request action + justification	reject justification + alternative suggestion	reject alternative suggestion + rephrase request	refuse
rephrase request	request clarification	clarification	comply

Figure 4 Request sequences: possible structures

These are just some of the sequences which can occur following a non-compliant response to a request for action. Each participant has available a series of options at each stage in the sequence. However, the selection of a given option is determined by the nature of the preceding move. That is, each participant constructs his move in relation to the other's preceding move and also in consideration of the potential consequences of his own current move. A model of discourse which seeks to capture the interactional processes involved in such sequences needs to take account of the ways in which participants make ongoing assessments about the current state of play and design their moves accordingly. We will see in chapter 5 how children of preschool age have gone some way towards mastery of these complex interactional strategies.

Throughout this and the preceding sections we have been looking at structural and pragmatic aspects of conversation. We have also emphasized the interactional 'work' involved in the initiation and management of conversation. In the next section we will focus specifically on some aspects of this interactional work, looking in particular at conversational turn-taking and the remedial devices used in cases of conversational breakdown.

Conversational processes

In the preceding section we made the point that a description of conversation should reflect its dynamic processes, showing how conversation is a joint production resulting from the interactional 'work' of the participants. We turn now to a more specific consideration of some aspects of these conversational processes. In particular, we will be focusing on conversational turn-taking and the repair of conversational breakdown.

Conversational turn-taking

We can observe from even a superficial analysis of conversation that participants regularly take turns, switching between the roles of speaker and listener. Generally one participant speaks at a time and the transition from one speaker to the next is usually accomplished with a minimum of gap between the turns as well as little overlapping between the current and the next speakers. What is not clear, however, is that the orderly and smooth transition of turns is the result of the collaborative activity of the current and next speakers and that this activity often involves extremely precise timing. In casual conversation the size of turns is not specified in advance. How then is the next speaker to know when the current speaker has completed his turn? Detailed analyses of conversational turn-taking have shown that it is not the case that potential next speakers wait until the current speaker has stopped talking before they begin their turn. If this were the case, then there would be regular, noticeable gaps between turns. Rather, what seems to happen is that potential next speakers anticipate the possible completion of the current turn and start up at that point.

Let us consider how potential next speakers anticipate points of possible turn completion. According to Sacks et al. (1974), speakers are allowed a turn consisting of one unit, which can be a word, phrase or sentence. The length of a unit is partially determined by sequential considerations. For example, a turn which is in answer to a preceding question will be potentially complete when the information requested in the question has been given. After completing their unit, speakers reach a possible turn completion point where a next speaker can legitimately start up to speak without being seen to be interrupting. Note that we talk of possible completion, because a current speaker may opt to continue at this point. Some evidence that participants are guided by this principle comes from the occurrence of overlap at points where the next speaker has falsely predicted completion. For example (Daden 1975:20):

(30) K: I saw 'em last night <u>at uhm school</u>
    J: <u>they're a riot</u>

Here overlap has occurred because J has predicted a possible turn completion point after *last night* in K's utterance and starts his turn at this point. However, K continues and overlap occurs.

Both participants are involved in the work of ensuring smooth transition between turns. The speaker constructs his turn in such a way that the listener can project its possible completion. One potential indication is the completion of a grammatical clause. Others include the use of response-eliciting devices such as tag questions, and exit devices such as falling intonation contours, as well as non-verbal cues such as the termination of any hand signal gesticulation used during the turn (Duncan 1972). Speakers can also construct their turn in such a way that possible completion points are delayed. One way is to use a subordinating conjunction such as *if*, which ensures that the speaker will be allowed at least one subordinate and one main clause before reaching a possible completion point. Speakers also use non-verbal within-turn signals as attempts to prevent transition to a next speaker at points of possible completion (Duncan 1973).

The listener who wishes to become the next speaker is also involved in the 'work' of avoiding gap and overlap. A potential next speaker must analyse the ongoing talk in order to be able to produce a relevant next utterance at the appropriate point. Jefferson (1973) has demonstrated that conversationalists display precision timing in starting to talk no sooner and no later than the appropriate point. For example, a next speaker can propose a completion to an utterance which is as yet incomplete by predicting what the current speaker is likely to say and by starting up at the precise point with a word or phrase which fits into the syntax of the ongoing turn (Jefferson 1973):

(31) Louise: no a Soshe is someone who <u>is a carbon copy</u>
              of their friend
     Roger: <u>drinks Pepsi</u>

To summarize: turn-taking is a good example of the dynamic processes of conversation in which participants negotiate speaker transition on a moment-by-moment basis at each transition relevance place. Turn-taking is *locally managed*, because it operates with one transition at a time. It is also *interactionally managed* as it depends on the collaborative activities of the participants for its smooth functioning (Sacks et al. 1974). As we shall see in chapter 7, even young children have acquired some aspects of this complex process before reaching school age.

Conversational breakdown and repair

There are often points in the course of a conversation where breakdown occurs and the participants perform interactional work to repair this breakdown. The most obvious examples are where a listener has failed to hear or understand part or the whole of a preceding utterance and uses the next turn to make a request for clarification, as in the following example from the child data:

(32) Siobhan: I see shells on that lorry?
     Heather: what lorry?
     Siobhan: that one that's blue

We can divide repairs into four main types, according to whether the repair is initiated by the current or other speaker and according to who carries out the repair (Schegloff et al. 1977). Thus the four types are:

1 Self-initiated self-repair
2 Other-initiated self-repair
3 Self-initiated other-repair
4 Other-initiated other-repair.

Example (32) illustrates type 2 as the repair is initiated by the next speaker but carried out by the current speaker. We will refer to this type as request for clarification. Type 4 involves other-correction, where the next speaker takes up some aspect of the speaker's talk and repairs it, as in the following example:

(33) Siobhan: I'm going to put mine in my basket so I nam
    Heather: I
        so I nam
        say I am

Here rather than continuing with a relevant next utterance Heather picks up Siobhan's *I nam* and corrects it to *I am*.

Type 3, where the current speaker initiates a repair but the repair is carried out by the next speaker, is illustrated by the following example:

(34) Siobhan: you have to have . um hard numbers and I have to have (0.4)
    Heather: easy numbers
    Siobhan: yea

Here Siobhan initiates a repair by pausing before a point of possible completion. Heather offers a candidate repair which Siobhan accepts. As this type of repair usually involves some aspect of turn-taking, we will deal with its developmental aspects in the section on children's conversational turn-taking in chapter 7.

The first type of repair, which is both initiated and carried out by the current speaker, will be referred to as *self-repair*. The following is an example:

(35) Heather: so your na- so your name hasn't got . um
        so your . so . so you aren't a girl .
        you're a boy

Here Heather initiates the repair by cutting off *name* after *na-* and restarting the clause. After *got* there is a brief pause followed by *um*, then another restart, broken off after *your*. The solution to the repair in this case is a complete restructuring of the originally projected sentence.

Repairs are interesting developmentally for several reasons. Clarification requests show how children can diagnose causes of conversational break-down and propose remedies, ranging from non-specific requests for repetition to specific queries about particular constituents of the preceding utterance (Garvey 1979). The child who carries out the repair has to be able to recognize what the problem is and then carry out the appropriate solution. It would not, for instance, be appropriate to simply repeat when more specific information is requested (as in (32)). Clarification requests interrupt the conversation and so it is possible to see them as embedded within an ongoing sequence. In some descriptions they have been referred to as 'insertion' or 'side sequences'. It is interesting to note how the ongoing conversation is resumed following the clarification request sequence. One way which is often used by adults is to resume with *so* or *and*, as if incorporating the content of the embedded sequence into the syntax of the ongoing sequence. A detailed consideration of the data in chapter 7 will indicate the extent to which preschool children can cope with these sequential aspects of conversation.

Other-corrections are similar to clarification requests, as the speaker who initiates the repair has to diagnose a problem. Here, however, the same person carries out the repair. One particularly important aspect of other-corrections concerns their social implications. Overt correction of another conversationalist is a potential face-threatening act (Brown and Levinson 1978) and so is often avoided in polite adult conversation. Where other-correction is unavoidable, the correction is often mitigated in various ways or presented as an invitation to self-correct, that is, as a request for clarification (Schegloff et al. 1977). It will be interesting to note how far children have developed this aspect of socially skilled behaviour in their conversations.

Finally, we come to self-repairs. Self-repairs can be occasioned by various factors. They can be related to speech planning and production processes, to affective factors such as emotional state, tiredness and so on, to memory lapses and other degeneracies of performance. They can also be related to interactional factors, such as the anticipation of problems of identifying referents sufficiently for the listener. Goodwin (1981), for example, has shown how various interactional phenomena, such as the extent of eye contact between the participants, the speaker's assessment of the degree of informativity of the content of his utterance in relation to its addressee, and his modifications of the ongoing utterance during the course of its production as a means of more adequate *recipient design*, can all contribute to the occurrence of self-repairs. We will also see that self-repairs by children are interesting in that they indicate the development of children's ability to monitor their own speech and correct it, where necessary.

Conversational principles

The final aspect of conversation which we will consider in this chapter concerns general conversational principles or maxims. Here we are concerned with general principles to which participants in conversation usually adhere. Grice (1975) describes a set of such principles for co-operative conversation. These include maxims such as being relevant, informative, orderly and truthful. Grice sees the purpose of talk as being 'a maximally effective exchange of information' (Grice 1975:47). As we have emphasized throughout, however, conversational interaction involves more than the exchange of information and indeed, in many cases, a maximally effective exchange of information is not considered desirable from a social point of view. So, in addition to Gricean maxims we need a set of principles to account for socially skilled aspects of conversation. One such proposal has been made by Lakoff (1973a), who describes rules of politeness in conversation. These include the following:

1 Don't impose – remain aloof.
2 Give options.
3 Make the other feel good.

The first rule can be explained in terms of free and non-free goods in conversation. Generally speaking, information such as the time or street directions are considered free goods – that is, if requested, the addressee is obliged to supply this information if possible. Other information is often considered non-free – such as a person's age, income, sex life and so on. To request information about these would be to violate the first maxim of politeness. Here again it is important to note that the distinction between free and non-free is context dependent. For example, asking the time of late-staying guests, or during a lecture, would not necessarily be seen as a free goods transaction. On the other hand, asking about age and income, and perhaps even sex, could be seen as free goods in, for example, Social Security interviews.[3] As far as the second rule is concerned, one way in which speakers can appear to give options can be seen in the choice of request forms which we were considering earlier. The use of a form such as *would you mind opening the door* as opposed to *open the door* is considered more polite as it appears to give the addressee the option of refusing. Finally, the third rule can be related to the avoidance of face-threatening acts but also to more positive behaviours such as the appropriate offering of compliments, or congratulations.

Towards a profile of conversational ability?

Having looked in some detail at various aspects of conversation, it might be helpful to bring together the main points in preparation for the detailed empirical analysis which is to follow. We must emphasize that the aspects of conversation that we have been describing are only suggestive of what is involved in socially skilled conversational interaction. We do not know enough about the nature of conversation to enable us to present a model of the mature adult conversationalist against which we can measure conversational development in children. For this reason a profile of conversational development, which might form investigations of conversational disorders on analogy with similar profiles for the areas of phonology, prosody, syntax and semantics (see Crystal 1982), would be premature. We can, however, present a preliminary checklist based on our discussion so far, against which we can assess the development of the children to be analysed in the course of this book. Each of the behaviours can be analysed according to their rate of occurrence in the data. For the present, we will make a rough division between rates of occurrence: regularly, occasionally, rarely and never.

We can begin with turn-taking. The first step is to note the extent to which the subject takes turns in conversation. Obviously this will depend crucially on the nature of the interaction and the efforts of the child's interlocutors. However, some assessment of the degree of turn-taking is an initial indication of whether a child can engage in conversation or not. The next stage is to consider interturn gap. As we will see later, development proceeds from long gaps of more than 5 seconds in very young children to minimal gaps of less than 1 second. Following this, we can consider the occurrence of overlaps which are due to attempts to predict possible turn completion points. We are treating this type of overlap as a positive indicator of development as it depends on the ability to process and analyse ongoing turns. Overlap is accidental and is due to the speaker continuing beyond possible turn completion points, as opposed to the overlap which occurs when a listener interrupts before a possible completion point. Finally we can consider ways in which overlapped turns are repaired. These points can be summarized as in figure 5.

	Regularly	*Occasionally*	*Rarely*	*Never*
Takes turns in conversation				

Gaps between turns:
    more than 5 seconds
    more than 1 second but
    less than 5 seconds
    less than 1 second				

Overlaps due to attempts to predict possible completion points				
Repairs of overlaps				

Figure 5 Turn-taking

Turning now to conversational structure, we will distinguish between responses and initiations. As far as responses are concerned, we will look at five subdivisions. The first two of these, *no response* and *inappropriate or irrelevant response*, are indicators of conversational immaturity or disability. A more extensive analysis might seek to investigate the nature of such inappropriacy or irrelevance and make further more delicate distinctions within this category. Next come *minimal predicted responses*, where the subject responds according to the expectations set up by the preceding utterance but does not add anything which would contribute to the continuation of the conversation. Obviously this can occur in any conversation for a variety of reasons. However, a tendency to make such responses most of the time to the exclusion of other possibilities would suggest either an unwillingness or an inability to participate in conversation. The converse of this option is the regular usage of the fourth category, *response plus additional content*, which refers to those responses which go beyond the minimal expectations set up by the preceding initiation. These are responses which simultaneously initiate or provide for a further response and which we have coded as R/I and R/(I) respectively in our examples. Finally, the fifth category, *other appropriate response*, allows for any other type of appropriate response which is not analysable in terms of the other categories. Obviously the type of response depends on the preceding initiation. Here we make a basic distinction between the three main types of initiation: question, request for action and statement, fully aware that these are crude and poorly defined categories. A fuller account of the possible relations between types of initiation and types of response awaits more extensive research in this area. We can summarize these points as in figure 6.

	Regularly	Occasionally	Rarely	Never
Initiation type				
Question/request for action/statement				
Response				
No response				
Inappropriate or irrelevant response				
Minimal predicted response				
Response plus additional content				
Other appropriate response				

Figure 6 Responses

Initiations are subdivided in several ways. Firstly, we look at the use of *attention-getters*, distinguishing between non-verbal and verbal devices. The same distinction is applied to *attention-directing* and some of the more common verbal devices are specified. We divide initiation types into the three categories already mentioned: *questions, requests for action* and *statements*. Reinitiations include four types: *repeats, repeats with prosodic shift, repeats with attention-getting or attention-directing devices*, and *rephrasings*. Reinitiations which involve rephrasing together with prosodic shifts and the use of attention-getting and attention-directing devices are subsumed under this category. These can be summarized as in figure 7.

As far as discourse content is concerned, we will be highly selective and focus mainly on surface devices for establishing and linking topics. More problematic aspects of discourse content, such as we will see in some of the examples of conversational disability to be presented in chapter 9, cannot be categorized adequately by means of a simple checklist and require more elaborate description. Accordingly, we will be looking in our data for the discourse devices in figure 8.

	Regularly	Occasionally	Rarely	Never
Attention-getting				
Use of non-verbal devices:				
Eye contact				
Physical (approach, touch, etc.)				
Pointing, showing				
Use of verbal devices:				
Vocatives				
Words (e.g. *hey, look, see*)				
Prosodic				
Attention-directing				
Present referents:				
Pointing				
Looking				
Non-present referents:				
Locating devices (e.g.				
do you know/remember)				
Relative clauses				
Appropriate use of articles				
Types of initiation				
Question				
Request for action				
Statement				
Reinitiations				
Repeats				
Repeats with prosodic shift				
Repeats with attention-getting/				
direction				
Rephrasing				

Figure 7 Initiations

	Regularly	Occasionally	Rarely	Never
Discourse connectors				
And				
But				
Because/so				
Well				
Others				
Ellipsis				
Anaphoric reference				
Misplacement prefaces				
(e.g. *by the way, to*				
change the topic)				

Figure 8 Discourse devices for establishing and linking topics

Our next main area of concern is appropriacy. Here we will be looking at the ability of a speaker to use speech acts appropriately. We will restrict our account to requests for action, although other speech acts such as greeting, promising, conveying sympathy, expressing gratitude, could have been included. We have decided to focus on requests for action as these are a commonly used speech act by young children and they are a useful indicator of the development of social and linguistic competence. The subdivisions which we propose concern firstly the formal devices used to accomplish the speech act, whether non-verbal or verbal, and then the dimension of politeness. Obviously there will be problems in the empirical analysis of politeness, as the estimation of what is polite is often subjectively determined and depends on features of the situation which may not be available to the analyst. Notwithstanding these problems, we proceed on the assumption that it will generally be possible to make fairly reliable judgements in this area based on the analyst's intuitions of what normally counts as polite behaviour. The dimension of indirectness, which can include the use of a wide range of strategies, is covered by the category *hint*. As we will see, this is clearly too imprecise and crude a category to cover the immense subtlety which can be involved in the use of indirect speech acts. Again, there seems to be no straightforward way of capturing this aspect of conversational competence in a simple checklist of behaviours. We can summarize our categories for appropriacy as in figure 9.

	Regularly	Occasionally	Rarely	Never
Non-verbal requests				
Pointing				
Pointing with vocalization				
Verbal requests				
Direct imperatives				
Embedded imperatives				
Question directives				
Need statements				
Hints				
Politeness markers				
Please				
Embedded forms				
Appropriacy of polite forms				

Figure 9 Appropriacy (requests for action)

Finally we turn to repairs. These are divided into the types which were discussed earlier – *clarification requests*, and their responses, *other-corrections* and *self-repairs*. We can summarize these categories, together with their subdivisions, as in figure 10.

	Regularly	Occasionally	Rarely	Never
Requests for clarification				
Responses to:				
Requests for repetition				
Requests for confirmation				
Requests for specification				
Production of:				
Requests for repetition				
Requests for confirmation				
Requests for specification				
Other-corrections of:				
Pronunciation				
Grammar				
Lexis				
Pragmatics				
Self-repairs to:				
Pronunciation				
Grammar				
Lexis				
Pragmatics				

Figure 10 Repairs

These categories will be illustrated in detail in our analysis of conversational data which will take up much of the remainder of this book. We will begin with an investigation of the origins of conversational ability in early infancy. This will lead to a detailed analysis of the empirical research data described in chapter 1, in which we will look at the following: the initiation of conversational exchanges, the use of request forms, the construction of coherent dialogue, and the development of turn-taking and repair devices.

3

Early conversational development

We defined conversation in chapter 1 as naturally occurring talk between two or more participants, taking care to emphasize the non-verbal aspects of this talk. Although our main purpose in this book will be to describe the development of children's ability to use *language* as a means of participating in conversations, it is important to note that the origins of conversation can be found in early infancy in the prelinguistic stage, before children have acquired language at all. It is here, for example, in the interactions between infants and their caregivers, that we find the first signs of the reciprocal behaviour on which later conversational development depends. We can see how, in these early interactions, babies learn to take turns to respond to their partner's elicitations and to expect predictable responses to their own behaviours. All this takes place before the development of language, and for this reason these early conversation-like interactions have often been referred to as proto-conversations. In what follows we will look at the nature of these proto-conversations. Firstly we will consider what infants have to learn in order to become participants in conversation, noting that they are equipped with some of the prerequisites for communication at birth. We will then examine the nature of early child–caregiver interaction, looking in particular at the behaviour of the child's caregiver. Finally, as the main part of our book will be devoted to an empirical investigation of conversations between peers, we will compare and contrast peer and caregiver interaction and assess their respective roles in conversational development.

Social and cognitive prerequisites of conversation

We can begin by considering what children have to learn in order to participate in conversations. We have noted that conversation involves the ability to take and assign turns and to engage in the reciprocal acts of initiating and responding. But underlying these abilities are various social and cognitive requirements. Communication presupposes a need or desire to interact with others. At the cognitive level infants have to learn to differentiate themselves from others, to develop the ability to co-ordinate actions and purposes and to predict the consequences of their own actions. But even more crucially, they have to be able to represent to themselves the internal representations of others in order to recognize that the intentions of others can differ from their own and to be able to interpret these intentions. This sharing of the other's perspective is often referred to as *inter-subjectivity*. We shall consider the development of intersubjectivity in early infancy shortly.

It has often been assumed that newly born babies are devoid of any basic social motivation and that their requirements are purely physiological. Recent studies of the behaviour of neonates would tend to refute this view. Indeed, it is now often claimed that infants are biologically predisposed for communication from the moment of birth. If we observe very young babies, we can see that, even in their first days, they spend their waking time moving their limbs, changing their facial expressions, attending to people and objects around them, and vocalizing. It has been shown that infants display an interest in the human face before they become interested in objects (Fantz 1965). It seems that neonates are biologically predisposed to develop this interest in the human face as their focal distance at birth is roughly equivalent to the distance of the mother's face during breast-feeding. Likewise, babies attend selectively to the sound of the human voice. They also display within hours of birth the type of motor activity, called *inter-actional synchrony*, which involves subtle movements in synchronization with the rhythm of another's speech. In infants this behaviour can only be elicited by human speech. Thus, it is claimed, 'the neonate participates immediately and deeply in communication and is not at birth a social isolate' (Condon and Sander 1974). We can briefly cite other evidence in support of this view. For instance, the crying of young babies, although often a reflex of physiological causes such as the pains of hunger, can in other circumstances be quieted if the baby is picked up. In this case crying displays a basic social need for attachment. In addition to such evidence of predisposition for social communication, it has also been shown that babies are equipped with many of the motor abilities which will later be utilized in conversation. For example, it has been observed from photographs and films of neonates that babies display at birth adult-like facial expressions and make various speech-like movements involving the lips and tongue (Trevarthen 1979). In sum, as Richards (1974) has put it, babies are equipped at birth with the potentiality of becoming social beings.

It is important, however, if we are to understand and appreciate the origins and nature of the development of conversation, that we recognize that the behaviours of neonates, such as crying and smiling, are reflex motor actions which are only later used with the intention of communicating. How do babies develop the ability to use these behaviours intentionally? The most obvious answer is that communicative behaviour develops as a result of the child's social experiences, in particular his interactions with his caregivers. We shall return to a description of this experience in the following sections. But first we will focus specifically on how these behaviours develop from the perspective of the child.

Let us consider first the development of smiling. Smiling is one of the most basic and widely recognized social behaviours. Caregivers sometimes only first recognize their babies as social beings as a result of the first smile. Indeed, a baby's first smile is usually seen as an important developmental milestone. However, as we have already mentioned, it is important to realize that a baby's early smiling does not carry the same communicative function as adult smiling. In the first few weeks of life, smiles are endogenous or reflexive – that is, they are related to cycles of neurophysiological excitation and discharges within the brain. The subsequent development of smiling has been documented by Stern (1977). By about six weeks, the baby's smile becomes exogenous – that is, it can now be elicited by external events such as gentle tickling around the area of the mouth. At this stage babies also smile in response to the human face and voice. By three months the smile has become instrumental and the baby produces a smile in order to elicit a similar response from others. By four months the smile can be co-ordinated with other facial expressions to produce more complex meanings.

A similar development from a reflex motor action to a communicative intention has been described by Lock (1978) in relation to a child's arm-raising when being picked up. The first developmental stage is simply a response to the stimulation of the caregiver's hands. Later the child anticipates this stimulation and raises his arms. The final stage comes when the child uses the action of arm-raising to request being picked up.

So far we have been looking at examples of the development of intentional communication in early non-verbal behaviour. We can now turn to the origins of basic conversational acts such as requests and statements. It has been suggested that intentional acts such as these develop around ten months as gestural performatives (Bates et al. 1979). This development corresponds in cognitive terms to Piaget's sensori-motor stage 5. Before this stage, the infant's schemes for interacting with objects and his schemes for interacting with adults are separate. For example, he is unable to secure an adult's help in attempts to reach a desired object, nor does he use objects to obtain the adult's attention. At this stage the baby has acquired *primary intersubjectivity*. The integration of attention to objects and attention to persons, together with the development of indirect causality which permits recognition that the adult is an agent of action independent of the child's control, has been called *secondary intersubjectivity* (Trevarthen and Hubley 1978). An example will help illustrate this development. Observations of a baby at 25 weeks showed that the baby displayed extreme interest in objects to the neglect of the mother. The baby did not combine attention to objects and mother. By 45 weeks, however, the infant was able to integrate attention to mother and objects (Trevarthen and Hubley 1978:210).

We can see how these cognitive developments underlie the ability to make speech acts such as requests and statements. Requests involve the ability to use human agents to operate on or obtain objects. Similarly, statements involve the use of objects to operate on human attention. The early gestural manifestations of requests and statements have been described as *proto-imperatives* and *proto-declaratives* respectively (Bates et al. 1979). The following is an example of a proto-imperative from a child aged 12 months (Bates et al. 1979:121):

> C. is sitting on her mother's lap, while M. shows her the telephone and pretends to talk. M. tries to press the receiver against C's ear and have her 'speak', but C. pushes the receiver back and presses it against her mother's ear. This is repeated several times. When M. refuses to speak into the receiver, C. bats her hand against M.'s knee, waits a moment longer, watches M.'s face, and then, uttering a sharp aspirated sound *ha.* touches her mother's mouth.

Here we can see how the child combines attention to her mother with attention to an object in order to elicit an action from the mother. A similar development is described for proto-declaratives, where the child uses an object to attract the adult's attention.

In looking at the development of communicative intention in early infancy, we have so far focused on the child. It is clear, however, that this development takes place within the context of interaction with mothers and other caregivers. We shall examine presently the nature of this interaction. Firstly, we will briefly survey the way mothers behave in these early interactions with their infants.

Early infant–caregiver interaction

Conversation is a co-operative activity. It involves two or more participants who take turns and jointly construct a text. How far can we apply the notion of conversation to the early interactions between babies and their caregivers? Here the situation is obviously asymmetrical. The caregiver is a competent adult conversationalist, while the baby has not yet developed language. Furthermore, conversation presupposes an intention to communicate. However, as we saw in the preceding section, it is only at about nine months or so that we can begin to reliably attribute the intention to communicate meanings to a baby's behaviours. Before this stage, it is safer to regard the baby's looks, gestures, cries and vocalizations as essentially non-communicative. For these reasons, we cannot realistically describe early interactions between infants and their caregivers as conversations. Yet detailed analyses of such interactions have shown that they have the appearance of mature conversations. We can find turn-taking with minimal overlap, and the baby and caregiver seem to be producing conversation-like exchanges in which one participant initiates and the other responds. These early interactions have been referred to as *proto-conversations* (Bateson 1975). The use of this term captures our impression that the interactions exhibit conversational properties, while at the same time recognizing the limitations of the child's contributions. In this section we will be looking at some aspects of these proto-conversations and will suggest that they form a basis for subsequent conversational development.

Because conversation is a co-operative activity, it can only be adequately described if we take into account the behaviours of each participant and show how they interact with one another. Sometimes, however, it is useful to consider these behaviours separately, in order to appreciate the distinct role of each participant. In what follows, we will consider the caregiver's behaviours in proto-conversations before returning to an analysis of the joint interaction of caregiver and child.

The role of the caregiver in proto-conversations

It is now widely accepted that mothers and other caregivers adapt their behaviour when interacting with babies and young children. Considerable attention has been focused on mothers' linguistic adaptations and their potential significance for the child's language development (Snow and Ferguson 1977). Caregivers also exhibit special behaviours when interacting with babies and infants. Facial expressions are exaggerated and performed frequently with much stereotypy. The most common of these are the mock-surprise, the frown and the smile. The mock-surprise, for example, has been described as follows (Stern 1977:18).

> When a mother is trying to get an infant's attention and he turns to look at her, the instant he does so, she is most likely to perform a mock-surprise expression. Her eyes open very wide, her eyebrows go up, her mouth opens wide, and her head is raised and tilted very slightly. At the same time, she usually says something like 'oooooh' or 'aaaaah'.

Maternal vocalizations to their infants differ from adult-directed vocalizations. The pitch is raised, stress is more pronounced, and speech is slower. Mothers maintain mutual gaze with their babies for long periods and will gaze and vocalize simultaneously. This contrasts with patterns of gaze behaviour in adult conversation, where the speaker looks away from the listener for most of the turn and only looks at particular points of the turn, for example, at the point of its possible completion (Kendon 1967). Generally, these maternal behaviours in interaction with their babies have been described as 'infant-elicited social behaviour' (Stern 1977:17). It is suggested that their prime function is to assist in the initiation and regulation of interaction with immature interactional partners.

If we consider a little more closely how mothers achieve this regulation of interaction with their babies, we will see that two elements are involved: selectivity and co-ordination. Mothers respond selectively to their infant's gestures and vocalizations, focusing on those which are meaningful in adult communication and treating them *as if* they were intended to communicate an intention by the child. So, for example, changes of facial expression are taken as indications of discomfort; if the child cries, the mother tries out various hypotheses to discover the reason for the crying, such as feeding, winding, changing, nursing, and so on; if the baby vocalizes or smiles following the approach of the adult, this is treated as a greeting and receives an appropriate response such as 'oh, hello then'. In other words, the mother selects those behaviours from the child's stream of behaviour which can be interpreted as having a communicative function and she treats them as if they were communicative. It is suggested that babies learn to become communicators on the basis of this experience. As Newson (1979:208) puts it, 'human babies become human beings because they are treated as if they were already human beings'.

But mothers do not just select aspects of their baby's behaviour and respond as if it were communicative. They also time their own behaviours precisely to co-ordinate with what the baby is doing. Vocalizations are phased within the child's sequences of vocalization/gesture and pause to create the appearance of turn-taking (Schaffer et al. 1977). Mothers follow their infant's vocalizations and gestures with a vocalization but often insert a pause between their own vocalizations as if waiting for the child to take a turn (Bateson 1975). Similarly, with the regulation of the child's gaze as a means of establishing joint attention, it has been shown that mothers will point where their babies are already looking (Murphy and Messer 1977) or will follow their babies' line of gaze and name objects the baby is looking at (Collis 1977).

Having considered how mothers respond selectively to their children's behaviours and how they co-ordinate their own behaviours with those of the child to give the appearance of conversational turn-taking, we can now turn to the ways in which mothers build a conversational structure around their children's contributions. As we saw in chapter 2, the basic elements of a conversational exchange are an initiation and a response. In what way can the gestures and vocalizations of babies and young infants be seen as constituting initiations and responses within conversational exchanges? Snow (1977) has analysed conversations between mothers and babies at several points between three and 18 months. She shows how mothers respond to and attempt to elicit contributions from their babies which can be interpreted as if they were intentional communications. The nature of the babies' contributions changed qualitively over time. At three months the child produced burps, yawns, sneezes and vocalizations which the mother incorporated into a proto-conversation. For example (Snow 1977:12):

(1) Ann: (smiles)
    Mother: oh what a nice little smile
              yes, isn't that nice?
              there
              there's a nice little smile
    Ann: (burps)
    Mother: what a nice little wind as well
              yes, that's better, isn't it?
              yes
              yes
    Ann: (vocalizes)
    Mother: there's a nice noise

We can see how many of the mother's utterances in this extract are responses to the child's behaviour. The mother takes the second part of a conversational exchange and treats the baby's smiles, burps and vocalizations as initiations to which she makes an appropriate response. As the child developed, the mother came to expect higher-quality contributions. For example, by seven months vocalizations and consonantal babble were expected, by 18 months words. The following example is taken from the same child at 1;6 (Snow 1977:18):

(2) Ann: (blowing noises)
    Mother: that's a bit rude
    Ann: mouth
    Mother: mouth, that's right
    Ann: face
    Mother: face, yes, mouth is in your face
              what else have you got in your face?
    Ann: face (closing eyes)
    Mother: you're making a face, aren't you?

Here, as in the previous example, we can analyse the basic exchange structure as IR (initiation–response). The child's contributions are treated by the mother as initiations and she responds to these. Often the mother initiates herself, as in (2): *what else have your got in your face?* Ann fails to respond. Instead, her next utterance is treated as a further occasion for the mother to respond. In this way, the mother defines the child's contributions retrospectively as initiations and thus constitutes them as first pair parts in a conversational exchange. Note that we are not ascribing to the child the intention to elicit a response. Rather, we are emphasizing the role of the mother in structuring the conversational exchange. As MacLure (1981) puts it, 'the conversational initiate still comes from the mother, . . . though one of her major achievements is to make it look as if it comes from the child'.

As well as responding to their child's behaviours, mothers attempt to elicit responses from the child. For example, a great proportion of inter- action in early infancy consists in the adult trying to elicit a smile from the baby. Snow (1977) reports how Ann's mother, when Ann was 0;3, devoted 124 consecutive utterances to the topic of burping and only shifted to the topic of what Ann was looking at after she had burped. We noted earlier that mothers often pause between their own vocalizations as if giving the baby a chance to take a turn. But the conversational role of mothers is even more elaborate than this. Mothers often synchronize their turns with what the child is doing or is likely to do next in such a way that the child's actions can be seen as responses. To take a further example from Ann at 0;3:

(3)   (mother has been feeding Ann; she removes the bottle)
      Mother: are you finished?
                yes? (removing bottle)
                well, was that nice?

MacLure (1981) has shown in a detailed reanalysis of this example that the mother's first utterance is an initiation to which *yes* or *no* would be appropriate responses. Whatever the child does next can be interpreted by the mother as such a response. If the baby cries, the answer is *no*. If she does nothing, the answer is *yes*. In this way the mother predicts the child's next action and produces an initiating utterance to which the child's action can be seen as an interactionally relevant response.

The role of mothers and other caregivers in structuring conversational exchanges involving their infants extends into later stages. Söderbergh (1974) describes how at 21 months a parent used the child's utterance and developed it to keep the dialogue going as well as prompting the conver- sation by asking questions and providing frames for the child's response. In this way some account was taken of formal deficiencies in the child's language. Similarly, Corsaro (1979a) shows how adults exert control over discourse with children by using forms which restrict the children's choice of responses. The forms used by adults for this purpose include polar interrogatives and tag questions. Adults often match their utterance to what the child has just said in order to establish a common reference situation. This provides the child with an opportunity for a further response. Shugar

(1978) refers to this process as *joint text construction*. Often this occurs where a child produces an utterance unrelated to the ongoing topic and the adult retrospectively constitutes the child's utterance as a relevant turn by providing an appropriate response. The following is an example from Siobhan at 3;8:

(4)   (Siobhan, Heather and the author are driving past the docks and
      Siobhan notices some boats. The preceding utterances had been about
      a local landmark)
      Siobhan: I wish I was on the other boat
      Author: yes
                 do you remember when we went in a boat?
                 we'll have to go in a boat again some time

Siobhan's utterance is not related to the preceding talk. She initiates a new topic but does so inappropriately by failing to provide sufficient identification of the referent *the other boat*. However, the author treats her utterance as if it were relevant and makes it so retrospectively with his response. He also provides her with the opportunity to continue with this topic (which, as it happened, was not taken up in this case).

MacLure (1981) has provided a detailed account of how mothers build a complex conversational structure around their child's behaviours. In order to illustrate this, we can examine the supportive role of adults in getting talk started following an initiation by the child. A widely used initiating conversational device is the summons–answer sequence (Schegloff 1968). The following is a typical example:

(5)   A: hey John
      B: what?
      A: what do you think you're doing?

The first part of this sequence is a *summons*, which has the function of getting the attention of the intended addressee. The usual response to a summons is something like B's *what?* Following this, A is constrained to continue by initiating the topic for which attention has been elicited. In fact, we can test the obligatory nature of this third part in the sequence by looking at the type of sequence often produced by children exploiting the rules of such a sequence for their own interactional ends, for example, as a joke:

(6)   Child: daddy
      Father: yes
      Child: nothing

Here the child's second turn is deviant as topic initiation ought to follow the summons–answer pair.

As far as child–adult conversation is concerned, MacLure (1981) shows how preschool children often violate the sequential constraints operating in summons–answer sequences by failing to take the third turn. Typically the adult will remedy the situation by taking the turn and attempting to define the topic. For example, following an attention-getting vocalization by the child, the adult will respond with something like *what's the matter?* or *what do you want?*, which are more explicit that the simple *what?* which respects the summoner's right to define the topic. In this way, the adult is already helping the child to structure the conversation. If, however, the child then fails to take the third turn, the adult will often continue with a further question aimed at establishing more precisely the topic of the child's concern. This question will usually be tailored to the child's ongoing activity and will be in the form of a yes/no question. If still no response is forthcoming, the adult will often continue with a follow-up utterance as if the child had indeed responded. The following is a typical example (MacLure 1981:120):

(7)   Child: daddy
      Father: what?
      Child: daddy
      Father: what've you done?
               broken a toy?
               (1.2)
               eh?
               (0.8)
               little scamp
      Child: (laughs)

As we can see, the adult progressively provides more content and thus reduces the cognitive and interactional demands on the child, concluding the sequence by treating the child's non-response as if a response had occurred. In this way, as MacLure shows, adults compensate for children's conversational deficiencies and ensure that conversational exchanges with their infants have the appearance of being well formed.

Infant–caregiver interaction in proto-conversations

So far we have been considering the role of caregivers in the structuring of proto-conversations involving babies and young infants. However, as we stressed earlier, an account of interaction should look at the behaviours of each participant and should consider the ways in which they co-ordinate their separate behaviours into a single social activity.

There are several ways of studying early infant–caregiver interaction. We can simply observe the interaction and note how each participant behaves.

Even this basic approach would enable us to observe the types of maternal behaviour which we have been describing as well as the development of the infant's social-communicative repertoire. However, a more common approach, which permits more detailed observation, involves the use of video or film recordings. Even greater insight into the subtleties of the interaction can be obtained from a frame-by-frame analysis of filmed interaction, in which the precise timing of behaviours can be established. This type of observation can focus on the interaction as a whole or can select particular behaviours such as patterns of gazing and vocalization.

Analyses of very early infant–caregiver interaction have isolated two distinct patterns of behaviour. The first has been described by Trevarthen (1979:343) as 'states of closely synchronized activity', in which infant and caregiver time their behaviours precisely to give the impression of a closely co-ordinated activity. Rather than taking turns, the participants will vocalize together (Stern et al. 1975). The other pattern is one of 'reciprocal or complementary activity' (Trevarthen 1979:343), in which the participants take turns and the turns are complementary to one another. For example, the following set of interactional exchanges were observed in a study of baby–mother dyads (Whiten 1977):

1 Baby vocalizes: mother replies.
2 Baby smiles: mother talks, smiles or laughs.
3 Mother touches or smiles: baby smiles or vocalizes.

As we can see, we have the basis at this very early stage of an exchange structure consisting of the complementary units of initiation and response.

We have emphasized the role of the mother in the structuring of these early exchanges. It is important, however, to consider the behaviour of the other participant, the child. The behaviour of the child is often determined by and given meaning by what the mother does, as we saw in the preceding section; what the mother does is similarly influenced by the child's behaviour. Mothers can be seen to respond to their child's gestures, looks and vocalizations; but equally, infants adapt to their mother's expressions, for example, by imitating their smiles and speech movements (Trevarthen 1979). Indeed, close analysis of infant–caregiver interaction by Trevarthen and others has shown that infants often attempt to take the lead in the interaction. Frequently it is the child who sets the pace while the mother replies (Schaffer et al. 1977). This pattern has been observed at a very early age during breast-feeding where mothers jiggle during pauses in the baby's sucking but the duration of the jiggling is controlled by the baby (Kaye 1977). Similarly, at a slightly later age (about nine months), children can be observed employing various strategies to initiate topics (Foster 1979; see also chapter 4). Later we will see how children initiate and sustain conversation without adult assistance. It is important, however, to note that the origins of this ability can be traced to early infancy.

At this point it might be helpful to consider what the child learns about conversation from his experience of interaction with caregivers. One of the earliest principles of communication to be acquired is that particular behaviours receive predictable responses. The child emits various signals such as looks, gestures and vocalizations. These are subject to a fairly restricted set of responses by the caregiver, as we saw from the basic exchange patterns described earlier. In time the child learns to produce a behaviour of a constant form and to expect a predictable response. Similarly, on the basis of a limited set of experiences, the child learns to make appropriate responses to the caregiver's elicitations. The clearest examples of such experiences are to be found in games such as 'give-and-take' and 'peekabo', in which the infant learns to take turns, to perform actions and to insert them in the appropriate slot in the episode. An early example would be the child's laughter following tickling at the end of the rhyme 'Round and round the garden'. Eventually the child learns to anticipate the sequence and laughs before the physical act of tickling or holds out an open palm to initiate the game. Bruner (1975) described a game of peekabo in which the child first learns to respond but soon moves to the role of initiating the game (Bruner 1975:15–16):

> M. initiates game while drying C.'s hair after bath, covering baby's face with towel, saying *boo* twice on uncovering. Both laugh. Ten minutes later, C. initiates, M. says *boo*. Laughs and lowers petticoat. C. repeats three times, M. maintaining excitement by varying time to say *boo*, and C. does not lower until signal *boo* is given.

Bruner notes further that before the game the initiator is in eye-to-eye contact which is steady and more than a glance and that similar eye-to-eye contact occurred after unmasking. Thus, as we can see, there is an analogy between the behaviours which the child learns in early child–caregiver interactions and games and those which form the basis of conversational interaction. The question, which remains unresolved, is whether the child's experiences of proto-conversations and games facilitate the learning of the principles of conversation.

Peer relations and the development of conversation

So far in this chapter we have been considering the possible role of caregivers in the development of children's conversational ability. We have shown how caregivers provided a structured interactional environment for their children which might facilitate the development of turn-taking and the reciprocity of conversation. However, most children also spend considerable time with other children. The actual amount is obviously subject to great variation, both within families and between cultures with different expectations regarding child-rearing. One estimate puts the amount of peer interaction as a proportion of total daily interaction as follows: 10 per cent at age two years, 30 per cent for preschool children, and 50 per cent for school-aged children (Barker and Wright 1955). This book will be concerned mainly with the analysis of children's conversational abilities in peer interactions. This has the advantage of allowing us to estimate the extent to which children can manage conversation without the assistance of mature adult speakers and can utilize skills which, in some cases, are still in the process of development. It is appropriate then at this point to consider the possible role of peers in the development of children's conversational ability.

The literature on peer relations provides conflicting views. Bates (1975) has reviewed a wide range of studies of the effects of peer relations on the acquisition of language. The general impression gained from this review is that the linguistic performance of children who are exposed mainly to their peers is depressed in relation to children whose linguistic input is mainly from adults. Children's speech to adults has also been found to be more complex than that addressed to their peers on a variety of linguistic measures. The subjects of peer studies include children who are twins and those raised in institutions as well as birth-order effects in families. These studies are confounded by many variables such as the sex of siblings and size of family in the birth-order studies, and the general effects of institutionalization in studies of children raised in institutions. There is also the question whether the issue involved is that peer input is inferior to adult input or whether simply the proportion of adult input is so reduced in cases of increased peer input that its potential benefits remain unexploited. It is difficult to ascertain in what ways peer input might be deficient. As we saw in chapter 1, even very young children make similar adjustments in their speech to younger listeners to the adjustments made by mothers and other caregivers, although it is by no means clear whether children's adjustments are as extensive, effective or supportive as those documented for adults. Bates suggests that the main differences lie in the extent to which young children's speech is egocentric. If young children fail to take account of their listeners' perspective, then this will have an effect on their use of language involving mastery of presuppositions. For example, pronouns might be used inappropriately (as in *he hit me*, where the referent of *he* is unknown to the listener). Furthermore, children seem to be less aware of listener cues indicating communicative breakdown (Peterson et al. 1972) and of using these cues themselves (Dittman 1972).

It is important to note that much of the evidence cited by Bates relates to the acquisition of language rather than the development of conversational abilities. The following chapters in this book will provide strong counter-evidence to the theory that children's communication is egocentric. Indeed, we will see that children display considerable ability to repair conversational breakdowns from an early age (see chapter 7).

The other side of the coin views peer relations as beneficial. Some studies are concerned with children's social-communicative development in general. It seems that children who have managed successful peer relations are less likely to have subsequent social problems in adolescence such as behaviour disorders as well as learning disabilities (Field 1981). The ability to interact satisfactorily with peers seems to depend on experience of peer interaction, and even those children who have been diagnosed as withdrawn can become more prosocial as a result of increased peer interaction (Guralnick 1981).

If we look at the nature of peer interaction, we can see that it differs in many important ways from child–caregiver interaction. Peer relations are more symmetrical; reciprocity and mutuality are encouraged. In peer groups children have to negotiate friendship, whereas in families relationships and norms are imposed from above. Accordingly, in peer situations children have to learn the principles of negotiation. A common situation, which is less likely to arise in families, is where a child attempts to gain access to an ongoing activity in a nursery where rules of access are negotiated by peers rather than imposed by adults. Such a situation gives considerable scope for the development of the child's communicative competence (Corsaro 1979b; see also the negotiation of non-compliant responses to requests in Chapter 5).

Peer situations also facilitate fantasy play, in which children are able to explore relations and concepts unhindered by the constraints imposed on everyday behaviour. It has also been suggested that peer interaction facilitates a decline in egocentric thinking (Piaget 1959). Finally, with regard to the development of conversational repairs, peer interaction affords children greater opportunities for developing these skills precisely because ambiguity and breakdown is more likely on account of their communicative immaturity.

In assessing the respective roles of peers and adult caregivers in the development of conversation we can contrast two viewpoints, both put by Bates (1975). The first stresses deficiencies in peer language (Bates 1975: 269–70):

> If peer language tends to be more egocentric – hence less easily understood – then children not only misunderstand one another, but do not possess sufficient tools to recover or force repetition of misfired messages. The greater competency of adults in both giving and receiving listener cues may account in part for the fact that children

are pulled into more explicit, less egocentric speech in their conversations with adults.

This view contrasts with the following account of the deficiencies of adult language (Bates 1975:285):

> Further comparisons of peer versus adult input may indicate . . . that for some kinds of presuppositions adults may be *too* helpful. Adults are so good at retrieving the child's presuppositions that they may fail to force him to confront his communicative inefficiency. A doting mother who second-guesses all her child's needs, acting on even the most minimal requests, may retard the child's progress towards greater explicitness in speech. At the same time, peers, by failing to retrieve information from requests or other matters that are important to the speaker, may pressure the egocentric child towards a greater mastery of conversational principles.

How can we reconcile these two viewpoints? Bates goes some way towards proposing a solution by suggesting that the role of peers versus adults may be related to the child's developmental level. We can perhaps put this more explicitly and suggest that adult input and support in conversational structuring is an essential element in the early stages. Babies are equipped at birth with a predisposition to engage in social interaction. But at this early stage the role of the adult in structuring the interaction and socializing the infant into the conventions of communication is crucial. At this stage peers would hardly be of assistance. Consider, for example, the situation where two babies are left to interact. We would anticipate, on the basis of the work described in this chapter, that little interaction would ensue as there would be no mature partner to make sense of the babies' behaviours and to build a complex conversational structure around them. At a later stage, however, perhaps around the age of three years, children have already mastered some of the basic principles of conversation. They can now engage successfully in conversation, taking turns, initiating and responding. They already have the building blocks which they can utilize for further development. At this stage, it may be that situations which evoke those very behaviours which are in the process of emerging might provide the optimal environment for their development. Thus the deficiencies of young children's communication, its ambiguity and egocentrism, might provide the child with opportunities to learn about conversational breakdown and how to deal with it.

Much of this is, of course, speculative and further detailed research is required to substantiate the hypotheses outlined here. We can, however, conclude by accepting that the roles of peers and adults are complementary. The present evidence suggests that children learn best to communicate if exposed to a reasonably wide range of interactive partners and situations.

We shall return to some practical implications of this discussion in our final chapter. In the meantime, we will present a detailed account of the development of conversation in two preschool children. We begin with an analysis of the devices they used to initiate conversational exchanges.

4

Initiating conversational exchanges

It is widely recognized that beginnings are often fraught with difficulty. This applies to many activities. As far as conversation is concerned, people frequently experience problems when they try to start up a conversation or gain access to one which is already under way. This is the most obvious aspect of conversational initiations. There are also problems, however, which occur during the course of conversation. These are more subtle and less obvious. They also involve the issue of initiation, if we define this term (as we did in chapter 2) as referring to utterances which predict or set up expectations for responses. We can examine whether and how speakers elicit further talk from their conversational partners. Some utterances are more clearly initiating than others. Requests for information and action demand responses, for example. Other utterances, such as statements, frequently only provide for the possibility of further talk but do not necessarily constrain the addressee to a particular response type. It will be interesting to see the extent to which children are aware of the discourse expectations of their utterances and how they pursue responses which are not forthcoming in the first place, when, for example, the addressee fails to respond.

A further important consideration is how the content of the initiating utterance is structured. This is particularly at issue in the case of new discourse topics, when the referents of the utterance, the persons, objects and events being discussed, have to be introduced to the addressee. As we shall see, the establishing of a discourse topic involves making assumptions about what the addressee does and does not know. Referents which are new to the conversation and potentially unfamiliar to the addressee must be introduced differently from those which have been already established in the course of the conversation. Children frequently experience problems with this aspect of conversational initiation, as we can see from inappropriate usage of pronouns and articles (for example, in utterances such as *he hit me* and *where's the book?*, where the addressee does not know who *he* is or which book is involved).

Let us look more closely at what is involved in the initiation of conversational exchanges. We described two activities in chapter 2: attention-getting and attention-directing. Attention-getting is essential where the attention of the addressee cannot be assumed, as at the beginning of a conversational encounter or following a lapse in the interaction. Attention-getters are also used following unsuccessful initiations. Both non-verbal and verbal devices can be used. Non-verbal attention-getters include the establishment of eye contact, touching or approaching the addressee. Verbal devices include vocatives, greeting and expressive particles such as *hey* or *oh*. Directing the addressee's attention to the referents of the initiation can also involve non-verbal as well as verbal devices. Speakers can show, hold up or point to a referent. Referents which are not in the immediate physical context, however, require more elaborate verbal devices.

In what follows, we will begin by reviewing briefly the literature on the development of initiations in children's conversations. This will provide the background for a detailed account of initiations based on the empirical data described in chapter 1. We will then look at the remedial devices which children use to reinitiate conversation following initially unsatisfactory or absent responses.

Initiating conversation: a review of the developmental literature

Various studies have illustrated the use of attention-getting devices by young children (Keenan and Schieffelin 1976; Ochs et al. 1979; McTear 1979; Umiker-Sebeok 1976). Verbal and non-verbal attention-getters are used by children as young as two years (Wellman and Lempers 1977). In studies of peer interaction Mueller (1972) and Mueller et al. (1977) have shown that the frequency of occurrence of attention-getting devices increased with age and suggest that this increase is a function of children's developing communicative competence. Wootton (1981) studied the use of vocatives by four-year-olds to their parents. He found that vocatives not only had a speaker selection function but were also used to elicit an appropriate next utterance when used in utterance-final position (see later).

Carter (1978) made a case study of the development of attention-directing behaviour in the second year. Before the child in her study learned conventional attention-directing words such as *look*, he used prelinguistic devices which generally involved the co-ordination of a gesture with a vocalization. So, for example, in order to draw the addressee's attention to an object, he would hold out or point at the object and utter a vocalization in which the main stable feature was an initial [l] or [d]. Carter traces the development of these prelinguistic devices to the use of conventionalized vocalizations. Thus *look* developed out of [l]-initial vocalizations, while those which were [d]-initial developed into words sharing phonetic similarity such as [diz] *(these)* and [dIs] *(this)*. At a later stage, children often use common nouns as an attention-directing strategy (Atkinson 1979). It is easy to overlook the function of this use of common nouns and interpret the child's intention simply as labelling objects. Contextual evidence is important here. To take an example: a child held up a toy car and said *car*. The adult acknowledged by repeating *car* and then the child said *broken*. As Atkinson points out, what the child seems to be doing here is not making a statement or labelling the object but drawing the adult's attention to the object. Once the adult had acknowledged attention, the child went on to predicate something about the object. In fact, this type of sequence has been widely reported. In many cases much conversational space can be devoted to such attention-drawing activity with the child repeating the noun until the other participant indicates attention (Keenan and Schieffelin 1976). It has been suggested that this means of encoding propositions such as *the car is broken* precedes the more mature syntactic means in which encoding takes place within a single sentence (Ochs et al. 1979; Scollon 1979).

In reviewing the development of children's initiating strategies, the question also arises of when children begin to use looks, gestures and vocalizations as a means of eliciting responses. As we saw in the previous chapter, mothers and other caregivers often treat children's behaviours as if they were communicative and so establish them as initiations to which they provide an appropriate response. There is, as we have seen, the problem of when we can attribute to the child the intention to communicate and to elicit a predictable response. It seems that we can find fairly clear cases of intentional initiations from about nine months. What about the cries and gestures of younger children? Foster (1979) has studied the development of initiations in children aged from 0;1 to 2;6. She found that the earliest strategic initiations (that is, those in which it might be possible to ascribe some communicative intention to the child) involved *self-topics*, where the child would try to direct attention to himself with something like a cry. In the case of self-topics, it suffices for the child to attract the adult's attention. The adult's task is to find the appropriate response. Foster found that children's early initiations were all of this type and that these were used (albeit infrequently) by even the youngest children in the sample (ages 0;1 and 0;5). A later development was the ability to direct attention to objects in the immediate physical environment (environmental topics). Early examples could be found in reaching behaviours at age 0;5, but clearer cases involved pointing at 1;3 and, later still, the use of attention-directing words. The ability to refer to topics not in the immediate environment *(abstract topics)* developed even later. The earliest signs appeared around 1;10, but clearer cases were to be found at about 2;6. One of the problems of abstract topics is that non-verbal devices, on which children rely heavily in their initiations, are not appropriate. A further factor is the late development of grammatical elements which are used in the establishment of abstract topics. These include the use of the definite article as a marker of old information, anaphoric pronouns as a means of referring to previously mentioned objects and persons, relative clauses as a means of specifying referents more clearly, and tense markers as a means of indicating time relations. The following example from Siobhan at age 2;6 illustrates these problems:

(1)   Siobhan: ['daɪmŋ] ['daɪmŋ]
      Mother: what's a [daɪmŋ]?
                 (exchange repeated several times)
      Siobhan: [ʌpa'tɛps] bus in house
      Mother: oh Stephen
      Siobhan: ['daɪmŋ]

Siobhan wants to refer to a child called Stephen but her mother is unable to identify the referent of ['daɪmn]. After several unsuccessful attempts Siobhan continues with further information which can be glossed in the adult language as 'up the steps and there is a bus in the house', referring to the fact that Stephen lives in a house up some steps and that he has a toy bus in the house. At this point the mother is able to identify Stephen. Siobhan acknowledges this identification to terminate the exchange. Here we can see that in addition to Siobhan's undeveloped phonological system she lacks devices such as fully developed relative clauses to say things like 'the boy who lives in a house which is up some steps and who has a toy bus in his house'.

We have treated attention-getting and attention-directing as if they were two distinct steps. Often however it is possible for a speaker to accomplish both steps at the same time by, for example, using a referring expression to direct the hearer's attention and getting his attention at the same time. In fact, Foster (1979) found that this was the more usual case for children at the prelinguistic stage. Children typically did not pause to check whether they had attention, unlike the slightly older children described by Keenan. Foster sees the use of separate steps as unnecessary given the particular attentional characteristics of mother–child interaction, but also suggests that it is related to an earlier stage in the child's conversational development and is not just a case of the child's egocentrism. Atkinson (1979) points out interestingly that the phenomenon of attention-getting and directing has largely gone unnoticed in studies of child language because adult researchers have been motivated to attend to everything the child says. This is not the case however in more natural situations where the child often has to go to great trouble to secure the attention of a busy adult.

Initiating devices in the data

Perhaps it would be helpful at this point to give some examples of devices used by the children to get and direct attention. This will illustrate the range of devices used and show how the children evidenced considerable communicative intent and ability.

Gaze direction was used as a means of getting attention, of indicating to a potential listener that he was being addressed, of differentiating between possible addressees and of checking that the addressee was attending. In short, it was used to check that the channels of communication were open. The clearest examples were when the children shifted gaze at the point of initiating a new topic:

(2)   Heather: why do you always do that and make me angry?
                      (7.8)
                      (turns to face author)
                      some day when I come here can I have a bath with Siobhan?
         Siobhan: uh? (looks up at Heather)
         Author: uhmmm
                      (6.0) (during this time Siobhan looks at author)
         Siobhan: what? (looks at Heather)
         Heather: a bath

         (Heather 4;0, Siobhan 3;8)   (I:1:103–8)[1]

Heather has been talking to Siobhan. After a pause of almost 8 seconds, she initiates a new topic but addresses this to the author. In order to ensure his attention, she directs her gaze at him. Siobhan indicates her attention by first looking at Heather, then at the author following his responses. When she addresses her *what?* to Heather she shifts her gaze away from the author and back to Heather. Similarly, with the following example in which Heather first addresses the author and looks at him, then, on receiving no response, looks at Siobhan and addresses her:

(3)   Heather: (looks at author)
                      can you make a whole lot of wee men?
                      (0.6)
                      can you?
                      (1.0)
                      (shifts gaze to Siobhan)
                      will you make a wee man will you and a wee lady?

         (4;0)   (I:1:213–15)

A more exaggerated means of indicating addressee was to lean over and face the conversational partner or to go over to him and initiate eye contact. One particularly clear example of this widely used device occurred when the children were seated side by side pretending to be driving in a care:

(4) Siobhan: you 'tend to be a baby (leans over to face Heather)
     Heather: umhmm
     Siobhan: and I'm a mummy
     Heather: umhmmm
     Siobhan: where do you want to go baby? (leans over to face Heather)

     (Siobhan 4;3, Heather 4;7)   (II:6:201–5)

Often verbal and non-verbal devices were combined, as in the following example where Siobhan uses a vocative as well as the device of leaning over to face Heather:

(5) Siobhan: baby (leans over to face Heather)
               baby (vowel lengthened)
     Heather: what?

     (Siobhan 4;3, Heather 4;7)   (II:6:247–9)

This example also illustrates the use of vowel lengthening in the reinitiation of *baby*. Another device was to increase volume as a means of indicating talk addressed to the partner. A particularly clear example occurred following talk to self by Heather. Talk to self was often untranscribable due to low volume, lack of clarity and either lower or higher pitch than usual. However, when Heather addresses the author following talk to self, she increases the volume, raises the pitch and speaks with more careful articulation:

(6) Heather: these are all the slippers
               these are all the slipper slip together
               there's a wee man
               that goes there
               can you make a whole lot of wee men (turns to face the author, increases volume, raises pitch, more careful articulation)

     (4;0)   (I:1:208–12)

A final example illustrates the use of attention-getting words such as *hey*, in this case in combination with a vocative:

(7) Heather: hey Siobhan
     Siobhan: what?
     Heather: do these stickers stick to your feet?

     (Heather 5;9, Siobhan 5;4)   (VI:16:181–3)

Examples (5) and (7) also illustrate how vocatives and attention-getting words can be used in a summons–answer sequence (Schegloff 1968), which is a presequence subsidiary to a subsequent main exchange. The speaker elicits the addressee's attention and then goes on to say something or ask a question after he has secured attention. Summons–answer sequences can also be used to direct or draw attention, typically by the use of *you know what?, you remember X?* questions:

(8) (Heather is telling story from book)
     Heather: and then you know what?
     Siobhan: what?
     Heather: they all standed up

     (Heather 4;7, Siobhan 4;3)   (II:6:390–2)

As far as drawing attention to objects is concerned, the easiest and most frequently used devices were non-verbal, particularly pointing and showing. These were appropriate as they were used in the context of reference to objects in the immediate environment which were thus readily identifiable. The use of *see*, particularly common in Scots English (Atkinson 1979) and in Ulster English, is interesting. In one case it was used with a pause allowing a possible response:

(9) Heather: see this one here?
               (0.8) (shows Siobhan a picture)
               I've got it in my comic

     (5;5)   (V:14:25–6)

but shortly after there was no gap between the utterances and the second was latched directly on to the first:

(10) Heather: see that big purple writing= (shows Siobhan)
               =well I've got that big story

     (5;5)   (V:14:30–1)

A combination of *see* and pointing was used in a longer sequence in which Siobhan was trying to identify the birthday card she had sent to her father:

(11) (Siobhan goes to the mantelpiece to point out the card)
     Siobhan: see that see that very first one (points to card)
               just beside the racing car one?
     Heather: uhhuh
     Siobhan: see that one with the little girl in it (points)
                                        that's a little car
     Siobhan: see this one? (points)
     Heather: I'll sh- I'll tell

Siobhan: no see that one (points)
Heather: that one? (points)
Siobhan: uhhuh
          well that is the one I gived him

(Siobhan 5;1, Heather 5;5)   (V:14:198–208)

It is interesting to look at examples of reference to objects and persons not present in the immediate context. Such references were in fact rare, as the children's talk was mainly concerned with the here and now. However, the children showed that they were able to refer to absent objects without difficulty (all the following examples are from session I) by using relative clauses in order to identify the objects they refer to. In addition, Heather uses an appositive noun phrase *wee streety things* in (12) for further identification:

(12) (Heather refers to plasticine)
     Heather: did you bring some of this to playschool?
               uh things that's got wee things on wee streety things

     (4;0)   (I:1:230–1)

(13) (Heather is looking for a dice)
     Heather: I think it's another one that's lost

     (4;0)   (I:1:252)

(14) (Siobhan is referring to a house being demolished)
     Siobhan: daddy I sawed the house that was broken

     (3;8)   (I:4:201)

It is interesting to look at an example from a later transcript (session IV), where Siobhan uses a relative clause to refer to an object (a shawl) which is however identifiable from the context:

(15) Siobhan: Heather won't take this thing that you be the queen for away
               from the bed

     (4;9)   (IV:11:29)

In this case the use of the relative clause appears redundant for identification of the shawl. Reference to the use of the shawl for dressing up as a queen may have served other interactional ends such as role allocation in pretend play.

Reference to persons was more problematic, as we saw in (1). Similarly in (16), except that here the other participant, Heather, aids identification with a request for clarification:

(16) Siobhan: well these are going to be for Emily instead of you then
     Heather: who are they going to be for?
     Siobhan: at the playschool
     Heather: Emily?
     Siobhan: yes
     Heather: who's she?
     Siobhan: the teacher at my playschool

    (Siobhan 4;6, Heather 4;10)   (III:7:46–52)

Here the identification of Emily as *the teacher at my playschool* takes place over several turns, elicited by Heather's clarification requests. There is, however, some indication in Siobhan's response *at the playschool* to Heather's first clarification request that Siobhan, rather than directly answering the question *who are they going to be for?* is doing the work of identifying Emily.

It is interesting to note that the children coped with such identification problems by the next session (IV):

(17) Siobhan: and my wee friend Andrea doesn't let me play with her toys

    (4;6)   (IV:9:263)

(18) Heather: guess what I was doing for Emma um Siobhan's teacher

    (4;10)   (IV:10:19)

In (17) Siobhan specifies Andrea with the appositive phrase *my wee friend*. Example (18) is particularly interesting as Heather self-corrects from the potentially inadequate identification and repairs with *Siobhan's teacher*. The decision as to which term to use in reference to persons (for example name, job description) is based on an assessment of the addressee's state of knowledge, for example, whether and in what capacity they know the person referred to. The complexities of this system of reference have been described by Sacks and Schegloff (1979) and it constitutes a recurring problem in everyday adult conversation. It is little wonder then that the more complex aspects of reference to persons should prove problematic for children too.

We have seen how attention-directing creates problems for children. Few such problems arose in the data as most reference was to objects in the physical environment and was achieved by non-verbal devices such as pointing and showing. Where problems arose with reference to non-present objects and persons, the addressee usually initiated a repair sequence as in (16) (see chapter 7 for more examples and a discussion of repairs). The speaker was then usually able to specify the referent more adequately. This suggests then that the children in this study were able to cope with the problems of attention-directing which arose in their talk. However, as we have seen, the demands placed on the children were limited by the spontaneous nature of their talk and it would be necessary to observe the children in more closely structured situations to see whether and how they coped with the more complex aspects of attention-directing.

It is difficult to evaluate the extent to which the children's initiating techniques were successful. Generally speaking, they managed to get their addressee's attention and to achieve uptake; that is, to get the addressee to recognize the illocutionary force of their utterances. To quantify this ability would involve identifying those initiations which were unsuccessful in securing uptake and assessing whether such instances decreased with age. The problem is to identify such cases. The clearest are those where the speaker reinitiates following no response, as these are quite clearly cases where the speaker has expected a response and takes action to secure one. Where there is no reinitiation, then it is difficult to determine whether a response was expected. This applies equally to adult conversation. While we expect responses to requests for information and generally some sort of acknowledgement to statements, there are often cases where an utterance is not followed by a contingent response and where this is not seen as exceptional. In the data, there were some utterances which appeared to require responses but did not receive any and the speaker did not treat this absence as noticeable. Interrogatives and tags would seem to be the clearest cases. For example:

(19) Heather: why do you always do that and make me angry?

    (4;0)   (I:1:103)

(20) Siobhan: they're awful aren't they?
     Heather: give me it

    (Siobhan 3;8, Heather 4;0)   (I:2:66–7)

Following (19) we would expect a response to the question *why?* (The context was that Siobhan had lifted up a toy which could be wound up and let it unwind without putting it back on the floor to 'walk'.) Instead Heather picked up the toy and played with it herself, then, following a pause of about 7 seconds, addressed a question to the author on a completely different topic. Although a literal response could have been given to (19), it was also possible to take it not as a request for information but as a rejection of Siobhan's prior action. As such, no response was necessary. In the case of (20) we might have expected Heather to reply *yes* before continuing. Again it is not clear that an explicit response was required and uptake may have been indicated implicitly by Heather's request for the object referred to by Siobhan.

With statements our intuitions are even more shaky, as there are many cases in adult conversation where statements do not receive an explicit acknowledgement but this absence is not taken to be unusual. Looking at one example from the data, we can see how Siobhan does not respond to Heather's statement but addresses a different concern:

(21) Heather: look out there you see . . . your house out there
ha ha ha
you missed it
(1.0)
you missed it
    Siobhan: when I when I come back-
    Heather: -no
I mi- I seen it when we were a wee bit far away
you didn't
    Siobhan: why are-
daddy I don't want to go to Heather's house

(Heather 4;0, Siobhan 3;8)   (I:4:32–41)

Here we can see how Siobhan does not respond to Heather's *you missed it*. In this case Heather reinitiates after a pause of 1 second, presumably in order to get indication of uptake. Siobhan begins to address a different topic but Heather cuts in and continues her topic. Her *you didn't* would again seem to be a candidate for a response by Siobhan but Siobhan continues with her own different topic.

Such examples pose problems for any attempt to quantify the extent to which participants in conversation elicit responses and respond to each other's initiations, as it is not possible to distinguish in any clear-cut way between those utterances which we described in chapter 2 as strongly prospective (expecting a response) and those which are less strongly prospective and simply provide for the possibility of a further response. As far as conversation between fully competent participants is concerned, we can adopt the analytic resource suggested by the conversational analysts of appealing to the ways in which participants display to each other their understanding of each other's utterances (Schegloff and Sacks 1973; Sacks et al. 1974). Thus, if an expected response is not forthcoming to the first pair part of an adjacency pair, the speaker of the first pair part will notice its absence and can take steps to seek a response. In other words, the occurrence of a reinitiation is taken as crucial evidence that a response had been expected in the first place. This is not, however, a sufficient condition, as there is, of course, the option of letting the absent response pass. In this case it would not be possible to mark the first utterance as strongly prospective.

This approach relies on the assumption that the intentions of speakers in conversations are not directly available to the analyst, or indeed to the other participants, but that they can only be inferred on the basis of the ways in which the participants display to each other their understandings of each other's utterances and reach a 'working consensus' of what is going on in the conversation (McDermott et al. 1978). This degree of indeterminacy may be a necessary consequence of the nature of conversation, based as it is on the interaction and joint construction of two or more participants, each with their own separate aims, intentions and strategies. However, there are clearly problems in a developmental study where the aim is to show whether children are successful at eliciting responses as well as responding to preceding initiations. It is not satisfactory to code an utterance as not expecting a response on the basis of the absence of a response and of the absence of a subsequent reinitiation or attempt to elicit one. This would be begging the very question that we are asking. Thus examples such as those discussed earlier must remain indeterminate. This being the case, it would be misleading, however, to classify the children's speech as egocentric, as would have been the case in Piaget's analysis (Piaget 1959). In other words, an assessment of the extent to which participants engage in conversation must be based on a close and principled analysis of the text as well as an appreciation of the ultimately indeterminate nature of conversational inter-action.

Fortunately, such cases as those discussed here were relatively infrequent. In the majority of cases, the children achieved some indication of uptake for their initiations, either at the first attempt or following a reinitiation. Reinitiations are a clear indication that children understand the discourse expectations of their utterances and are in active pursuit of a response. I will now turn to a detailed consideration of the children's reinitiations, showing the devices used and the extent to which these were successful, and looking for some indications of the development of the children's ability to initiate conversational exchanges.

Reinitiations

Reinitiations occur when either no response or an unsatisfactory response has been received. A reinitiation indicates that a response is sought and that its absence is 'noticeable' (Sacks 1968). Thus reinitiations are an indication that children are aware of the discourse expectations of their utterances.

Children display an ability to reinitiate from an early age. Halliday (1979) reports that his son at age nine months used a vocalization [ə] meaning roughly 'do that again'. When the child realized that this act of meaning was no longer eliciting a response, he replaced it with a loud [m̃n] which functioned as a more intensified form. Similarly, at 15 months, he used intonation to distinguish a reinitiated form. While reading a book he would say [á::dà] (mid-rise + mid-fall, no upjump), but on turning to the next page he would say [á::dǎ] (mid-rise + upjump to high fall). Halliday glosses these forms as 'what's that?' and 'and what's that?' respectively. The second utterance is related to the first by this special intonation pattern.

Keenan (1974) shows how twin boys aged 2;9 used repetition as a means of eliciting a response. Where a comment was not acknowledged by the conversation partner, it would be repeated until the acknowledgement was forthcoming. For example:

(22) A: ee moth (repeated twice)
     B: goosey goosey gander, where shall I wander?
     A: ee moth (repeated four times)
     B: up, downstairs, Lady's chamber
     A: ee moth (repeated three times)
     B: ee (lay) moth

In this example the speaker A repeats the utterance over and over again until it is acknowledged. Similar findings have been reported by Scollon (1979).

Reinitiations are usually not simple repetitions, as we saw in Halliday's examples. As well as changing prosodic patterns, the children can also use various eliciting devices such as attention-getting words, vocatives and gaze to make a reinitiation more likely to succeed. In a naturalistic study of the communication of two-year-olds, Wellman and Lempers (1977) found that the children reinitiated 54 per cent of the time following no response. They also found that the children often adapted the original message by using more initiating devices. Later we would also expect various rephrasings and paraphrasings of utterances. These will be illustrated later in the discussion of the data.

Garvey and Berninger (1981) have studied reinitiations in dyads of children ranging from 2;10 to 5;7. They looked in particular at the length of time that a child will wait to receive an expected response and the way children handled their partner's failure to respond. The pause between an initiating utterance and its reinitiation was usually within 2 seconds. This pause exceeded the usual interval between turns for these children, which suggests that the children waited for a response and only reinitiated when they noticed its absence. Different types of initiating utterance were more likely to be followed by absent responses. The most common were declaratives, followed by exclamatives, interrogatives, imperatives, declaratives with question tags and, finally, verbal routines which demanded a simple, conventionalized response. These results indicate the response expectancies of different initiation types for children of this age. Those initiations which are realized by interrogative forms (including tags) and imperatives are more likely to receive responses than declaratives. This bias is also supported by evidence from the tactics used to secure a response, as the device which was most successful was to change the form of the initiating utterance to an interrogative.

Similar results were obtained in the data from Siobhan and Heather. The children were generally successful in obtaining a response to their re-initiations, though often the response was not to the first attempt and considerable persistence was required. However, the success rate of their reinitiations, if we count the ultimate outcome rather than the first response, was high, ranging from 80 per cent in some sessions to 100 per cent in others.

Let us look at how reinitiations were accomplished, as this will give us some insight into the children's ability to pinpoint the possible reasons for the failure of their utterances to secure a response and the means they took to remedy this. If lack of attention was diagnosed as the source of the problem, then subsequent use of an attention-getting device often proved effective, as in the example which we quoted in chapter 2:

(23) Heather: (turns to face author)
               I want a biscuit and a drink
     Siobhan: I wanta get a drink (turns to face author)
     Heather: I want a drink and a biscuit
     Siobhan: I want a drink and a biscuit
     Heather: hey
               I want a drink and a biscuit
     Author: okay

(Heather 4;0, Siobhan 3;8)   (I:1:129–38)

At first the children simply repeat their request. This sometimes was sufficient to elicit a response. However, in this particular case, Heather had to go further and used the attention-getter *hey* in addition to repeating. This attempt was successful.

Often combinations of verbal and non-verbal devices were used to elicit a response. In the following example, Siobhan fails to respond to Heather's request for information. After a pause of 5 seconds, Heather tries again with a vocative. She repeats this strategy after a further 1 second. This time she increases volume and leans over towards Siobhan. Siobhan responds, but Heather rejects the response and reinitiates this rejection after a further 7 seconds, rephrasing her utterance and adding Siobhan's name. This strategy elicits a terminating response:

(24) Heather: they why do you not look for them?
               (5.0)
               Siobhan
               (1.0)

```
         Siobhan (increases volume, leans over to face Siobhan)
Siobhan: I'm too busy to talk
Heather: you are not
         (7.0)
         you aren't Siobhan
Siobhan: yes I am
         (22.0)
```

(Heather 4;10, Siobhan 4;6)   (III:7:8–14)

In addition to repeating an utterance, the children could also rephrase. Rephrasings were particularly interesting as they showed the children's ability to modify their utterances in various ways, for example by isolating, reducing, expanding or reordering sentence constituents. The function of the rephrasing could be either to make a response more likely or, as in the following example, to identify a referent more adequately, in this case by substituting a noun for a pronoun:

(25) Siobhan: she's not making it go forward daddy
               she's not making it go forward daddy
               she's not putting the bus forward daddy

     (3;8)   (I:1:148–50)

Reinitiations then could be accomplished by the following means:

1 Whole or partial repetition of initiation with or without initiating devices such as gaze, pointing, volume increase, vocatives, attention-getting words
2 Rephrasing of initiation with or without initiating devices.

The use of rephrasings rather than repeats would appear to be an indicator of greater flexibility on the children's part, as they show the ability to paraphrase and adapt the original initiation. In actual practice, however, it was difficult to identify pure repeats of prior initiations, as most utterances which were verbal repeats were modified prosodically. We can illustrate the complexity of the children's prosodic modifications by looking at two examples from session I. In (26), Heather is holding a donkey and making clicking noises. Siobhan rejects Heather's noises by saying *that's a donkey*. She repeats this twice but fails to get Heather to change her noises. The sequence runs as follows:

```
(26) 1  Siobhan:  that's a donkey
     2            (1.0)
     3            she's saying cluck (to author)
     4  Heather:  I amn't
     5            I'm saying (clicking noises)
```

6 Siobhan: that's a donkey
7 Heather: donkeys say this
8 Siobhan: no they don't

(Siobhan 3;8, Heather 4;0)   (I:2:112–19)

Let us look at a representation of the prosody of lines 1, 2 and 6 from this sequence, which would normally be treated at straightforward verbal repeats (see figure 11). In the first utterance, Siobhan uses high pitch, indicating disagreement. This is contrasted with a marked step down in

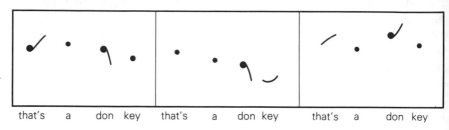

that's   a   don key   that's   a   don key   that's   a   don key

Figure 11 Intonation patterns in example (26), chapter 4

pitch in utterance 2, which would appear to have the function of reiterating her point. However, when it is clear that Heather is not prepared to change her noise, Siobhan repeats in line 6 with a marked step up in pitch, again indicating disagreement.

Our second example occurred a few lines later in the same session, when Heather announced that she had found some Plasticine. On receiving no response, she repeated:

(27) 1 Heather: I found some Plasticine
     2   I found some Plasticine

If we inspect the prosodic representation of this example, we again find marked prosodic modification between the two utterances (see figure 12). In line 1, there is a complex nucleus placed on the first and final syllables of

I   found   some   plas ti   cine   I   found   some   plas   ti cine

Figure 12 Intonation patterns in example (27), chapter 4

Plasticine. The same pitch sequence (falling, then rising) is carried over to the second utterance, but the first part of the nucleus is now placed on *found* and there is a marked step up in pitch height on *Plasticine* with a continuing upward direction through to the final syllable of the word. One possible interpretation of this modification is that Heather is demanding an urgent response to her utterance.

These examples will suffice to make the point that the notion of an exact repetition is difficult to support empirically, as even utterances which are exact verbal repetitions may have undergone complex prosodic modifications. It is beyond the scope of our analysis to dwell further on the range and extent of this complexity, except to recommend that a detailed investigation of the development of children's use of prosody in interactive discourse would be a worthwhile topic for future research. Certainly, to ignore such modifications would be to underestimate the level of children's conversational skills.

We turn now to the devices used by the children to accomplish rephrasings. The following is a selection of the devices used:

Ellipsis
(28) Heather: is it a toy seesaw?
              (1.0)
              is it?

(4;0)   (I:1:161–2)

Reduce, for example, contract auxiliary
(29) Heather: you are not
              you aren't Siobhan

(4;10)   (III:7:12–13)

Expand
(30) Heather: where's the spoon?
              where is that spoon?

(5;1)   (IV:12:96–7)

Add constituents
(31) Heather: I have
              I have got a basket (+ object noun phrase)
              I've got a basket in the house so (+ prepositional phrase,
              + so tag, auxiliary contraction)

(4;0)   (I:4:288–90)

Add tag
(32) Heather: they're going in the water
              (1.6)
              aren't they?

     (4;0)   (I:4:172)

Change sentence mood
(33) Heather: she's a little girl (declarative)
              isn't she a little girl? (negative interrogative)

     (5;1)   (IV:12:346–7)

Explicit demand for response
(34) Siobhan: going to put this underneath your pillow
              very special for you
              do you listen . . . not hear that?

     (4;3)   (II:6:432–3)

Often these devices were combined as in the following examples:

(35) Heather: Siobhan you ARE 'posed to cut THOSE things out (vocative;
              contrastive stress)
              you ARE 'posed to (contrastive stress; ellipsis)
              Siobhan you ARE 'posed to (vocative; contrastive stress)
              do you know that? (explicit demand for response)

     (4;10)   (III:7:309–13)

(36) Siobhan: (talking about alarm clock)
              that's that's what . what can wake you up very hard . early in
              the mornings
              (0.6)
              um it could (elliptical)
              (0.6)
              couldn't it daddy? (change addressee; negative interrogative;
              vocative)
              (1.4)
              couldn't that one daddy (it – that one)
              (0.6)
              could that sort . couldn't that sort of one wake you up very
              early (expand: add sort of + verb phrase)

     (4;6)   (III:7:387–91)

Several of these devices were being used from session I, although here the most frequently used devices were ellipsis and tags. By session IV there was a greater variety of devices being used, particularly with request forms, with direct imperatives being replaced by interrogative and embedded imperative forms. The use of interrogatives is interesting as it was a widely used means of securing a response following a previously unsuccessful initiation in declarative or imperative form. Various types of interrogative were possible, including tags, or *see?* and full positive and negative interrogatives. Interrogatives in reinitiations almost invariably secured a response.

One aspect of development which became increasingly apparent from session IV onwards was that it was becoming more difficult to identify reinitiations. This was because utterances following unsuccessful initiations seemed designed to elicit a response but were not addressing exactly the same proposition as their priors. Justifications of statements were a case in point. For example:

(37) (the children are disputing the number of cards they have on the floor)
```
Heather:  both have eight
          (2.2)
          if you put one away-
Siobhan:                      -umhmm-
Heather:                              -both have eight
          sixteen of them
          (1.4)
          cos eight and eight's sixteen
Siobhan:  uh uh (disagreeing)
```
(Heather 5;5, Siobhan 5;1)   (V:14:133–9)

This dispute continues for some time but this example illustrates the point. Heather is trying to get Siobhan to agree to her calculation of the number of cards. She is eliciting a positive acknowledgement. Her first utterance *both have eight* receives no response so she continues with an explanation. (Siobhan's *umhmm* which interrupts this explanation is probably an indication of attention rather than an acknowledgement of agreement.) Heather's *sixteen of them* also fails to elicit a response so she continues with a justification. At this point Siobhan responds with a disagreement marker.

This example also illustrates a second point which became more apparent in the later sessions, that is, attempts to seek confirmation or agreement following statements. Statements had a much higher rate of failure than other reinitiated forms, which suggests that young children do not perceive a need to respond to these forms – a finding which is supported by Garvey and Berninger's (1981) study described earlier. However, by session IV there was some evidence that the children were becoming more actively engaged in eliciting an explicit acknowledgement of their statements, which indicates a change in the discourse expectations which these utterances now carried for the children. Where these statements had the function of rejecting a prior utterance of the other participant, then the reinitiation was also seeking to elicit agreement. For example:

(38) (the children notice a lorry from the car)
      Heather: dump lorry
      Siobhan: uh got stones
      Heather: no it's not
                it's cement
      Siobhan: no it's stones and cement
      Heather: I know
                mixed together
                into grey
                (2.0)
                isn't that right?
      Siobhan: umhmm

      (Heather 5;1, Siobhan 4;9)   (IV:9:149–58)

Following this discussion about the lorry, Heather offers a compromise solution *mixed together/into grey*. She gets no response and could leave it there but she actively pursues a response with her explicit *isn't that right?* Sometimes this pursuit of a response exceeded the expectations of its recipient:

(39) Siobhan: and there's the biggest garden
      Heather: what?
      Siobhan: the biggest garden in the world
      Heather: where is the biggest garden?
      Siobhan: at the Poly playschool outside
                see?
                (1.0)
                see? (louder)
      Heather: yes
                you don't have to shout

      (Heather 5;1, Siobhan 4;9)   (IV:9:349–57)

Most of the examples discussed so far have involved cases of no response to an initiation. Reinitiations could also follow unsatisfactory responses. In these cases the sequences were often longer as the speaker attempted to get the desired response but the addressee persisted with her own response. Two examples will illustrate the range of devices used by the children in such sequences, the first from session I and the second from session III:

(40) (Heather has found a small bottle among Siobhan's toys)

  1 Heather: what's that? (elicits name of object)
  2   whose is that? (elicits ownership)
  3 Siobhan: that's mine (response to 2)
  4 (louder)   that's mine (repeats 3)
  5 Heather: what's it called? (elicits name)
  6 Siobhan: it's a bottle (response to 5)
  7   it's mine (repeats ownership response)
  8 Heather: what's it called but? (re-elicits name)
  9 Siobhan: it's . it hasn't got a other name (response: rejects 8)
10 Heather: what's it called but? (repeats 8)
11 Siobhan: but it hasn't got a other name (rejects 10)
12 Heather: ah but what's it called? (rejects 11, re-elicits name)
13 Siobhan: it's a bottle (response to 12)
14 Heather: ah but what's inside it? (elicits contents)
15 Siobhan: nothing (response to 14)
16 Heather: no what what pretends something's in it (elicits 'pretend' contents)
17   what is it? (paraphrases 16)
18 Siobhan: there's nothing (response to 16 and 17)   (I:2:156–73)

Here we have a clear case of a breakdown in communiction, with Heather persistently questioning Siobhan about the bottle and Siobhan becoming increasingly annoyed that her response is not accepted as satisfactory. Sometimes Heather reinitiates with repetitions (line 10), in other cases she paraphrases, changing the content from eliciting the name of the object (lines 1, 5, 8, 10, 12), to its ownership (line 2), its contents (line 14), and its pretend contents (line 16). Notice how Heather is forced to become more explicit as the sequence develops, although it is not clear whether her initial purpose was to elicit a response within a pretend game or whether she changes the content of her elicitations following responses which are for her unsatisfactory. Note too the use of *but* in lines 8, 10, 12 and 14. *But* indicates that a response has been received but is unsatisfactory. Heather shifts its position from sentence-final position (which is grammatical in her dialect of Ulster English) to a more salient sentence-initial position and strengthens it with *ah*. Her *no* in line 16 is a stronger indication that the preceding response was not satisfactory.

(41) (Siobhan is cutting pictures out and offers one to Heather)

  1 Siobhan: this is one of your favourite things to give to mummy
               (9.0)
  2   this is her thing right? (reduce; tag)
  3 Heather: let me see
  4   no

   5 Siobhan: sure you have to give it to her (rephrase; <u>sure</u>)
   6 Heather: I don't want it
   7 Siobhan: sure sure you have to take it home and give it to your
              mummy
              right? (rephrase: expand; <u>sure</u>; tag)
   8 Heather: I don't want it
              (3.0)
   9   look Siobhan I don't want it (repeat + <u>look</u> + vocative)
10 Siobhan: sure you only . only
11   you only have to carry it home to your mummy (rephrase)
12 Heather: I don't want it
             (1.2)
13 Siobhan: sure it's only your wee picture what you have to give to
             mummy (rephrase)
14 Heather: I know but I don't want to have it
15 Siobhan: sure it's your favourite picture (rephrase)
16 Heather: it isn't
17 Siobhan: it is
18 Heather: it isn't
19 Siobhan: it is your favourite picture (expand auxiliary; expand 17)
             (1.8)
20   yes it is cos that . that's . that's
21   sure spoons are your favourite things aren't they?
             (rephrase; <u>sure</u>; tag)
             (1.2)
22   aren't they <u>Heather</u>? (repeat tag; vocative)
                 <u>no</u>
             (2.2)
24   they're not (expand: elliptical)
25 Siobhan: they are
26 Heather: they aren't
             (2.2)
27 Siobhan: what ones are your favourite? (interrogative)
28 Heather: nothing
             (Siobhan changes topic)

  Siobhan 4;6, Heather 4;10)   (III:7:259–86)

Here we can see a range of devices used by both children to achieve their interactional goals, Siobhan to get Heather to accept the picture and Heather to refuse it. Siobhan makes various appeals – for example, to the idea that it is Heather's favourite picture, that it is suitable for her mother, that Heather likes spoons and so on. She also tries to minimize the demands put on Heather by using forms such as *only* (lines 11, 13). She finishes with a question about Heather's favourite things to which Heather is able to reply negatively. Siobhan uses various reinitiating devices such as tags (lines 2, 7, 21, 22), vocative (line 22), initial *sure* (used in Ulster English in an utterance reversing the polarity or contradicting a preceding utterance) (lines 5, 7, 10, 13, 15, 21). At one stage she gets into a dead-end sequence (lines 16–18, also 24–26), but she resolves this by expanding (line 21) with a further justification (lines 20–21) or by rephrasing (line 27). Heather for her part resorts mainly to the device of denying that she wants the picture (lines 6, 8, 9, 12, 14) but also of rejecting Siobhan's claims (lines 16, 18, 23, 24, 26). She also reinitiates to try and make her point. In line 9 she reinitiates with *look* and a vocative, as well as repeating line 8. In line 24 she expands on 23 by adding subject and verb.

Both these examples are typical of many lengthy sequences in the data; in both cases the initiator of the sequence was unsuccessful, but this derives less from the devices used and more from the obstinacy of the addressee. Other cases ended in compliance (see the discussion of initially non-compliant requests in chapter 5).

Vocatives in initiations and reinitiations

We have been referring to vocatives as attention-getting devices, though, as Wootton (1981) has shown, they can also be used to signal that a response is being elicited, especially when they are used in utterance-final position. As vocatives are clearly recognizable discourse devices, it will be interesting to examine the ways they were used in the data.

The most obvious function is to signal the intended addressee of an utterance. This is particularly useful in the case of a change of addressee. However, vocatives seem to be used in many cases where there is no doubt about the potential addressee. Sometimes they may have been used to signal endearment, as in Siobhan's use of *little baby* in her role of mother in pretend play. Vocatives were also used in cases of urgency as a means of ensuring attention as well as eliciting a response. The clearest examples were summons–answer sequences where the addressee has to signal attention before the speaker continues.

These functions can be related to the position of vocatives in utterances. If we take summons–answer sequences as examples of utterance-initial position, we can see that utterance-initial vocatives are used to signify addressee and to get attention. For example:

(42) Heather: (to author) there's a whole lot of Plasticine isn't there?
              (to Siobhan) Siobhan isn't there a whole lot of Plasticine?

(4;0)   (I:1:177–8)

Sequential evidence supports this claim. If we look at cases where a speaker reinitiates and has to get attention, the position of the vocative shifts from utterance-final to initial position. For example:

(43) Siobhan: you just do them things in the school
                see?
                (2.0)
                see Heather?
                (2.0)
                Heather you just do them things=
     Heather: =right we'll be in the school

(Siobhan 4;9, Heather 5;1)   (IV:8:297–302)

Siobhan is unable to elicit a response from Heather. She uses *see*, then adds a vocative. Finally she uses initial vocative to summon Heather. In fact, in sequences such as this where several attempts are made to elicit a response, the trend was to shift vocatives from final to initial position or even to use the vocative alone as a summoning device, which seemed to be a powerful attention-getter:

(44) Siobhan: (to author) Heather won't let me be the baby
                (1.6)
                daddy
                (1.6)
                daddy=
                =Heather won't let me be the baby
                (1.0)
                (whining) daddy
     Author: what is it?

(Siobhan 4;9)   (IV:8:585–90)

Vocatives in utterance-final position seemed to have the function primarily of eliciting a response, with the assumption that attention had already been secured. In the following example, Heather is disputing a prior claim by Siobhan but cannot get Siobhan to respond. Her use of a final-positioned vocative elicits a response:

(45) Heather: yes it was
                (2.8)
                it was so
                (1.1)
                it was so Siobhan
     Siobhan: no it wasn't

(Heather 4;0, Siobhan 3;8)   (I:1:238–41)

We can also draw on sequential evidence to support this claim. In cases where the speaker assumed that the addressee had both attended and heard, the reinitiation was frequently elliptical, as a full repetition was not necessary. In fact the function of the reinitiation was solely to elicit a response and the vocative would be placed in final position:

(46) Siobhan: sure spoons are your favourite things aren't they?
          (1.2)
          aren't they Heather?
    Heather: no

(Siobhan 4;6, Heather 4;10)   (III:7:279–81)

Further evidence is provided here by Heather's overlapping of Siobhan's vocative. Heather is able to respond before Siobhan completes her utterance, so that the reinitiation has the function of eliciting a response.

To sum up, vocatives are used for a variety of functions. Initially placed vocatives are primarily used for attention-getting while finally placed vocatives are response eliciting. Vocatives were a powerful initiating device and generally secured attention and responses. The children in the study displayed sensitivity towards the differential placement of vocatives, espccially in their reinitiated utterances.

Concluding remarks

We have seen in this chapter how children's communication is generally successful and that it has *recipient design*. Children use the variety of devices described in chapter 2 to secure their listener's attention and to direct the listener's attention to the objects, events and persons they refer to, both in the immediate physical context and, with older children, outside the physical context. In addition, they are able to recognize communicative breakdown and apply a variety of repair devices as remedies.

The devices we have described have illustrated this aspect of children's conversational development. The observations from this study support those of similar studies (for example, Keenan and Schieffelin 1976; Wootton 1981) which suggests the possibility of universality for the devices children use to get and direct attention. Some of these devices are, however, restricted. Tapping a potential addressee is more typical of a small child and would be considered marked behaviour among unfamiliar adults. Various devices are also culture specific. Milroy (1980), for example, reports a high degree of physical contact such as tapping and hugging among working-class adults as a part of conversational behaviour, which suggests that there are differences in cultural norms. Devices such as gaze would seem to be fairly universal as an important feature in face-to-face interaction, which is learnt from an early age in the first months of interaction between infants and caretakers (Stern 1977). Vocatives would also seem to be a primary initiating device with various functions, which may also be culture specific and which are subject to various constraints on their selection and usage (Ervin-Tripp 1972; Brown and Gilman 1970).

The devices we have described for initiating and reinitiating conversational exchanges are intimately related to various aspects of the children's linguistic development. We have seen how the ability to refer to objects and persons outside the physical context depends to a great extent for its realization on the prior acquisition of grammatical competence, for example definiteness, relative clauses and tense markers. Reinitiations which involve rephrasing also frequently display aspects of grammatical competence, such as the ability to paraphrase by reordering sentence constituents, reduce by ellipsis and substitution and change sentence mood. The interactional requirements of designing utterances for successful communication would thus seem to be an important stimulus for the development of linguistic competence.

We have seen how the children in this study used a variety of devices to initiate and reinitiate conversation. It has been more difficult to pinpoint areas of development. Partly this is due to the nature of the object of enquiry. To be more specific: it is not possible to rank the various initiating devices in terms of their complexity. Obviously, for a child at the pre-linguistic stage, the use of preverbal attention-getters precedes verbal devices. But for the child who has developed a range of verbal and non-verbal devices, as for the adult, the choice of any given device does not necessarily reflect conversational maturity but can depend on the specific demands of the situation. Thus, in some cases, a non-verbal device might be more appropriate than a verbal device. Ranking in terms of complexity is only appropriate in cases where some devices have not yet emerged. Given that the children in this study were using all the devices described by session I, we must conclude that their acquisition of the basic skills of initiating preceded this time.

We can, however, look at cases of unsuccessful initiations as possible indications of areas of subsequent development, although we must bear in mind that we are now concerned with a very small number of examples. For instance, there were signs that reference to non-present persons was still problematic by session III, although it was being negotiated successfully be session IV. As far as reinitiations were concerned, we saw that success rate was high over all the sessions, but that a greater range of devices was being used by session IV and that children were becoming more actively concerned with eliciting acknowledgements of their statements. We also saw how, in an example from session III, the children were able to proceed beyond the repetitive dead-end sequences more typical of session I. These aspects of development will be taken up in chapter 5, where we will examine the ways in which children negotiate request sequences and how they develop more elaborate means of reinitiating their requests following non-compliant responses.

5

Request sequences

Requests for action (often referred to as directives) have been widely studied as one of the basic units of conversational interaction. There are several reasons for this, as we saw in chapter 2. The choice of a particular request form is determined by social considerations such as the age and rank of the addressee and the degree of politeness to be conveyed. We can also consider the conditions which underlie the felicitous performance of speech acts, such as requests, and the extent to which speaker and addressee refer to these conditions as a means of indirectly conveying requests and expressing non-compliance. As requests may involve conflict between the wishes of the requester and those of their recipient, request sequences are a potential arena for the negotiation of social and psychological issues such as rights and obligations, willingness and ability.

In this chapter we will see how these issues are articulated in the requests of young children. We will begin with a general overview of the development of the production and comprehension of requests by children. We will then examine the extent to which children display social sensitivity in their choice of request forms as well as an awareness of the conditions underlying this particular speech act. This will lead to a discussion of request sequences in which the initial response is non-compliant. We will see how the requests, the responses they receive and other related material are often negotiated over extended sequences. A detailed examination of these sequences will show that it is important to consider various non-linguistic phenomena such as the interactional aims of the participants and the extent to which the requests carry high or low 'costs and benefits' for one or other of the participants.

Children's production and comprehension of requests

We can trace the development of requests for action back to the early prelinguistic stage during the child's first year. As we saw in chapter 3, children's gestures and vocalizations can be interpreted with some reliability as intentional requesting schemas from about the age of nine months. Carter (1978) described a range of different communicative schemata including requests based on a detailed and careful observation of one child between 12 and 16 months. One of the most common schemata was the request for action which was realized by an open-handed reaching gesture towards an object together with a vocalization which took the form of an [m]-initial monosyllable. The main criterion for establishing the child's intentionality involved examining the child's behaviour subsequent to the request. Following compliance the child would become quiet or change to another activity, but would persist with the request following initial indifference or refusal on the part of the recipient of the request. Similarly, Halliday (1975) reports the use of vocalizations such as [nā] at 0;9–0;10½ and [mnŋ] at 1;1½–1;3 which he glosses respectively as 'I want that' and 'give me that'. Children also use prelinguistic communicative schemes to request the performance of an action, as we can see in the following extract from a study by Dore (1975):

> J. tries to push a peg through a hole and when he cannot succeed he looks up at his mother, keeping his finger on the peg, and utters [ʌʔʌʔʌʔ]; his mother then helps him push the peg, saying *OK*.

At a slightly later stage words such as *more* are used frequently to request repetition of an activity (Gopnik 1977).

Ervin-Tripp (1977b) reviews a number of accounts of the early use and development of verbal requests. The first requests, early in the second year, are realized by combinations of gestures with names of desired objects and words such as *more, want, gimme*. By the third year children are using more elaborate forms such as embedded imperatives (for example, *would you push this?*). Newcombe and Zaslow (1981) found that children as young as two and one-half years used indirect forms such as *question directives* and *hints* (see chapter 2). However, these forms were used generally to identify problems which adults might be expected to remedy and so are unlike the more mature use of these indirect request forms by adults and older children, where indirect requesting strategies have the function either of providing the addressee with the option of non-compliance or of concealing the directive intent in order to avoid loss of face in the event of non-compliance. In a study of children aged 3;6 to 5;7, Garvey (1975) found that few indirect requests were used by the younger children. The older children, however, produced on average twice as many successful indirect requests as the younger children. Garvey also reports cases of more complex requesting strategies where the directive intent is concealed in order to manipulate a greater likelihood of compliance. Some of these strategies require several steps for their successful accomplishment.

It seems that mothers and other caretakes are sensitive to differences in the forms of requests and use more indirect forms as a funcion of the child's increasing age (Bellinger 1979). Tollefson (1976) found that in early mother –child interaction with children under two years, 69 per cent of mothers' requests were defective in that they failed to fulfil one or more of the preconditions on requests. For example, the child might already be carrying out the action prior to the request or the mother may have carried out the action herself. It is suggested that one of the functions of these requests is to present situations in which responses are possible and in which the older child will in fact be expected to respond. Likewise, Garnica (1978) shows how mothers provide non-verbal cues to enable their children to respond to their requests. Comparisons of requests to a one-year-old and a three-year-old child showed that the mother used more gestures to the younger child and modelled the required action for the child. The mother of the three-year-old relied more on verbal instructions and less on gestures. Thus it would seem that mothers use various devices to aid their children's comprehension of requests and to shape compliance, and that these change in accordance with the developing linguistic competence of the child.

We have seen that some indirect requests are likely to provide more difficulty for children's comprehension. Various factors are involved, such as the degree of explicitness of the surface form, for example, whether the agent and intended act are mentioned or whether the action refers to routines and rules that are part of the child's everyday experience. Children as young as two years can respond appropriately to requests in the form *can you find me a truck?* and even to requests in which the desired act is not stated, as in *are there any more suitcases?* (Shatz 1975; 1978b). However, they also respond with actions to utterances in forms rarely used conventionally to convey requests, such as *may you find me a truck?* Thus, Shatz argues on the basis of a discrimination experiment that children operate an action-based rule of the form 'mother says – child does'. The children were presented with utterances containing *can you* + feasible act in two discourse contexts, one following a series of directives and one following an information exchange. It was found that, even in the information exchange context, children showed a bias towards action responses. It is argued that older children develop away from this action-based strategy by learning the appropriate linguistic and contextual markers for various illocutionary acts. Some support for an early ability to discriminate illocutionary force is provided by experimental data from Reeder (1980), who tested the ability of children aged 2;6 and 3;0 to discriminate offers from requests, when they were worded ambiguously, as in

(1)   would you like to play on the bicycle?

Reeder found that the 2;6- and three-year-olds were equally adept at discriminating offers but that the three-year-olds were more reliable at discriminating requests. He concludes that the children appear to be aware of the appropriate felicity conditions associated with different illocutionary acts and are also able to utilize general inferential skills about the functions of utterances addressed to them. Thus it seems that by about age three children have the ability to comprehend requests for action realized indirectly by forms such as question directives and hints, although it may require considerable social knowledge to make reliable inferences about more opaquely expressed directive intentions.

Children's requests as social acts

There is now quite a lot of evidence, mainly from observational studies, that young children's choice of request forms takes account of social features of the speech situation. Andersen (1978) shows how four-year-olds in role play displayed sensitivity to rank of addressee in their choice of request type. Similarly, in an experimental study of Italian children aged 2;10 to 6;2, Bates (1976) found that children were able to select more polite forms in requests addressed to adults. Ervin-Tripp (1977b) has reviewed a number of studies of social variation in children's request forms, the main conclusion being that children's choice of forms is governed by their understanding of features of the situation such as age, rank and sex of addressee as well as the nature of the task required by the request. Children as young as two years differentiated age and rank by addressing simple imperatives to peers but desire statements, question directives and permission directives to adults. In a study involving four-year-olds, it was found that the choice of request form was also determined by the task. Embedded imperatives were used for wheedling goods whereas direct imperatives were used for behaviour control. Task and addressee interacted so that need statements were more typically used when requesting goods from adults, presumably because with adults the child was not in competition for the goods. Hints referring to aversive conditions requiring remedy were also more commonly addressed to adults. The interaction of situation and age of addressee was studied in an experimental study by James (1978). Situations were distinguished according to whether requests were concerned with rejecting intrusions (for example, where addressee occupied speaker's territory or took her possessions), or with requesting goods and services. Addressees were adults, peers and juniors. It was found that the children, aged 4;5 to five years, distinguished according to age of addressee particularly in the rejection of intrusion requests, using direct imperatives to juniors but modified imperatives to peers and adults.

One of the main problems in studying variation in the use of request forms is that the choice of a particular form can be based on extremely subtle and often culture-specific considerations. For instance, in a study of the pragmatic determinants of directive choice by a group of black American children aged seven to twelve years (Mitchell-Kernan and Kernan 1977), it was shown that, as well as taking into consideration the various inter-personal functions of requests, the children also used requests not to obtain goods and services but to define, reaffirm, challenge, manipulate and redefine status and rank. Requests were a means of establishing power over an addressee. Compliance with a direct imperative was often taken as an indication of submission and addressees of requests frequently insisted on more polite embedded forms to counter this effect.

The evidence suggests that children display a considerable degree of social competence in their use of request forms (see Becker 1982 for a recent review of children's requesting strategies). The question arises of whether and how their requests differ from adult forms. Ervin-Tripp (1977b) suggests that adults have available more subtle forms of deviousness, although these are already present to some extent in the early years. Generally however children have yet to learn how to make requests which do not explicitly identify what is wanted, or to engage in strategies which allow for withdrawal from embarrassing situations, by retreating to a more literal meaning if exception is taken to the indirectly conveyed meaning. Thus children have to learn to conceal their purposes. As Ervin-Tripp (1977b:188) puts it: 'Wide use of tactful deviousness is a late accomplishment.'

We can turn now to a detailed examination of children's requests based on data from the two children, Siobhan and Heather. The requests were coded according to Ervin-Tripp's categories (see chapter 2), ignoring permission requests which were rare. It was found that the children displayed a command of the various request types described by Ervin-Tripp and that they varied these according to their addressee. More personal need statements and hints were used to the copresent adult while more direct imperatives were used to each other. These results confirm those reported elsewhere, for example, in Andersen (1978) and Ervin-Tripp (1977b).

There was no evidence in the limited sample of a developmental trend away from direct imperatives to more indirect forms. This can be explained, however, in terms of the context of the requests. Given that most of the requests were directed to a peer in play, we would expect on the basis of other studies (for example, Ervin-Tripp 1977b) that direct imperatives would predominate. This is not an indication of immaturity. There would need to be a wider range of contexts, with variation of addressees according to age and familiarity and greater variation in tasks, in order to assess the development of a wider range of forms reflecting a more mature understanding of the social features of requests. The category of hints is also problematic. In some cases there were not especially indirect, yet in other cases they displayed evidence of strategic ploys on the part of the requester. This category would have to be broken down further in order to distinguish levels of indirectness and degrees of politeness.

It is interesting to examine the use of embedded imperatives by the children. We would predict that these would occur typically in the case of difficult tasks, when directed to unfamiliar addressees or those differing in rank. If we examine some examples of embedded imperatives, we can see that the dimension of the nature of the task had a bearing on their use:

(2) Heather: will you make a wee man, will you, and a wee lady?

(4;0)   (I:1:215)

(3) Heather: would you show me?

(4;0)   (I:1:387)

(4) Heather: would you give me that?

(4;0)   (I:1:295)

(5) Siobhan: will you give me the scissors for a wee minute?

(4;6)   (III:7:73)

(6) Siobhan: will you please give me the scissors and then I can have the stool and you have this?

(4;6)   (III:7:216)

The first two examples involved the addressee in leaving an activity in which she was engaged to carry out the requested action. Example (5) was a request for the addressee to hand over one of her own possessions. The requests for the scissors occurred in the context of both children wanting to do cutting-out activities where only one pair of scissors was available. In each of these cases, we can judge that the request involved high cost to the addressee in that she had to leave an activity in which she was engaged or yield a prized possession. The 'scissors request' also involved high benefits for the requester, as she stood to benefit highly from compliance. Interestingly, only (3) resulted in compliance, a further indication that the requests involved high costs to their addressees. So it would seem that there is a relationship between the children's choice of more polite forms and the nature of the task. This point will be taken up in more detail later when we look at the issue of costs, benefits and variation in request forms in more extended request sequences.

Conversely, if we examine those occasions where direct imperatives were used almost exclusively, we can see that these were generally cases of role allocation among the children or of regulating the course of play. Here requests were typically low cost, as in:

(7)   Heather: just throw it in there

       (5;5)   (V:13:586)

This was spoken while putting toys into a doll's house, where the nature of the request did not carry high costs or benefits to the participants.

A speech act approach to children's requests

There is also evidence that children are aware of the conditions underlying speech acts, as proposed in speech act theory. Garvey (1975), analysing the requests of children aged 3;6 to 5;7, found that these conditions, which she describes as *meaning factors*, were often made explicit in *adjuncts* to requests (that is, utterances giving the reason for the request or supporting it in some way) as well as in non-compliant responses. Thus, in making a request, children would often state the reason for the request, for example:

(8)   stop it. You hurt my head

express their desire or need for the outcome of the act, for example:

(9)   hey come here. I want to show you something

or query the willingness of the hearer to perform the action, for example:

(10) here, do that. Do the rest of that OK?

Responses also made these meaning factors explicit. Temporizing acknowledgements, for example:

(11) A: come on, get on
     B: as soon as I finish putting out this roaring fire

indicated that the hearer acknowledged the request and was aware of the time-based condition that requests should normally be carried out at the earliest available opportunity. Non-compliant responses made reference to various conditions on requests. For example, the hearer could assert his inability or unwillingness to carry out the action, claim that he did not need or want its outcome, wasn't obliged to carry out the action, was not the appropriate person to do the action, had a prior or conflicting right to requested goods, and so on. For example:

(12) A: get the table
     B: no, I don't want to do that

Reference to hearer's inability proved to be the most effective deterrent of repeated requests, indicating that speakers normally assume hearer's ability to perform the action when making a request. Other non-compliant responses such as the denial of obligations were less effective in deterring repetition of the request.

Garvey also examined the children's indirect request forms and found evidence that children were addressing the conditions underlying requests by querying the hearer's ability and willingness or referring to his obligations (for example, *you have to X*). Here however there is the problem of determining whether the children were really referring to ability and willingness with forms such as *can you* and *will you* or whether these forms had simply become conventionalized formulae for mitigating requests or expressing politeness.

The data from Siobhan and Heather supports Garvey's findings. The children often accompanied requests with an utterance justifying the request, for example:

(13) Heather: give me the wee bus
               it's going in the car wash

    (4;0)   (I:1:151–2)

Such justifications could also appear in the slot following a non-compliant response as a means of reinitiating the request:

(14) Heather: change lunch boxes
     Siobhan: no
     Heather: you'll have a bigger one so you will

    (Heather 4;0, Siobhan 3;8)   (I:4:489–91)

In this case Heather is supporting her request by referring to the consequences of the action – in particular, its benefits for the hearer. In other cases, children referred to their own rights or benefits, for example:

(15) Siobhan: no let's change over puppets
                please
                cos cos I want the dog

    (4;9)   (IV:10:5–7)

Other requests made reference to ability. In one case, Heather requested Siobhan to carry out an action which she was unable to do herself:

(16) Heather: do it for me
               I can't reach up

    (4;0)   (I:5:157–8)

while in another case Siobhan requested Heather not to do an act because she could do it herself:

(17) Siobhan: no don't
     I can do all that

   (5;1)   (V:13:446–7)

Looking at responses, we can see that there is some support for the taxonomy of conditions specified by Labov and Fanshel (1977) (see chapter 2), as the following examples indicate:

Existential status of the act
(18) Siobhan: um now you be the baby
   Heather: no I've been the baby

  (Siobhan 4;9, Heather 5;1)   (IV:8:384–5)

Consequences of the act
(19) Siobhan: you sit in that chair
       this this is the chair
       and that's the working chair well
   Heather: ah but you can't reach away over there . . . do your work
       you have to sit on that stool if you're going to do your
       working work

  (Siobhan 5;1, Heather 5;5)   (V:14:249–53)

Time referents
(20) Heather: well go and get some nappies
   Siobhan: I'll do it in a minute now

  (Heather 4;7, Siobhan 4;3)   (II:6:265–6)

Need for action (including appropriacy of act)
(21) Siobhan: you rub your head
   Heather: my head- my head isn't itchy

  (Siobhan 4;9, Heather 5;1)   (IV:8:71–2)

(22) Heather: pretend this is in the hospital
   Siobhan: you don't do those things in a hospital

  (Heather 5;1, Siobhan 4;9)   (IV:8:295–6)

Query need for action or need for request
(23) Heather: you lie down there
   Siobhan: why?
   Heather: cos you're dead

  (Heather 5;5, Siobhan 5;1)   (V:13:796–8)

Deny ability
(24) (Heather wants Siobhan to fasten cover of toy pram)
    Heather: would you do the things?
    Siobhan: I can't do them either

    (Heather 5;1, Siobhan 4;9)   (IV:11:110–12)

Willingness (including alternative wishes)
(25) Heather: help me to put them in
    Siobhan: no no
             we're not going to do the same as we did

    (Heather 5;5, Siobhan 5;1)   (V:13:187–9)

(26) Heather: but you have to tidy the box up don't you?
    Siobhan: I'm bored of tidying up
             I'm going to put my belt on

    (Heather 5;9, Siobhan 5;5)   (VI:16:373–6)

Obligation (including assertions of alternative obligations)
(27) Heather: now would you give me that?
    Siobhan: don't have to give you my Plasticine

    (Heather 4;0, Siobhan 3;8)   (I:4:295–6)

(28) Heather: waken up
    Siobhan: no cos I have to go to sleep

    (Heather 4;7, Siobhan 4;3)   (II:6:109–10)

There were no cases of a hearer making reference to the speaker's right to make a request as a means of indicating non-compliance. However, in addition, it was also possible to refuse by asserting that addressee was not the appropriate person to do the action, for example:

(29) Heather: you start this time
    Siobhan: no you
             whoever has the snap has . can go again

    (Heather 5;1, Siobhan 4;9)   (IV:14:574–6)

or by rejecting some aspect of the content of the request, for example:

(30) Siobhan: you've got to count up to sixty right?
    Heather: but I thought we were at thirty a minute ago

    (Siobhan 5;1, Heather 5;5)   (V:14:347–8)

Indirect requests also provided some evidence of children's awareness of the conditions associated with requests, particularly those associated with willingness and obligations. Children could question if the addressee wanted to perform an act:

(31) Siobhan: do you want to come out in my car?
    Heather: in a minute

    (Siobhan 4;6, Heather 4;10)   (III:6:180–1)

Children also used utterances beginning with *I want* or *I need* as an indirect means of requesting, where the required act had to be inferred:

(32) Heather: I want a biscuit and a drink

    (4;0)   (1:1:129)

In some cases, a request with *want* was an indirect means of getting the other child to stop doing something, for example:

(33) Siobhan: I want to count the cards

    (3;8)   (I:1:72)

Here Siobhan indirectly requested Heather to stop counting the cards so that she herself could count them. Finally, there were *want* requests addressed to the copresent adult which indirectly requested the adult to get the other child to perform an act, for example:

(34) Siobhan: I want Heather to play with me

    (3;8)   (I:1:353)

(35) Heather: I want Siobhan to come up with me

    (4;0)   (I:1:420)

There were no recorded examples explicitly asserting the speaker-based condition of the form *I want you to X*.

  Indirect requests addressing the condition of obligation were realized usually by the form *you have to X* and frequently concerned requests about role-play actions, for example:

(36) Heather: you have to do my operation

    (5;1)   (IV:8:485)

Negated obligation was used as an indirect means of requesting to stop doing an act, for example:

(37) Heather: you don't have to do it everywhere
             that's enough

    (5;1)   (IV:12:189–90)

In some cases the response made reference to additional conditions:

(38) Heather: you don't have to shout
     Siobhan: yes I can if I want to

    (Heather 4;10, Siobhan 4;6)   (III:7:209–10)

There was one example of a request prefaced by *don't forget,* which addresses the condition that it is not obvious to the speaker that the hearer will carry out the act in the absence of the request (Searle 1969:66):

(39) Heather: Siobhan don't forget to bring your bikini round to my house

    (5;1)   (IV:10:225)

Finally, one request, which followed a direct imperative, queries the existential state of the action:

(40) Heather: well get a nappy
             have you got the nappies for me?

    (4;10)   (III:6:262–3)

From the examples presented in this section we have seen how there is some evidence that the children were aware of the conditions underlying the felicitous production and comprehension of action requests. It was not possible to analyse frequency of occurrence due to the small numbers of such examples. It is however interesting to note the emergence of these *meaning factors* in the data by examining the first occurrences of references to conditions on requests made explicit in responses, as in figure 13.

	I	II	III	IV	V	VI
Existential status				X		
Circumstances					X	
Time referents		X				
Need for action		X				
Need for request	X					
Ability				X		
Willingness					X	
Obligation	X					
Rights						

Figure 13 First occurrence of reference to conditions underlying requests in non-compliant responses to requests

Bearing in mind the usual reservation about problems of sampling and representativeness of the data, we see that figure 13 gives some indication that the development of the awareness of the conditions underlying requests is a gradual process. Complex conditions such as reference to the possible consequences of a request act develop late, whereas querying the need for the request or the action using a simple *why* question occurs earlier. Some of the other results are more difficult to explain. Denial of obligation occurred early (see (34)), but did not occur again until session IV. Denial of willingness occurred late. Perhaps it takes children some time before they realize that the denial of willingness is a means of expressing non-compliance. Further speculation is unwarranted and we must await the results from larger samples in longitudinal studies for a more comprehensive description of the development of the meaning factors underlying requests for action.

Request sequences

It was argued in chapter 2 that it is important to go beyond a description of requests as isolated speech acts to a consideration of their function in the context of the sequences in which they occur. The most interesting cases are likely to be those in which the initial responses to the request is non-compliant, as these are a potential arena for further negotiation between the participants. We turn now to a detailed analysis of such sequences, looking in particular at the following:

1. How the requester behaves following initial non-compliance, that is, what means are used to reinstate the request and persist with it as well as reasons for withdrawing requests and how this is accomplished
2. How the requestee behaves in initially non-compliant sequences, that is, what means are used to persist with non-compliance and why the requestee occasionally switches to being compliant.

A total of 576 request sequences, that is, sequences of interaction initiated by a request for action, were identified. Of these, 122 (21 per cent) received responses which were initially non-compliant (this excludes responses which request clarification or which delayed compliance, for example, *wait a minute*). Of these 122 non-compliant sequences, 25 (20 per cent) eventually terminated with compliance on the part of the recipient of the request.

Non-compliance can be expressed in various ways. We can distinguish between simple refusals, usually expressed by *no*, and refusals with accounting, in which the non-compliant participant justifies the refusal, for example, by negating or questioning one of the preconditions of the request (Labov and Fanshel 1977) or by rejecting part or all of the propositional content of the request. In addition, responses could be requests for clarification or delays (that is, postponements of the action response).

The form of the request seemed to have little bearing on the form of the non-compliant response, apart from the predictable discourse constraints related to the request forms; for example, interrogative forms usually received *yes/no* responses, although these could be implicit. Direct imperatives usually received *no* as a non-compliant response, while compliance was realized non-verbally with an occasional verbal acknowledgement (for example, *yes, OK*). Non-compliant responses to need statements and hints either rejected the proposition asserted by the request or provided a justification for the refusal.

The length of non-compliant request sequences varied, ranging from a minimum of two turns, where the requester accepted the non-compliance and either initiated another topic or allowed the requestee to do so, to a maximum of 33 turns.

Behaviour following initially non-compliant responses

Following a non-compliant response, the requester has the choice of persisting with the request or allowing the sequence to terminate. In this study, non-compliance did not seem to deter requesters and they were more likely to persist rather than withdraw. Let us look at some of the ways in which they continued with their request. Requests could be reinitiated either by simply repeating them or by rephrasing. Repetitions could include minor modifications such as the addition of address terms or attention-getting devices (see chapter 4). Rephrasings included syntactic reordering of constituents, change of request type (for example, from direct imperative to embedded imperative), providing a justification for the request, or rejecting a prior justification for a refusal. These distinctions are similar to those between 'rigid' and 'flexible' reinitiations of requests (Levin and Rubin 1984). The following example, typical of non-compliant sequences from session II onwards, illustrates a more flexible reinitiating behaviour:

(41)   (Siobhan wants to wear a jacket)
    1 Heather: right you play with all those toys
    2 Siobhan: no I've to um go out on holidays today now
    3 Heather: no it's not- no you don't always wear that every day
    4 Siobhan: no cos um today I'm <u>going</u>
    5 Heather: <u>tomorrow</u> it isn't holidays
    6   isn't it the party?
    7   so you don't you don't wear that sure you don't?

(Heather 4;10, Siobhan 4;6)   (III:6:132–7)

Heather takes up Siobhan's justification of a refusal and rejects it (line 3). This provides further material for Siobhan to reject (line 4). Heather cuts in and continues her rejection of Siobhan's line 2. An analysis of reinitiation types suggests that the use of more complex means of reinitiating requests increased with age, especially in the case of Heather. This supports the findings of Levin and Rubin that older children used more flexible means and that younger children showed greater rigidity, being less able to monitor the reasons for the failure of their request.

A further distinction can be drawn between aggravated and mitigated reinitiations of requests (Labov and Fanshel 1977). Aggravated forms include repeats, often with a higher pitch level, indicating annoyance. They also tend to focus on the speaker's wishes at the expense of those of the recipient of the request. Mitigated request forms attempt to soften the costs of the request to its recipient and are often accompanied by justifications. We will examine the children's use of aggravated and mitigated forms in the following sections and in the more detailed analysis of the 'scissors request'.

Costs and benefits in requests

We have noted that the degree to which requesters persisted with a request and to which requestees refused compliance seemed to be related to the value the participants put on the requested action. Thus we would predict longer sequences where the request carried high benefits for the requester or high costs for the requestee. High-benefit requests are for goods or services valued by the requester. High-cost requests are those which require the requestee to give up valued goods or to leave an ongoing activity to perform the requested action. High-cost and high-benefit requests would combine both sets of conditions.

The issue of costs and benefits of requests has implications for the choice of request forms. Ervin-Tripp (1976) predicts the use of embedded imperatives in the case of a request for a 'special task', and Mitchell-Kernan and Kernan (1977) discuss how aspects of a request, such as its difficulty or cost to the addressee, are registered in the greater use of embedded imperatives. Similarly, in our discussion of the children's use of embedded imperatives in the data, we were able to explain the choice of request form in terms of costs and benefits.

Unfortunately, however, it does not seem possible for the analyst to determine the costs and benefits attached to a particular request independently. The question of whether goods or services are valued at any given time is not predictable but is determined and negotiated by the participants themselves and depends on a variety of factors. One of these (perhaps one of the more important, though intangible, ones) is their mood at that particular time. It is possible to make a *post hoc* examination of longer non-compliant sequences and rationalize that their length and the extent of the participants' persistence is related to the high costs and benefits attached to the request. But the fact that a request for goods, for example, produces a long argumentative sequence on one occasion does not predict the same for a subsequent occasion. To take the example of the 'scissors request' (example (51)), which will be discussed in detail later, the persistence of the children can be explained by reference to the situation where both children want to cut out pictures from books but only one pair of scissors is available. However, other requests, which appeared to the outsider to be made in similar circumstances, were granted without any fuss.

While the question of determining costs and benefits as an independent and objective measure remains problematic, there is no doubt that costs and benefits are an issue for the children in their requests. Children often stressed that they wanted an action to be carried out, for example:

(42) (Siobhan wants Heather to select a particular card)
    Siobhan: put this one down
              no
              you could have put that one down
              I wanted you to

    (5;1)   (V:14:610–13)

As well as explicitly stressing their wishes, children would indicate that they valued compliance and offered benefits in return.

(43) (Siobhan wants Heather to agree)
    Siobhan: say yes
    Heather: no
    Siobhan: I'll be your best friend if you say yes

    (Siobhan 4;6, Heather 4;10)   (III:7:342–4)

The children also showed an awareness that requests carried high costs for their recipient and were prepared to take account of these to gain compliance, for example, by stressing the benefit to the addressee:

(44) Heather: change lunch boxes
    Siobhan: no
    Heather: you'll have a bigger one so you will

    (Heather 4;0, Siobhan 3;8)   (I:4:489–91)

or by taking account of their objections:

(45) (Heather wants to gather in the cards)
    Heather: Siobhan get them back to me
    Siobhan: I'll have no cards
    Heather: I'll give you a whole puzzle
    Siobhan: umhmm

    (Heather 5;5, Siobhan 5;1)   (V:14:76–9)

Thus reducing the costs of a request was a ploy used to wheedle compliance from an initially non-compliant partner.

Sequential aspects of requests

We have seen how the realization of a request and its response are not isolated events but can occur over an extended sequence. In order to ensure compliance or to persist with non-compliance, children use a variety of devices. Comparison of request sequences for the purposes of quantification or to measure development is difficult, as each sequence develops according to which option is selected by a participant from a large range of options at each stage in the sequence. For this reason, the analysis of sequences will have to be descriptive with the aim of shedding light on aspects of the children's requesting behaviours and how they develop.

Looking first at the requester's behaviour, we have seen how the children used different request forms to initiate requests, depending on factors such as the nature of the task and the addressee. However, different request forms were also used within the same sequence. Here the use of a different form is similar to a repair device (chapter 7) as the speaker discards one form which has been unsuccessful and tries with another. We might expect intuitively that the natural progression for a speaker wishing to ensure compliance would be towards more polite forms such as embedded imperatives. However, although more polite forms can be elicited on explicit demand (see experiments by Bates 1976), they were rare as subsequent attempts in request sequences in the data. In the 'scissors' request (example (51)) embedded imperatives were used to reinitiate the request after intervening exchanges on unrelated topics (see (51), lines 29, 36) and also in the following example, following a gap of three seconds:

(46) Heather: Siobhan don't forget to bring your bikini round to my house
            (3.2)
            will you will you bring your bikini round to my house?
      Siobhan: umhmm

      (Heather 5;1, Siobhan 4;9)   (IV:10:225–7)

Instead, the tendency following non-compliance was to appeal to the copresent adult with hints (for example, *Heather won't change over*) or to return to more direct forms following the failure of polite forms. However, apart from changing request form, other means were used to cajole the partner into compliance. We have already seen that methods used include reducing the costs of the request or offering friendship. Other methods included the use of *please* or attempts at compromise. The following is an example of how a series of different request forms, supplemented by an attempt to stress the benefits for the addressee, were used to induce compliance (in this case, unsuccessfully):

(47) (Siobhan has a toy elephant and Heather a toy dog. Siobhan wants Heather to exchange the toys)
Siobhan: let's change over puppets
             please
             cos cos I want the dog
Heather: no
Siobhan: change over with me
(to author) Heather won't change over
(to author) change over
             (1.8)
             there
             the elephant is much more nicer
             (1.0)
(to author) Heather won't let me have the dog

  (Siobhan 4;9, Heather 5;1)   (IV:10:5–14)

As far as the development of these requesting behaviours is concerned, there seems to be a progression in later sessions towards the devices illustrated here. This compares with the first session where the children seemed to get themselves into 'dead-end' situations with repetitive rounds of *refuse/reject* responses:

(48) Heather: give me it
     Siobhan: no
     Heather: yes
     Siobhan: no
     Heather: yes
     Siobhan: no
     Heather: yes
     Siobhan: no
     Heather: yes
     Siobhan: no
     Heather: yes
     Siobhan: no
     Heather: yes
     Siobhan: no
     Heather: where is it?

  (Heather 4;0, Siobhan 3;8)   (I:2:266–80)

Here, as in several other examples, the situation is terminated only by one of the participants changing or extending the topic.

So, as far as requesting behaviours are concerned, the children show development from rigid to more flexible strategies with an increasing ability to justify their requests, take account of their partner's wishes and objections and to offer compromises and other more cunning strategies to cajole their partner into compliance.

The behaviours of a non-compliant participant depend on the prior utterance of the requester. There are various means of expressing non-compliance, ranging from simple refusal to rejecting some aspect of the request or the justification. The more requesters justified requests, the more material was available to incorporate into a non-compliant response. Thus, in (48), Siobhan did not use elaborate means to express non-compliance but this was partly due to the face that Heather's reinitiated requests were minimal in form. We can compare this example with more elaborate forms where the requestee rejects utterances supporting or justifying the request (see (51) lines 3 and 6) or with attempts to compromise, as in the following example:

(49) (The children are playing on the floor, colouring in a book. Siobhan wants Heather to move, as she hasn't enough room)
　　 Siobhan:　ah I haven't got enough room
　　 Heather:　neither have I
　　 Siobhan:　you use one side
　　 Heather:　ummm (inaudible)
　　 Siobhan:　no this is-
　　 Heather:　change over sides
　　 Siobhan:　no
　　 Heather:　it won't be so squashed if you do on that side
　　　　　　　(1.0)
　　　　　　　OK?
　　 Siobhan:　but you-
　　　　　　　look on your side
　　　　　　　that's a dot-to-dot and you can't colour in dot-to-dot
　　 Heather:　yea but you help me to do this one

(Siobhan 4;9, Heather 5;1)　　　　　　　　　　　　(IV:12:277–89)

Here Heather does not want to move but makes an alternative suggestion and states its advantages. Faced with Siobhan's objection, she counters with a further possible solution. In other cases an effective device was to change the topic. This was frequently used by requestees as a device for terminating a sequence and avoiding compliance. An example from session I:

(50) Heather:　have you finished the jigsaw?
　　 Siobhan:　no I haven't
　　 Heather:　have you finished it?
　　　　　　　(Heather tries to take book)

Siobhan: I want that
(Siobhan puts her arm over the book)
(Siobhan starts to sing)
hey little piggie

(Heather 4;0, Siobhan 3;8)   (I:1:119–21)

Taking the turns of both participants together, we can see how the development of a request sequence is the result of the joint construction of both participants, each pursuing their own interactional goals and utilizing a variety of strategies. We have seen some indication of development in the use of more elaborate strategies in the later sessions. These tend to give rise to longer and more complex sequences, although other factors are relevant such as the ability of a participant to persist with or terminate a sequence. This in turn depends on the values attached by the participants to the request in terms of its benefits to the requester and its costs to the requestee.

The scissors request

The following example of an extended request sequence is provided to illustrate the range of devices used by the children to request and refuse. The example is taken from session III and revolves around a request for a pair of scissors in a situation where both children want to cut out pictures but only one pair of scissors is available. The utterances are glossed, where appropriate, to illuminate the requesting and refusing behaviours:

(51) *The scissors request: Siobhan 4;6, Heather 4;10*
   (a)

1	Siobhan:	will you give me the scissors for a wee minute?	Embedded imperative
2		I won't be very long with them	Support: mitigating
3	Heather:	oh yes you will	Reject 2
4	Siobhan:	no I won't	Reject 3
5		sure I'll only cut this picture out	Support: mitigating
6	Heather:	that will take a very long time	Reject 5
7	Siobhan:	then I'll go mmmm very quick	Continue 5
8		you're taking a long time	Hint? link to 6
9	Heather:	* * * *	?

(Heather whispers. Siobhan gently taps her hand on the table, then addresses the author)

10	Siobhan:	take a picture of us sitting down	

(discussion with author, followed by argument with Heather over distribution of space)

(III:7:73–83)

(b) (50 utterances later)

11	Siobhan:	she's taking very long with my scissors	Hint to author
12		so she is (10)	Tag
13		Heather's taking very long with the scissors daddy	Rephrase 11
14		so she is	Tag
15		and I want them now daddy	Need statement
16	Heather:		* *?
17	Siobhan:	what?	Request clarification
18	Heather:	nothing (8)	Response to 17
19	Siobhan:	Heather's not letting me have the scissors	Hint to author
20	Author:	she'll give them to you in a minute	Delay
21	Siobhan:	I want to have them now (12)	Reject delay + need statement
22	Heather:	I'm nearly finished	Delay: mitigating
23	Siobhan:	let me have them now	Reject delay + direct imperative
24		cos I need them	Justification
25	Heather:	I'm nearly finished	Delay
26		just one more to do	Continue
27		that's the last one	Continue

(Siobhan holds up one of her cutouts)

28	Siobhan:	isn't that very good daddy?	

(III:7:134–52)

(c) (6 utterances later)

29	Siobhan:	will you give me the scissors for a wee minute?	Embedded imperative

30	* * scissors * for the table	Support?
31 Heather:	I have to cut these pieces out	Refuse with justification
32 Siobhan:	that's the same table as our one isn't it daddy?	

(discussion about pictures)

(III:7:158–61)

(d) (15 utterances later)

33 Siobhan:	och Heather's taking very long with the scissors	Hint to author
34	and hurry up	Direct imperative to Heather
35	Daddy I wanted the wee stool so I did	Hint to author (new topic)

(argument sequence about stool)

(III:7:176–8)

(e) (37 utterances later)

36 Siobhan:	will you please will you give me the scissors and then I can have the stool and you have this?	Embedded imperative
37	uh?	
38	yes and I'll be your best very friend	
39 Heather:	I'm cutting your pictures	Reject request
40	I am not	
41	that's my picture	
42 Siobhan:	this?	Request clarification
43 Heather:	not	?
44	this is my picture this	
45 Siobhan:	hope you won't cut this wee favourite picture out that I cut	
46	I'm gonna cut these ones out so you'd better give them to me very fast	Direct imperative
47 Heather:	you've cutted them then	?

(Heather hides the scissors)

48	haven't got them	Rejects request 46
(Siobhan looks on table for scissors)		
49 Siobhan:	(whining) uhh I want the scissors daddy	Need statement
50 Heather:	I haven't got them	Rejects request
51 Siobhan:	(louder) daddy Heather's not letting me have the scissors	Hint to author
52 Heather:	I haven't got them	Rejects request
53 Author:	where did you put them Heather?	
54	come on	
55 Heather:	I haven't got them	
56 Author:	don't be unfair	
57	now you stand up	
58	go on	
(Heather puts the scissors on the table and Siobhan takes them)		
59	are you teasing Siobhan?	
(Heather laughs)		
60	now you go over on to the other chair and Siobhan goes on the stool	
(Siobhan and Heather change places, laughing)		
61	watch how you carry the scissors now	
(Siobhan laughs)		

(III:7:216–42)

This lengthy request sequence, which reaches potential termination four times only to be reinitiated again, in one case with 50 utterances intervening, illustrates the variety of forms used to request as well as to express noncompliance. Siobhan begins with a polite form, an embedded imperative, which is appropriate to a high-cost request for valued goods. She attempts to reduce the cost of the request (line 2). However, this and her subsequent support (line 5) have the opposite effect and they provide Heather with further possibilities for refusing the request, in this case by rejecting Siobhan's supporting statements. So while Siobhan's justifications are potentially an effective means of reducing the cost of the request, they are two edged in that Heather can question them and thus further put off the request.

In section (b) Siobhan tries unsuccessfully to enlist her father's support and uses a variety of devices to attract his attention (for example, vocatives and tags), and to restructure her original request (line 11) by rephrasing with the name *Heather* in place of the pronoun *she* (line 13). She also changes from using a hint (lines 11 and 13) to a need statement (line 15). The hint is again rephrased in line 19 and the request restated with a need statement (line 21) which also has the function of rejecting her father's delaying tactics. Heather's behaviour is also interesting as at this stage she tries to divert and delay, first with an utterance which gives rise to a clarification request which she answers inappropriately (line 18) and then by promising impending compliance.

In section (c) the request is reinitiated, again with an embedded imperative. This time Heather supports her refusal/delay in compliance with a justification. This seems to satisfy Siobhan as she changes the topic (line 32). However, she subsequently shows her annoyance with Heather's failure to fulfil her promise of compliance by first appealing to her father (line 33) and then addressing a direct imperative to Heather. She changes the topic herself by introducing a different point of conflict.

Section (e) begins with a polite request in the form of an embedded imperative accompanied by an offer of exchange and of friendship, clearly an attempt to reduce the cost of the request. Heather's behaviour in lines 42–44 is not quite clear. She seems to be still delaying compliance but at the same time beginning to tease Siobhan, possibly in the hope of confusing her and diverting her attention from her main objective of obtaining the scissors. The teasing becomes explicit from line 47 onwards when Heather hides the scissors and can then subsequently reject any further requests by negating one of the basic preconditions of a request: that the hearer is able to carry out the action (more generally that the request is inappropriately addressed to her because she hasn't got the scissors in her possession). Siobhan's appeals to father become more aggravated, using first a need statement accompanied by whining (line 49) and then a hint, this time with louder whining (line 51), referring to aversive conditions which father is being requested to remedy. At this stage father mediates and the sequence terminates with Siobhan receiving the scissors and with laughter from both children.

Concluding remarks

In this chapter we have discussed two main aspects of requests:

1 The way in which children's choice from a variety of request forms displays a sensitivity towards the social features of speech situations.

2 How children's requests and responses evidence an awareness of the conditions which underlie the felicitous performance of this particular speech act.

Our data has exemplified and substantiated the findings of other studies (for example, Ervin-Tripp 1977b; Garvey 1975). We then looked at those sequences in which the initial response to a request was non-compliant. This led us to examine the variety of devices that recipients of requests can draw upon to express non-compliance and the means available to requesters to reinitiate and persist with the request. We saw that the children showed a development towards more flexible and more elaborate strategies.

The discussion of request sequences was seen to be fruitful as requests and their responses can often be negotiated over lengthy sequences of inter-action. An examination of these sequences has enabled us to make a more fine-grained analysis of the children's communicative skills by comparing the different requesting and responding behaviours used within sequences and by showing how, for example, the choice of a particular request form was determined by the failure of a previous form as well as by the partner's preceding response. We were also able to show a development in qualitative terms from repetitious behaviours to a more effective use of means of justifying requests and responses. The choices made by the children within sequences – for example, whether to continue or terminate following a non-compliant response – were shown to depend on the children's assessment of a variety of factors. These included the likelihood of eventual compliance as indicated by the type of response or by the children's subjective assessment of the costs and benefits attached to the requested action.

The uncontrolled nature of the study has yielded a qualitative rather than a quantitative analysis. This would seem to be particularly inevitable in the case of the discussion of sequences, since, as we have seen, comparability across sequences is rendered virtually impossible owing to the wide range of possible sequences resulting from the wide range of options available to each participant at each stage in the sequence. This type of analysis does, however, shed interesting light on the complexity of conversational inter-action and enables us to estimate the extent to which children have developed an ability to cope with some of this complexity.

6

The development of coherent dialogue

In this chapter we will be looking at the development of the ability to construct coherent sequences of dialogue. We will look first at various surface devices which are used to show cohesive ties between utterances; then we will look at the ways in which utterances are related as initiations and responses in conversational exchanges.

Cohesion is a linguistic device for creating text. When we hear or read a series of sentences, we are usually able to determine whether they are connected or not. Our recognition of this depends partly on the presence of properties in texts which have been referred to as *cohesive devices*. To take a simple example:

(1)   John and Mary met at a dance. A year later he married her

We would normally assumed from the juxtaposition of these two sentences that the pronouns *he* and *her* refer to *John* and *Mary* respectively. On its own the second sentence would not be understood as we would not know the referents of *he* and *her* (nor would we be able to locate *a year later*). Pronouns are a means of referring to previously mentioned persons and objects without repeating the original reference item (usually a noun phrase). As such, they enable us to make cohesive links within a text. Other devices include the following: substitution (the use of proforms), ellipsis, conjunction and lexical cohesion. Examples of these are as follows:

Substitution (verbal group)
she won't come – but she <u>did so</u> last time
Ellipsis
did you see her – no, I didn't (i.e. <u>see her</u>)
Conjunction
it always rains here – <u>yet</u> I wouldn't live anywhere else
Lexical cohesion
I like <u>fish</u> – I had some <u>trout</u> the other day

Although most discussion of cohesion makes reference to connections between sentences, the same devices can be used across speakers as a means of showing relations between their utterances. One common cohesive device in conversation involves the use of discourse connectors (Quirk et al. 1972; Crystal and Davy 1975). Discourse connectors fulfil a variety of functions. Some show semantic links with what has gone before, either supplementing or reinforcing the preceding discourse (for example, *in fact, as a matter of fact, in other words, that is*) or diminishing or retracting it (for example, *at least, or rather, actually, mind you*). Other connectors seem to have an attitudinal value (for example, *the trouble is, the question is, frankly, sadly*), while others function as *softeners* or markers of informality (for example, *you know, I mean, you see, mind you*). As we shall see, these connectors are relatively infrequent in the conversations of preschool children (Crystal et al. 1976:81).

It is important to note, however, that cohesion is not a necessary condition for coherent dialogue. Utterances can be interpreted as responses even when they contain no cohesive devices, as we can see in the following example from Widdowson (1978:29):

(2)   A: that's the telephone
      B: I'm in the bath
      A: OK

Although no cohesive devices are used here, we have no trouble in interpreting B's utterance as a response to A, and then A's second utterance as a response to B. In order to explicate this, we can appeal to Widdowson's term *coherence*. This contrasts with cohesion in that with cohesion the links are signalled overtly, whereas with coherence there are no formal signals. Instead, we have to go beyond the surface features of the utterances. To illustrate this point, we can cite Widdowson's explanation of (2). A's first utterance can be heard as an indirect request to B to answer the telephone. B's utterance can be heard as a response which puts off the request by providing a reason for being unable to fulfil it. A's next utterance acknowledges this and (possibly) undertakes to perform the action. In this case, it is fairly simple to recover the 'meaning' of the utterances by a process of expansion in which the missing propositional links are supplied. For example:

(3)   A: that's the telephone (can you answer it please)
      B: (no I can't answer it because) I'm in the bath
      A: OK (I'll answer it)

What we can note from this brief discussion of coherence is that participants in conversations rely on more than surface markers of cohesion in their construction of relevant dialogue. A first utterance sets up expectations concerning what type of utterance may follow. For example, a request for action predicts a response related to the request, which can be either compliant or non-compliant, as we saw in chapter 5. Responses are inspected for their relevance in the light of the discourse expectations set by preceding initiations (Coulthard and Brazil 1981). But how do we know that an utterance is related, when there are no formal markers such as pronouns to guide is? The answer is that relevance is basically intangible and that the extent to which an utterance is relevant is determined by the ability of the participants to interpret it as such. In some cases we have to go to great lengths to find the relevance of an utterance. This is what participants in conversations seem to do. Relevance is often negotiable within a conversation rather than being some sort of yardstick which can be applied to utterances. Moreover, the relevance of utterances often only becomes apparent later and speakers often suspend their interpretations in the expectation that the relevance of an utterance will become clear in the subsequent talk. Similarly, preceding talk can often be reinterpreted in the light of new utterances (Cicourel 1973). In the next chapter we will look at some of the ways in which children deal with misunderstandings and other types of communicative breakdown, while in chapter 9 we will examine in some detail cases of conversational disability, in which speakers appear unable to produce relevant contributions to dialogues. In sum: relevance is an important consideration when we examine relations between utterances, yet it cannot be measured in as clear cut a way as the surface cohesive devices used to exhibit links between utterances.

The development of cohesion in conversation

One of the earliest cohesive devices used by young children involves repetition of all or part of the preceding utterance. The development from this relatively immature to more adult-like conversational strategies has been explored in a series of papers by Ochs Keenan (1974; 1975; Keenan and Klein 1975). Repetition was used predominantly at age 2;9 as a means of responding, whereas by 3;0 strategies such as substitution were used. For example:

(4)   A: flower broken . flower ...
      B: many flowers broken

Often prosodic shifts and phonological substitutions were used to maintain long sequences of semantically coherent dialogue over several turns (in one case, up to 41 turns). For example (where ' indicates nuclear tone):

(5)   A: silly .. 'silly
      B: no Toby's 'silly

A: 'silly you! 'silly
B: no 'no silly! no not you 'silly

Later the children's dialogues were less repetitive and used devices which were formally and semantically more diverse. For example, by 3;0 they were using anaphoric pronouns instead of repeating preceding utterances:

(6) A: see battery
     B: I see it
     A: you see it?

(See also Benoit 1982 for similar findings.) Likewise, Siobhan at age 3;0 often used repetition to fulfil various communicative functions: as a means of acknowledging preceding utterances (as in Keenan's data), as a device for engaging in verbal play and as a device for responding to questions. For example, in verbal play, repetition accompanied by prosodic shift and a playful posture indicated the non-literal function of the repetition (McTear 1978:299):

(7) Father: you're a wee 'tough
     Siobhan: 'you wee tough

Siobhan often repeated adult's questions, sometimes going on to answer them. This did not seem to depend on whether she knew the answer or not, but rather on whether she wished to accept the role of respondent to the question or to reassign it to the questioner. For example, in (8) she responds following her repetition of father's question (McTear 1978:305):

(8) Father: what's that? (indicating tape recorder cable)
     Siobhan: what's that?
               that goes in there (points to socket)

In other cases, answers could be elicited from her after persistent prompting. Later (at 3;7) she stopped using repetition as a means of responding to questions and used the phrase *don't know*. This did not have its literal meaning but was a new device for rejecting the role of respondent, as we can see from the following example in which she shows that she can answer the question if prompted sufficiently (McTear 1978:308):

(9) Father: what's that?
     Siobhan: don't know
     Father: is it a basket?
     Siobhan: yes

The subsequent development of cohesion is only scantily documented. Ervin-Tripp (1978) reports the following developments in children between about 2;9 and 3;6:

1 The appearance of auxiliary ellipsis in responses, so that the subject is often pronominalized, the auxiliary (with tense and aspect) remains, but the remainder of the predicate is ellipted. For example, *John did, Bill was.*

2 The use of pronouns in replies to refer back to previously mentioned nouns.

3 The use of sentence connectives (or *conjunctions*) across turns. Development reflected the relative cognitive difficulty of the relationships indicated: addition was first expressed *(and, too, also)*, followed by temporal change *(then)*, causality *(so, because)*, adversative contrast *(but, though)* and then condition *(if)*. (See also Fine 1978.)

It is important to note that, as in many other areas of child language development, the usage of an item does not necessarily imply mastery. We can illustrate from Siobhan's use of *because* (reduced to *cos*) between 3;0 and 3;1. Although many examples were adult-like in that two events were related causally (as in *I can't go out – cos the gate's shut*), other uses did not correspond to adult usage. Sometimes *cos* was being used as an attention-directing device:

(10) Grandfather: look daddy, we're having all sorts of trouble here, all the cars are having crashes
     Siobhan: (to father, pointing at pretend cars) cos the car's broken

Even more clearly, *cos* could be substituted for a notice verb such as *see*:

(11) Siobhan: see – my engine's broken now
              see – my engine's broken now
              cos my engine's broken now

In other cases, *cos* was not related in any discernible way to the preceding discourse, as in the following two examples:

(12) Father: and what was the story about?
     Siobhan: (drawing in book) cos I drawing the trees

(13) Siobhan: my engine's broken
     Grandfather: is your carburettor broken?
     Siobhan: cos my engine's broken

From these examples we can see how the conjunction *because* was still in the course of being acquired and deviated in some cases from adult usage.

As we would expect, the children in the present study had acquired various surface markers of cohesion such as ellipsis, proforms and conjunctions such as *and, because* to mark relations across utterances and speakers by session I (although, as we shall see later, there were some cases where their failure to use cohesion resulted in more immature sounding talk). Other discourse markers acquired by session I were *well, sure, see* and framing devices such as *now* and *right*. *You know* was first used in session IV together with *neither* and *anyway*, and *otherwise* occurred in session V. We must however remember that in making this sort of analysis we are relying on the fact that these features happened to occur in particular sessions but that we have no way of knowing whether the children had acquired the features earlier or whether other features had also been acquired which didn't happen to appear in the data. In other words, we have to face the problem of drawing conclusions about the children's linguistic potential or competence on the basis of their actual performance.

Well is used in utterance-initial position with a variety of functions, one of which is to indicate that the preceding utterance has been acknowledged but the response is in some way inadequate; that is, it deviates from the intended perlocutionary effect (Lakoff 1973b; Hines 1978). For example:

(14) Siobhan: I want to play with all the Lego
     Heather: well you can't have that

     (Siobhan 3;8, Heather 4;0)   (I:2:98–9)

Here Heather is not going to grant Siobhan's request and indicates her reservation with *well*.

This use of *well* can also imply a degree of dissatisfaction with a preceding utterance with the meaning of something like *yes but*:

(15) Heather: why did we not go to get a drink in there?
     Author: it was shut
     Heather: oh
     Siobhan: well I wanted a wee drink

     (Heather 4;0, Siobhan 3;8)   (I:5:30–3)

There was no instance of the use of *well* as an indication of hesitancy or indecision on the part of the speaker (Crystal and Davy 1975).

Sure is used utterance initially in Ulster and Irish English to indicate contrastivity with a preceding utterance, again with roughly the meaning of *yes but*. It is also seemingly used as an agreement-eliciting device:

(16) Heather: I've got a basket in the house so
     Siobhan: well sure I got a basket here . with my lunch

     (I:4:290–1)

(17) Heather: well the rain won't get in
     Siobhan: sure it's not raining

     (Siobhan 3;8, Heather 4;0)   (I:4:508–9)

The response-eliciting function could be made more explicit by the use of question intonation or tag forms:

(18) (Heather has told Siobhan to leave her bag in the car so that the other children won't take it)
    Siobhan: sure sure the girls aren't allowed up the steps?
          (2.4)
          sure they aren't?

    (3;8)   (I:4:553–4)

You see, often shortened to *see*, has various functions. It can be used stylistically as a 'softener', reducing the force of the utterance, as a means of informing the listener that the speaker has information which he needs to be told about (Crystal and Davy 1975), or as an attention-drawing device in Scots and Ulster English (see chapter 4). In session I it seemed to be almost merged with its attention-getting function, as in (19) where Siobhan is explaining to Heather how to play with the Lego:

(19) Siobhan: and . and put that there
           see I got . two um
           you should have put them four wee * in the middle

    (3;8)   (I:2:4–6)

Used finally, it also had the function of requesting a response:

(20) Siobhan: you do that see (shows Heather how to separate pieces of Lego)

    (3;8)

although here too we can see the more literal sense with an attention-drawing function. The literal sense was less apparent by session III:

(21) Siobhan: and see you have to .
           see we can change over seats (louder)
    Heather: you don't have to shout

    (Siobhan 4;6, Heather 4;10)   (III:7:207–9)

Here the function seems to be expressing information which the speaker feels the listener ought to know. Heather's response supports this interpretation by showing annoyance with the intent conveyed by Siobhan's utterance.

    The three occurrences in session IV were all response-eliciting devices with rising intonation and separate tone groups; for example:

(22) Siobhan: you don't do those things in a hospital
              you just do them things in (1.4) in the school see?
              (2.0)
              see Heather?

   (4;9)   (IV:8:296–9)

By session VI *you see* was being used mainly with the information-express-
ing function; for example:

(23) (Siobhan is explaining to Heather about the calendar)
    Siobhan: no see all of the names .
              see January has the most numbers
              see it starts on Sunday (1.0) and ends on Saturday
              see January is the longest

   (5;5)   (VI:16:12–18)

There seemed little evidence of the use of *you see* as a 'softening' device.

The other discourse device which was already in evidence in session I was
the use of framing words such as *right* and *now*. As Sinclair and Coulthard
(1975) have shown, these words can be used to signal that a new unit of
discourse or a new activity is about to be initiated, as, for example, when a
teacher moves to a new topic during a lesson. In these cases, these words do
not have their literal meanings. For example:

(24) Heather: I know what colour that goes
    Siobhan: (high pitched) *
              (15)
    Heather: now would you give me that?
    Siobhan: don't have to give you my Plasticine
              (2.8)
              what do that .
              that's my battery
    Heather: now I make the dinner

   (Heather 4;0, Siobhan 3;8)   (I:1:293–9)

Here we can see how Heather uses *now* on two occasions as a means of
signalling that she is about to initiate a new discourse topic or activity.

Thus we can see that already in session I the children had available
various devices for marking surface relations in discourse. On scanning the
transcripts of the remaining sessions, we can see in session IV the use of
neither as a proform agreeing with a prior negative:

(25) Siobhan: I didn't get my head chopped off
    Heather: neither did I

   (Siobhan 4;9, Heather 5;1)   (IV:8:43–4)

and of the concessive conjunct *anyway*, although here the meaning of concession, signalling 'the unexpected, surprising nature of what is being said in view of what was said before' (Quirk et al. 1972:674), is not immediately apparent:

(26) Heather: I'm going to be out first
    Siobhan: I know that
              but I don't mind sure I don't
    Heather: no I don't mind anyway
              what's the matter with not not getting out first?

    (Heather 5;1, Siobhan 4;9)   (IV:9:239–43)

However, given that getting out of the car first had previously been a source of major contention between the girls on many occasions, Heather's use of *anyway* is perhaps not inappropriate.

In session V the inferential conjunct *otherwise* was used. This shows a link with a negative condition implicit in the preceding discourse (Quirk et al. 1972:670):

(27) (Heather is putting toy television into doll's house)
    Heather: just pretend that's the side
              cos otherwise that would have to be turned off

    (5;5)   (V:13:597–8)

You know, which also has a softening function, was first used in session IV, although here the example was not particularly clear. It reappeared in session VI, in final position with the meaning 'are you not aware?':

(28) Heather: you can colour it in you know
          (3.0)
          you can colour over the top you know

    (5;9)   (VI:15:154–5)

and in intial position as a sort of attention-getter:

(29) Siobhan: (goes across room and sits on her doll's house)
          (10)
          you know sometimes when I'm here I sit on my doll's house on the roof

    (5;5)   (VI:16:19)

Other discourse devices such as *mind you* and expressions of attitude such as *frankly* were not used by the children. However, as mentioned before, we are relying here on the unsatisfactory method of accounting for actual occurrences in a limited sample of interaction and are unable to make more general conclusions about the acquisition of discourse connectives by the children.

Constructing conversational exchanges

At the most elementary level the construction of conversational exchanges involves the ability to initiate and respond, or, as Halliday (1975) puts it, to assign and adopt the communicative roles of speaker and listener. We looked at the development of initiations in chapter 4. We turn now to the ways in which responses are used to construct coherent sequences of dialogue.

In a study of his son Nigel, Halliday (1975) located the onset of dialogue at about 18 months. At this age, Nigel's interactional repertoire was limited to the following:

1 Response to WH-questions (provided the answer was already known to the questioner).
2 Responses to commands.
3 Responses to statements, signalling attention and often continuing the conversation.
4 Responses to responses of others.
5 Initiations (but only *what's that?* questions at this stage).

As we can see, Nigel had already developed the ability to engage in elementary exchanges. Similar findings have been reported elsewhere. Crosby (1976) reports the differentiation of yes/no and WH-questions in a child at age 1;5 and Horgan (1978) discusses a similar ability in a child aged 1;3. It is not clear, however, whether such responses are appropriate from the perspective of the mature conversationalist. Steffenson (1978), for example, found that two-year-olds generally responded to questions, but that their responses were often inappropriate. They seemed to be following a rule such as: if there is a question, give an answer, even if you don't understand it. Dore (1977b), on the other hand, found that, in a sample of three-year-olds, 27 per cent of the questions addressed to the children received no response; he concludes that failure to respond did not appear to violate a social obligation for these children. Obviously the ability to respond interacts with the development of the comprehension of the question. The ability to respond to WH-questions, for example, develops between the ages of one and six years (Ervin-Tripp 1970; Cairns and Hsu 1978; Tyack and Ingram 1977). Children first learn to respond to *where* and *what* questions and later to *why, how* and *when* questions. This can be explained partially by appealing to the notion of conceptual complexity (for example, location is acquired earlier than concepts such as causality and time), but also by the type of response which the question requires. For example, *where* questions can often be answered non-verbally, whereas *when, how* and *why* questions generally require a verbal response. There seems, however, to be some support for distinguishing between the child's ability to respond as a result of comprehension of the question and the realization that questions impose a social obligation to respond. A similar distinction applies to statements which often require an acknowledgement of attention. As Dittmann (1972) has shown, children as old as seven years, in comparison with adolescents and adults, often fail to acknowledge statements even though they have clearly understood the content of the utterances addressed to them.

In general, then, the developmental trend is towards greater contingency in children's conversational contributions. Bloom et al. (1976) found that, in a study of adult–child dialogue, children's responses at 21 months were mainly non-contingent. Responses to questions seemed easier than responses to statements. Initially responses tended to be imitative of the adult utterance, but later the children added to or modified clause constituents in their responses. Mueller (1972), in a study of 3½- to 5½-year-olds, found that 62 per cent of utterances received a definite response while a further 23 per cent received at least a visual indication of attention. Moreover, contingency increased with age. Similar results have also been reported by Garvey and Hogan (1973).

What about the ability to produce exchanges longer than the two-part pairs discussed so far? The three-part exchange, in which the questioner follows the response with an evaluation, is an obvious candidate for investigation. We will recall that this type of exchange is common in classroom discourse, where teachers initiate with a question, a pupil responds, and the teacher follows this with a move which accepts and/or evaluates the pupil's response. A similar three-part exchange occurs frequently in doctor–patient interviews and in talk between speech therapists and clients. It can also be found in casual conversation. In children's conversations, such explicit feedback is rare. In a study of questions and responses in a sample of children aged 2;10 to 5;7 Berninger and Garvey (1981) found that only 5 per cent of responses received explicit feedback. In casual conversation, however, feedback is often marked implicitly by incorporating the response in the next utterance, as in the following (constructed) example:

(30) A: where did you go last night?
     B: the pub
     A: did you see Elaine?

Here the third utterance takes account of the response in the second turn without acknowledging it explicitly. Taking this wider view of feedback,

Berninger and Garvey (1981) found that 38 per cent of responses were acknowledged by a relevant next contribution. Similar findings for first graders in peer discourse and adults in adult–child dialogue, 52 per cent and 76 per cent respectively, suggest a developmental progression (Mishler 1978).

The type of conversational exchange illustrated in (30) is open ended in comparison with the question–answer pairs discussed earlier or the three-part initiation–response–follow-up exchanges, as the third turn provides for continuity by incorporating content from the preceding initiation–response pair into the next initiation. It is still possible, however, to divide such sequences structurally into two-part exchanges which are linked topically. The research evidence discussed earlier suggests that young children master these elementary types of exchange during the first three years of life. Following this, the next stage would appear to involve the use of utterances with a dual discourse function: that is, they respond to a preceding utterance as well as simultaneously setting up expectations for a further response. These are the utterances, coded R/I and R/(I), which we described in detail in chapter 2. We turn now to an investigation of the use of these utterance types in our empirical data, based on a detailed analysis of typical samples of dialogue from different stages of development.

The development of dialogue in the data

Four samples of extended dialogue have been selected from sessions I, II, IV and VI. The data is coded to show the following:

1 Exchange structure in terms of initiations and responses.
2 Links within initiating or responding moves as well as links across turns.

Figure 14 is an example of dialogue from session I in which the children were discussing Lego instructions. This extract exhibits many of the features of dialogue which we have been discussing. Reference is mainly exophoric to items which can be recovered from the context, for example, *that* (lines 4 and 5), *it* (line 7) and *that one* (line 10). It could be argued that *it* in line 13 and in lines 15 and 16 is anaphoric, referring back to previously mentioned referents in lines 10 and 14 respectively. Conjunctions are used to link turns. These are mainly *and* and *and then*, although *but* occurs twice (lines 10 and 17) and *well* is used to link line 14 back to line 10. *See* is used in utterance-final position (line 25) as an attention-drawing device, with the possible additional function of eliciting a response. Tags are also used with this latter function, often accompanied by high pitch termination, as in line 4. As far as conversational structure is concerned, the children take turns efficiently and in their turns take account of preceding talk by making relevant next contributions. Sometimes these are minimal markers of acknowledgement,

(The children are examining Lego instructions)

	Text		*Exchanges*
1	S:	see	
			Ex 1
2		and then=	I-
3	H:	=I see	R
4	S:	do that first don't we?	I
5		and do that	cont
			Ex 2
6		and then=	cont
7	H:	=and then do the wee things on it don't we?	R/I
			Ex 3
8	S:	yes	R
9	H:	put all the blues on	cont (I)
			Ex 4
		(1.2)	
10	S:	but here that one . that hasn't got white	I
			Ex 5
11	H:	I know	R
12		ha- has to have white	cont (I)
			Ex 6
13	S:	it should	R
		(3.6)	
14	H:	well that one's got white too hasn't it?	I
			Ex 7
15	S:	yes but it's broke	R/(I)
			Ex 8
16		I brokened it	cont
17		but I . have to take it all off	I
			Ex 9
18		I show you take the white ones off?	I
			Ex 10
19	H:	(nods)	R

```
20  S:  I know
21      you take it off at the sides don't you?              ⌐⌉}    I
                                          Ex 11                  )
                                                                 )R
22  H:  (nods)                                           ⌊⌋      ) cont I, 21
23  S:  look                                                    /
24  H:  it's very tight for me                                 ⌐    I
                                          Ex 12
        (1.0)
25  S:  you do that see                                        ⌐⌉    I
        (1.2)
                                          Ex 13    ⌊⌋}
26      and put them here                                       cont
        (1.0)
27  H:  I does the whites and you does the blues               ⌐     I
                                          Ex 14
28  S:  yes                                                    ⌊     R
29  H:  you have the wee blues chairs and I have
        that . I have that wee chairs don't I                  ⌐⌉}
                                          Ex 15
30      =I have the wee baby . chairs don't I?                 ⌊⌋     I
31  S:  yes                                                    ⌊      R
```

(I:2:36–67)

Figure 14 Coded extract from session I: Siobhan 3;8, Heather 4;0

as for example *I know* (line 11), *it should* (line 13) and *yes* (line 28). Sometimes, however, the children provide more than the minimally expected response, as for example when Heather in line 12 adds to her acknowledgement of Siobhan's line 10, or later when Siobhan in lines 15 and 16 adds to her response to Heather's line 14. This is a way of providing extra material for the next speaker to use in the next turn, which is, as we have seen, an important device for creating continuity in dialogue. There are, however, few examples of this type. Similarly, there are few cases of the turn type R/I, which respond and initiate at the same time and so provide links between exchanges. Most of the exchanges in this extract have the structure initiation + response; that is, they are *closed exchanges* with little linkage between them except at the general level of the overall topic or activity in which the children are engaged. This means that new exchanges have to be initiated at several points in order to keep the dialogue going, as for example at lines 4, 10, 17 and 18.

One interesting point which emerges from a prosodic analysis of this extract is that the children employ a wide pitch range, which might be interpreted as an expression of their excitement and enthusiasm. One discourse consequence of this is that utterances are often linked prosodically, as the next speaker echoes the pitch level of the previous speaker in a sort of *pitch concord*, which has the effect of marking continuity between utterances over and above formal syntactic and semantic links. We can illustrate with two examples. In the first (see figure 15) we can see that Heather's pitch termination on *things* is high and that this is echoed by the high pitch level

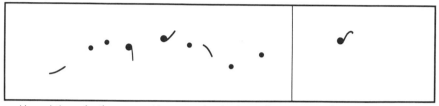

H: and then do the wee   things on   it don't we?   S: yes

Figures 15 Intonation pattern in figure 14, lines 7 and 8

and the rising pitch direction of Siobhan's *yes*. A similar example occurs later in lines 27–31, this time maintained across several turns (see figure 16). Much more detailed analysis is required of children's use of prosody as a discourse device than can be offered here and we also lack a detailed developmental account of discourse intonation. The present examples suggest, however, that preschool children play and experiment with prosody as a means of creating coherent stretches of dialogue.

We can move on to an example from session II, which revolves around Heather's assertion that 'Father Christmas is coming today' (figure 17). The main cohesive device to be noted is the anaphoric use of *he* to refer back to the previously mentioned Father Christmas (lines 2, 5, 6, 9 and 10). Siobhan's reference to *presents* in line 4 provides a link with Heather's line 1 which can be described in terms of *coherence* – that is, the retrieval of this linkage depends on shared knowledge that Father Christmas brings presents. It is important to note the development of children's ability to create coherence in this way, as its appropriate usage depends on the ability to make reasonable assumptions as to what knowledge is shared between speaker and listener. As we saw in chapter 4, this task sometimes proved difficult for the children, especially when they made reference to persons not present in the immediate situational context.

Figure 17 can be contrasted with figure 14 in terms of its conversational structure. We can illustrate this by examining the nature of the children's responses. In Siobhan's response (line 4) to Heather's line 1, she rejects

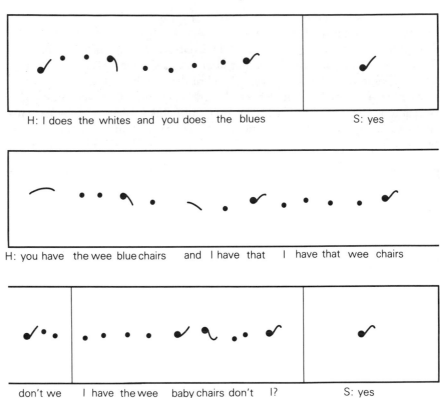

Figure 16 Intonation pattern in figure 14, lines 27–31

Heather's proposition but, in addition, provides extra material which Heather can take up in her next turn. Heather does so in line 5, first by acknowledging, then by qualifying her original assertion. Agreement is apparently reached by line 7 and the sequence could have terminated there with Heather's *yes*. However, Siobhan wishes to press home her point and reinitiates the topic in line 8 with *and that's all* and then adds further information in line 9 which links back thematically to her line 6. Heather rejects this and provides a justification (line 10), which Siobhan in turn rejects with a further counter-justification. The dialogue then enters a cycle of rejection/counter-rejection exchanges in which no new content is added *(there is – there isn't – there is)*. This is typical of earlier immature and repetitive cycles which often continued for up to 20 turns in session I. Siobhan provides the release from this cycle with a further justification in line 15, following which Heather changes the topic.

If we look at this extract from a structural point of view, we can see that most of the utterances are of the types R/I and R(I), which, respectively,

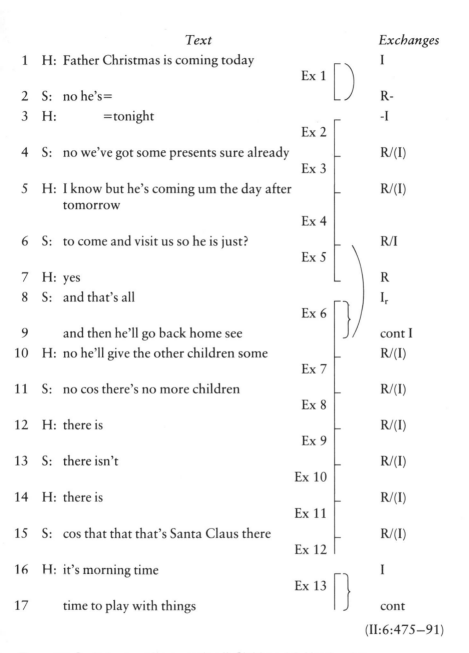

	Text	*Exchanges*
1	H: Father Christmas is coming today	I
	Ex 1	
2	S: no he's=	R-
3	H: =tonight	-I
	Ex 2	
4	S: no we've got some presents sure already	R/(I)
	Ex 3	
5	H: I know but he's coming um the day after tomorrow	R/(I)
	Ex 4	
6	S: to come and visit us so he is just?	R/I
	Ex 5	
7	H: yes	R
8	S: and that's all	I$_r$
	Ex 6	
9	and then he'll go back home see	cont I
10	H: no he'll give the other children some	R/(I)
	Ex 7	
11	S: no cos there's no more children	R/(I)
	Ex 8	
12	H: there is	R/(I)
	Ex 9	
13	S: there isn't	R/(I)
	Ex 10	
14	H: there is	R/(I)
	Ex 11	
15	S: cos that that that's Santa Claus there	R/(I)
	Ex 12	
16	H: it's morning time	I
	Ex 13	
17	time to play with things	cont

(II:6:475–91)

Figure 17 Coded extract from session II: Siobhan 4;3, Heather 4;7

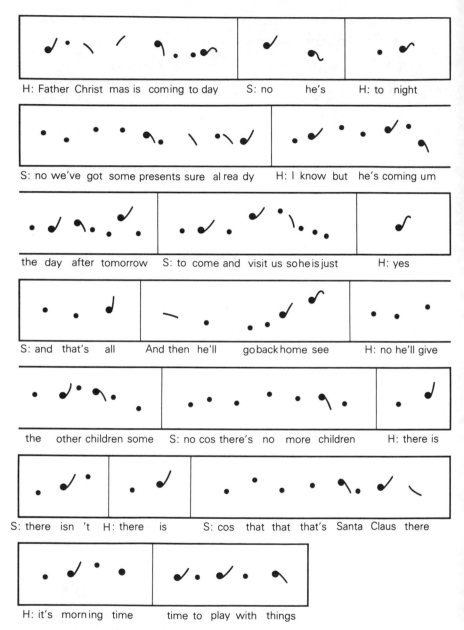

Figure 18 Intonation patterns in figure 17

respond and at the same time expect or at least provide for a further response. This function is also carried by the intonation, as we can see from the prosodic representation of this extract in figure 18. We can see how each of the utterances coded as R/I or R(I) is realized by mid-key termination, which signals possible continuation of the exchange. This continues until line 7, which is realized by low termination, accompanied by a voice quality adjustment to a lowered laryngeal setting. This signals that the utterance is setting no further constraints on the next speaker to continue the exchange. Siobhan's reopening of the exchange in line 8 is again realized by mid-key termination, while her line 9 has high termination, indicating that a further response is being demanded. This function is also carried by the response-eliciting tag *see*, which carries the nucleus.

Figure 19 illustrates a different way of creating continuity in dialogue. Here the children's turns often consist of more than one discourse act as they continue by justifying, adding further information or requesting additional related material. A good example is Heather's response in lines 4–6 to Siobhan's line 3. Here further material is provided which the next speaker can take up in the succeeding turn. This contrasts with the alternative option of terminating the exchange with a simple acknowledgement, which we found frequently in the extract from session I. For example, there are potential termination points at lines 2, 4, 8, 10, 13 and 15. Even where Siobhan initiates a new topic at line 12, Heather re-establishes the original topic, acknowledging Siobhan's line 11 and providing a further justification. Similarly, Heather allows the topic to close at line 10 but Siobhan reopens at line 11, linking back to line 9 (see also the links between lines 14 and 16). This structure has its realization in the prosodic patterns used by the children. As in the previous extract, most of the utterances have mid-pitch termination, allowing for continuation. Lines 8 and 9 have low-level termination and the sequence almost comes to an end at these points, only to be revived by Siobhan's line 11, which is marked by a rise in key and which has mid-level termination.

Looking at other discourse features in this figure, we can note the anaphoric use of *that* in Siobhan's line 2 to refer back not to a single noun phrase but to the whole proposition expressed in line 1. *Sure* occurs twice, first as a type of tag *(sure I don't)*, seeking agreement, and then with the same function and accompanied by a vocative (lines 3 and 7). Both children use *anyway*, which first occurs in this session (see earlier in this chapter).

Our final example (figure 20), taken from session VI, illustrates a combination of many of the devices we have been describing in a lengthy sequence which also exemplifies the children's developing ability to talk about hypothetical events. There are several markers of cohesion; for example, Heather's proform *so do I* (line 2), her *it* in line 4 which refers back to her preceding proposition *pity it wasn't our camera*, and the use of

(The children are travelling in the car)

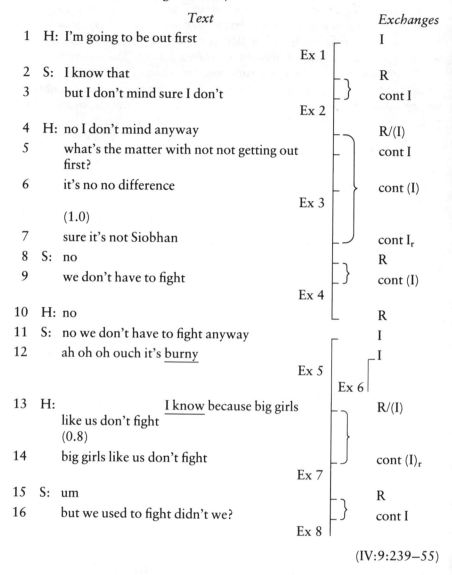

		Text		Exchanges

1   H: I'm going to be out first — I

Ex 1

2   S: I know that — R
3   but I don't mind sure I don't — cont I

Ex 2

4   H: no I don't mind anyway — R/(I)
5   what's the matter with not not getting out first? — cont I
6   it's no no difference — cont (I)

Ex 3

       (1.0)
7   sure it's not Siobhan — cont I$_r$
8   S: no — R
9   we don't have to fight — cont (I)

Ex 4

10 H: no — R
11 S: no we don't have to fight anyway — I
12   ah oh oh ouch it's <u>burny</u> — I

Ex 5   Ex 6

13 H: I know because big girls like us don't fight (0.8) — R/(I)
14   big girls like us don't fight — cont (I)$_r$

Ex 7

15 S: um — R
16   but we used to fight didn't we? — cont I

Ex 8

(IV:9:239–55)

Figure 19 Coded extract from session IV: Siobhan 4;9, Heather 5;1

(The children have been playing with the video camera)

		Text	Exchanges
1	S:	I like to do that	I
		Ex 1	
2	H:	so do I	R/(I)
3		pity it wasn't our camera	cont (I)
4		wouldn't it be good Siobhan	cont I
		Ex 2	
5	S:	yes and my daddy=	R/(I)-
6	H:	* *	?
7	S:	=if if you had a toy one and I had a toy one and he had a real one it'd be good	I
8		we'd all be taking pictures of Jason	cont I
		Ex 3	
		(sings)	
9		and my daddy	cont I
10	H:	yes and he'd be taking lots of pictures of us instead of us taking pictures of ourselves	R/(I)
		Ex 4	
11	S:	yes	R
12		how could we take pictures of ourselves?	cont I
13	H:	no I could take a picture of you and you could take a picture of me	R/(I)
		Ex 6	
14	S:	yea	R
15		but they wouldn't come out like real cameras	cont (I)
		Ex 7	
16	H:	they might	R/(I)
		Ex 8	
17	S:	no	R/(I)
		Ex 9	
18	H:	if we had a real one and your daddy had a real one it'd be good we=	R/(I)
		Ex 10	
19	S:	=well ours would have to be small	R/(I)
		Ex 11	

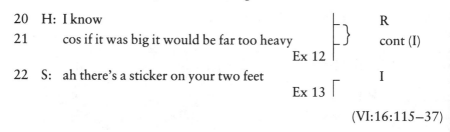

```
20   H:  I know                                                      R
21         cos if it was big it would be far too heavy        }     cont (I)
                                            Ex 12
22   S:  ah there's a sticker on your two feet                       I
                                            Ex 13
```

(VI:16:115–37)

Figure 20 Coded extract from session VI: Siobhan 5;5, Heather 5;9

but (line 15) and *well* (line 19) to acknowledge and at the same time qualify preceding utterances. One sign of immaturity is the repetitiveness of several of the utterances, for example, Siobhan's line 7 and Heather's line 18, in which complete propositions are repeated where a more mature speaker might use substitution, ellipsis or lexical cohesive devices.

As far as the conversational structure of this extract is concerned, the children use the two devices for creating continuity which we saw used separately in figures 17 and 19. Firstly, they use responses which provide for further talk. This includes utterances such as *they might* (line 16), which is realized by high-key termination, and *no* (line 17), which has mid-key termination. As these utterances reject preceding utterances, they provide for a further response by the next speaker over and above the cues expressed prosodically. The second device which the children use to create continuity is to link their utterances within their own turns, as in Siobhan's lines 7–9. Finally, we might note an example of precision timing in turn-taking at lines 18–19. Siobhan starts at a possible turn completion point after Heather's main clause *it'd be good*. However, we can see from Heather's *we* that she intended to continue the turn. She stops as Siobhan starts and relinquishes the floor to her. A fuller discussion of children's turn-taking can be found in chapter 7.

We are now in a position to summarize the main development which takes place in children's ability to structure their conversations. In the earlier stages, we find that children can initiate and respond to simple topics. However, their exchanges are usually fairly closed and do not combine into larger topically and interactionally related sequences. As a result, young children's conversations often come to a dead end and there is a continual need to initiate new topics. This means that topics are not pursued for any length of time but rather are rapidly exhausted. One aspect of development consists in the ability to structure longer sequences of dialogue. Here we are not concerned with the children's attentional span, which undoubtedly has an effect on their ability to engage in longer sequences, but on the devices they use to achieve this continuity. The major development comes when children learn to respond to a preceding turn and simultaneously set up expectations or provide for the possibility of a further response. This can be combined with the device of fitting more than one utterance into a turn. We can schematize these different structural possibilities as in figure 21.

I	*II(a)*	*or*	*II(b)*	*III*

A:⌐I
B:└R
A:⌐I
B:└R
	A:⌐I
	B:⊢R/I
	A:⊢R/I
	B:└R
			A:⌐I
			B:⊢R
			  ⊢cont I
			A:└R
				A:⌐I
				B:⊢R
				  ⊢cont I
				A:⊢R/I
				B:└R

Figure 21 Development of exchange structure

It should be emphasized that this is a preliminary account based on a fairly restricted set of data. More studies are needed of a larger sample of children engaged in a wide variety of activities. Moreover, we have limited our account to the most general aspect of conversational structuring – how utterances are related sequentially interms of prospective and retrospective constraints – and have not examined the speech acts used by the children within these structures or the propositional and topical links between their utterances. However, the perspective which we have taken has enabled us to isolate the ways in which children initiate conversational topics and then sustain these topics in coherent dialogue. We will see in chapter 9, when we examine some cases of conversational disability, how this perspective provides a useful framework for the analysis of such problematic cases.

The examples which we have been looking at so far have all involved referential talk, in which children have made requests, asked questions and discussed plans and activities. It is also informative to look at other speech events such as play dialogues and dispute sequences. We turn to these in the next section.

Play dialogue and dispute sequences

Garvey (1977a) describes play as a *non-literal* orientation to an activity. Children engage in much verbal play. We have already mentioned Keenan's twin study where the children engaged in sound play which had the ingredients of dialogue. The children took turns, expected a response from their partner, repeated until a response was forthcoming and attended to the other's turn by either repeating it or modifying it with phonological substitutions and prosodic shifts. The following example illustrates such a play dialogue (Keenan 1974):

(31) A: [apʃi:] [autʃi:] [o:tʃi:] [o: ʃabatʃ]
     B: [ʃa: ʃabatʃ:]
     A: [ʃo: babatʃ]
     B: [ʃo: babat] [ʃo babatʃ] (laughs)
     A: [ʃo: bababatʃ]
     B: [ʃo: batʃ] (laughs)

Garvey (1977a) also found play dialogue involving grammatical operations:

(32) F: cause it's fishy too
     (5;7)   cause it has fishes
     M: and it's snakey too cause it has snakes and it's beary too because
     (5;2)   it has bears
     F: and it's . . . and it's hatty cause it has hats

Here the children create new adjectives by the morphological process of adding -y to the noun giving the meaning of 'having the quality of the noun'. Peck (1977) found similar patterns of play in interaction between two children, one of whom was a native speaker and the other learning English as a second language. She found that in such play dialogue the expression of meaning was not the primary purpose of the exchange. The children's word play was rule governed but the rules were created by the children themselves in the course of the dialogue. She also suggests that such play with language provided a beneficial context for children's second-language learning as there were practice opportunities for phonological and grammatical substitutions.

One of the stylistic features of play dialogue is the rapid and rhythmic exchange of turns. Often children engage in ritual cycles of assertion/counter-assertion. Similar patterns were found in argument sequences by Brenneis and Lein (1977). As argument sequences proceeded, there was a general escalation of volume and reciprocal acceleration until turns were being taken simultaneously. In both play and argument sequences, then, the children engage in dialogue but the sequences differ from normal conversation stylistically in that turn-taking is more rapid and exchanges are often highly ritualized and repetitive. These sequences are nevertheless dialogue as the children take account of each other's turns. Play and argument are difficult to disentangle and often merge, although generally play is marked by laughter and argument by aggression, shouting and often crying.

Let us look now at some examples from the data. Play with dialogue occurred in the sessions recorded in the car, where, as in studies by Keenan (1974) and Iwamura (1980), the lack of toys and other stimuli threw the children back on their own resources for amusement. Some of these play dialogues involved sound play, as in Keenan's study. In these cases, there was no referential content, although conventional words were often used. For example:

(33) Siobhan: getting slower now aren't we?
that's why we're coming off the motorway
way why
way
Heather: (simultaneously with Siobhan)
why
way why
way why
(Siobhan laughs)

(Siobhan 4;9, Heather 5;1)   (IV:9:327–33)

Here Siobhan moves from referential discourse to sound play, picking up the similarities between *way* and *why* and contrasting them by juxtaposition. Heather soon notices the structure of this play and joins in after Siobhan's second *way*. Similarly, in (34), where a request for clarification *what?* became the object of sound play:

(34) Author: you two just watch out for things
Heather: what?
Author: see what you can see
Heather: what what what what
Siobhan: what what what
          what what what
Heather: what watch watch watch
Siobhan: say it loudly
Heather: what
Siobhan: what what what what what
Heather: what what (repeated together about 15
          times, getting louder each time)

(Siobhan 3;8, Heather 4;0)   (I:5:65–75)

By Heather's second turn the discourse has turned to sound play. Siobhan joins in, then Heather modifies *what* to *watch* as they speak simultaneously. Siobhan pauses to give instructions *(say it loudly)*, then they launch again into simultaneous talk escalating in loudness.

A different type of play dialogue occurred when the children constructed dialogue using conventional words but where the literal meaning was irrelevant:

(35) 1 Heather: horrible smell
      2   it's not my shoes
      3 Siobhan: it's not my shoes
      4 Heather: it's not my shoes
      5 Siobhan: uh?
      6 Heather: it's not my shoes

```
 7               it's
 8 Siobhan:  it's not my sandals
 9 Heather:  they're not my sandals
10 Siobhan:  it's not my bottle
11 Heather:  it's not my bottle (both laugh)
12 Siobhan:  it's not my head
13 Heather:  it's not my head
14 Siobhan:  it's not my um nose
15 heather:   it's not my nose
16 Siobhan:  it's not my mouth
17 Heather:  it's not my mouth
18 Siobhan:  it's not my=
19 Heather:             =cheeks
20 Siobhan:  cheeks
21 Heather:  cheeks
22 Siobhan:  it's not=
23 Heather:          =my eyes
24 Siobhan:  eyes
25 Heather:  not our ears
26 Siobhan:  no
27 Heather:  not your head
28 Siobhan:  it's not our head
29 Heather:                  it's not our hair
30 Siobhan:  it's not our hairs
31 Heather:  not our socks
32 Siobhan:  not our socks and not our sandals
33 Heather:                               sandals
34 Siobhan:  and not the seats=
35             =and this is the microphone
36 Heather:  microphone
37             and not our (4.2) um (1.0) not our (1.0) bottom
38 Siobhan:  not our bottom
39             not our tummy
40 Heather:  and not our tummy
41             and not our legs
42 Siobhan:  and not our legs
43 Heather:  and not our skin
44 Siobhan:  and not our skin
45 Heather:  and not our T shirts=
46             =and dress
47 Siobhan:  you've got a dress and I've got a T shirt
             don't put that on my seat
```

(Siobhan 3;8, Heather 4;0)   (I:5:341–88)

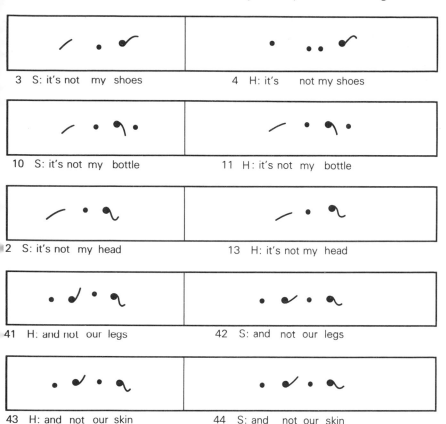

Figure 22 Intonation patterns in example (35), chapter 6

This extract also moves from referential discourse to dialogue play, initiated by Siobhan at line 8 where she substitutes *sandals* for *shoes*. At this point Heather takes up the game which is to find a new word to fit into the frame *it's not my –*, where the words can belong to the semantic fields of clothes, body parts (and, possibly, objects in the car such as seats and the microphone). The referential content is virtually irrelevant. The interaction gains its structure from the basic initiate/respond-by-repetition pattern, which is reinforced prosodically by identical intonation contours with heavy accentuation on the final substituted word (see figure 22), as well as by isochronous timing, where the children exploit the basic stress patterns of the English language in order to produce identical frames into which new words can be substituted. Both children orient to this mutually constructed pattern and are able to repair it when it threatens to break down. The first indication of 'trouble' occurs at line 14 when Siobhan hesitates before finding the word *nose*. She hesitates again at line 18 but Heather is able to supply *cheeks*. After a further hesitation at line 22, Heather takes over the initiative and supplies the words for Siobhan to repeat. Siobhan tries to regain control at line 32 by not only repeating but also adding her own new word. She is temporarily distracted from the game at 34 and 35 when she refers to the seat and microphone, but Heather returns to the game, although not without problems (see the filled and unfilled pauses in her line 37). From this point on both compete to supply the initiating utterance. By 46 the discourse becomes referential as Heather refers to their respective clothing and then Siobhan changes the topic in 48. The two points of overlap are also interesting as they are again indications of precision timing in turn-taking. At 28/29 Heather starts up before Siobhan completes *head* but this is entirely predictable as it is repeating Heather's preceding utterance. The overlap at 32/33 is a case of Heather predicting the word Siobhan is supplying on the basis of having heard only the first syllable. Her overlap may be an attempt (albeit unsuccessful) to regain the floor and the initiative at this stage.

These play sequences were generally marked by laughter or explicitly marked as play by the children. For example:

(36) Siobhan: we only pretending crying
　　　Heather: I know

　　　(Siobhan 3;8, Heather 4;0)　　　　　　　　　　　　　　　　(I:4:443–4)

(37) Siobhan: stop stop stop stop
　　　　　　　　I said stop
　　　　　　　　and that doesn't mean stop
　　　　　　　　.
　　　　　　　　.

　　　Siobhan
　　　and
　　　Heather: stop stop stop stop stop stop

　　　(Siobhan 4;7, Heather 5;1)　　　　　　　　　　　　　　　(IV:10:127–32)

Dispute sequences were another speech event with interesting characteristics. Sometimes the disputes were serious and resulted in fighting and crying. At other times they were almost ritualized and on occasions laughter ensued, so that they were difficult to distinguish from play dialogue. In session I, disputes were generally series of rounds of assertion/counter-assertion with highly repetitive patterns. The following is a brief example:

(38) Siobhan: that's not old Lego
　　　Heather: it is
　　　Siobhan: it isn't (crying)
　　　Heather: it is

Siobhan: no no no (bangs foot on floor)
Heather: yes
Siobhan: it isn't that Lego (gets louder each time)
Heather: it is
Siobhan: it isn't that Lego
Heather: it is
Siobhan: it isn't that Lego
Heather: it is
Siobhan: it isn't that Lego (shrieking and banging both feet on floor)
Heather: yes it is
Siobhan: no no no
Heather: it is
Siobhan: no (knocks over Lego)
Heather: stop that

(Siobhan 3;8, Heather 4;0)   (I:2:191–210)

This is typical of a repetitive dispute sequence from session I. Such sequences usually escalated until one of the participants managed to find a release by changing the topic. For example, on this occasion, Siobhan critized Heather's combinations of coloured Lego blocks: *it's blue that goes with yellow.* On other occasions one of the participants would issue a mock threat such as *you're not getting any of my lunch*, which could in turn lead to a series of ritualized rounds if, for example, the other child repeated the threat.

It was possible for the children to utilize the fairly predictable pattern of turns in such sequences to pull a trick on the other child. For example:

(39) Siobhan: give me that
     Heather: no
     Siobhan: yes
     Heather: no
     Siobhan: yes
              I'm going going to eat it
     Heather: no you aren't
     Siobhan: yes I am
              cos I sawed the bits
              she says no
     Heather: you said no
     Siobhan: no you said no and I said yes
     Heather: you said no
     Siobhan: no I said yes
     Heather: you said no again

(Siobhan 3;8, Heather 4;0)   (I:2:136–50)

Here Heather latches on to the fact that Siobhan uses *no* to reject her counter-assertion and uses this to reject Siobhan's assertion *I said yes*. This sequence illustrates a point of potential development as we can see that, in addition to the fairly repetitive rounds, we also have utterances by Siobhan justifying her assertions, for example, *I'm going to eat it, cos I sawed the bits*. This is the pattern which appears in later sessions, where children support their assertions and counter-assertions with justifications. The next speaker can then take issue with the justification and thus provide for a more varied sequence. One example from session III illustrates this. There is a danger of repetitive rounds but the children add further utterances and create more variety:

(40) Siobhan: sure it's your favourite picture
     Heather: it isn't
     Siobhan: it is
     Heather: it isn't
     Siobhan: it is your favourite picture
               (1.8)
               yes it is cos that . that's . that's
               sure spoons are your favourite things aren't they?
               (1.2)
               aren't they <u>Heather?</u>
     Heather: <u>no</u>
               they're not
     Siobhan: they are
     Heather: they aren't
               (2.2)
     Siobhan: what ones are your favourite?
     Heather: nothing

(Siobhan 4;6, Heather 4;10)   (III:7:273–86)

In this case Heather, who is otherwise occupied, makes minimal denials and it is left to Siobhan to do all the work to try to establish her argument. She falls at first into a repetitive assertion/counter-assertion cycle but then moves on by justifying her assertion.

Finally, a more advanced dispute from session VI, where both children are able to justify their arguments and resolve the dispute:

(41) Heather: do you like this big br- her big brother?
     Siobhan: no his br- his . that is his friend and he lives in a different
               house see?
     Heather: he lives in the same house
               (pointing) that wee boy lives in the same house and the big
               one lives in the same house

Siobhan: no
        see the one with the sort of curly hair and black hair well he
        lives in a different house
Heather: he doesn't
Siobhan: <u>*</u>
Heather: <u>then</u> how every day when we go to his house is he there?
Siobhan: look he just comes to visit
Heather: why every day?
Siobhan: maybe just=
Heather: =maybe he lives next door
        just like <u>*</u>
Siobhan: <u>no</u> he lives up at the end I think
        yes he do<u>es</u>
        in that green door
Heather: oh yes
        it's maybe just . just like Auntie Hilary comes into my house
        nearly every day
Siobhan: yes
Heather: that's more like it
Siobhan: yes
        but Julie=
Heather: =and that's what he does
Siobhan: yes

(Siobhan 5;5, Heather 5;9)   (VI:16:38–61)

Instead of getting tied up in repetitive rounds of *he does/he doesn't* the
children justify their positions by explanation or by querying the other's
position. They put forward various possible explanations, making comparisons with other similar situations, until they reach a solution by a
process of negotiated compromise.

The dispute sequences we have looked at show the same type of development as other dialogue in that there is a progression towards greater
thematic continuity and less repetitiveness. At the same time, utterances
come to fill the dual role of responding to a preceding utterance as well as
providing for further talk. The play dialogues are rather different as here the
literal meaning is less important and the sequence can revolve around the
phonological shapes of words and their semantic connotations. No doubt
more advanced word play is possible as the children learn various word
associations and connotations. Unfortunately the play dialogues only occurred in the early sessions, so we are unable to show any such development
on the basis of the recorded material.

Concluding remarks

This chapter has shown how preschool children are able to sustain dialogue over long stretches of interaction. This is a development from earlier stages when caretakers structure the interaction for the child and keep the dialogue going when it threatens to break down. We have looked at several ways in which the children in this study sustained dialogue. We looked first at the use of devices for showing connection in dialogue. These included cohesive devices, including discourse connectors, some of which involved local norms, which the children were using already by the first session. *Well* and *sure* were being used in session I, while *neither, anyway* and *otherwise* were first used in sessions IV and V. The children did not use more mature discourse connectors such as *mind you, frankly, actually, as a matter of fact*. We would have to look at a sample of older children in order to investigate the development of these devices. The children also used discourse framing devices to mark boundaries in the discourse, for example *right* and *now*.

We also looked at the structure of the children's dialogues and found a development from a tendency to use more closed exchanges consisting of initiation + response sequences to a more open exchange structure where exchanges were linked by utterances with the dual function of both responding to a preceding utterance and initiating or providing for a further response. Another development was towards longer turns where the children accomplished more than one act within their turn at talk. For example, they would add a justification to a preceding request within the same turn. This also provided more material which could be taken up by the other speaker. Finally, the children provided for thematic continuity by linking back to their own previous utterances as well as the utterances of their partner.

We have also seen that there is considerable variation in dialogue type. Play sequences differed from other dialogue in that there was the possibility of simultaneous turns and the propositional content was less relevant. Disputes also varied in that there was a wider range of prosodic features used, including loudness and variation in voice quality. In other respects disputes showed similar developments to other types of dialogue as the children developed from rather repetitive dispute sequences and became more able to respond to previous assertions with justifications and counter-assertions. What would be interesting now would be to investigate the ability of children to engage in a variety of conversational situations, ranging from the more informal spontaneous types described here to the more formal situations of the classroom. We will return to these issues in chapter 8. But first we will look at two aspects of conversational processes which we have only mentioned in passing in this chapter: the development of conversational turn-taking and of a range of remedial devices to be employed in the case of conversational breakdown.

7

Conversational processes:
turn-taking and repairs

Turn-taking is one of the basic ingredients of conversation. As we saw in chapter 3, infants learn some of the principles of conversational turn-taking as a result of their experience of interaction with caregivers in the pre-linguistic stage. Turn-taking in adult conversation is normally accomplished smoothly, with few overlaps and few gaps between turns. This smooth transition of turns can be attributed to the collaborative interactional work of the participants. The listener, who is the potential next speaker, monitors the current turn for its point of possible completion. (Recall from our discussion in chapter 2 that the size of turns in casual conversation is not specified in advance and that next speakers have to anticipate when the current turn is complete.) At the same time, the current speaker constructs the turn in such a way that the listener can project its possible completion. Various devices may be used such as tag questions, falling intonation contours and non-verbal cues. In this chapter, we will examine children's development of conversational turn-taking and assess the extent to which they approximate to the adult model that we have outlined.

The second concern of the present chapter will be with the repair of conversational breakdown. We will look first at cases where the listener diagnoses a problem and either requests clarification or offers a correction. Following this, we will look at self-repairs, in which the current speaker anticipates a potential problem and deals with it, as it were, before it occurs. We will see that young children display an early ability to deal with conversational breakdowns and that their repairs are a useful indicator of their interactional as well as their formal linguistic competence.

Turn-taking

It has been suggested that children's turn-taking differs from the model proposed by Sacks et al. (1974) in that there are fewer overlaps and longer gaps. This may be because children have not yet acquired the ability to project possible turn completion points (Gearhart and Newman 1977). This inability to process the turn in progress also results in more irrelevant next turns, particularly in multiparty talk or when attempting to intrude into an ongoing conversation. By three or four years, however, children have the ability to repair overlaps by stopping when interrupted or by repeating the overlapped portions when interrupting. By four and one-half years they are already able to make explicit observations about turn-taking procedures and types of talk (Ervin-Tripp 1979).

Let us look first at the question of the gap between turns. Studies of adult conversation have shown that interturn gaps are on average 0.40 seconds in telephone conversations (Brady 1968) and 0.77 seconds in interviews (Jaffe and Feldstein 1970). Lieberman and Garvey (1977) found that, in a study of 3½-year-olds, gaps averaged about 1.2 seconds over the entire dialogues, and in initiation–response pairs alone averaged 2.1 seconds with the most frequent duration being 1.5 seconds. In a more extensive study (Garvey and Berninger 1981) it was found that the mean length of interturn gap ranged from 1.1 to 1.8 seconds for the youngest dyads (aged 2;10 to 3;3) to 0.8 to 1.5 seconds for the older group (aged 4;7 to 5;7). Thus we can see that, while gaps are slightly longer than in adult conversation, they decrease in length with the older children.

One aspect which is potentially overlooked when we consider the average length of interturn gap is that the length of gap can vary according to the type of conversational exchange and/or the nature of the response expected. Garvey and Berninger (1981) addressed this issue in their study. They restricted their analysis to exchanges initiated by means of questions or other clearly initiating moves such as summons–answer routines and requests for repetition. They then determined the extent to which responses were predictable and/or complex. A response which was highly predictable was one which followed a summons, a request for repetition and other initiations with which the response was closely linked. Less predictable responses followed initiations such as yes/no and WH-questions. The measure of complexity reflected the extent to which new propositional content was encoded in the response. Responses with a low level of complexity included answers to a summons (e.g. *John – what?*) and to requests for requests for repetition (e.g. *this is my book – what? – this is my book*), as the response did not require any new propositional content. Other responses, after WH-questions, for example, were coded as being more complex. They were often marked by a greater frequency of hesitations, false starts and rephrasings.

It was predicted on the basis of these measures that responses of low predictability and high complexity would follow longer interturn pauses than other responses. This prediction was supported by the data and accounts for the range of average length of pause reported earlier. It was noted, however, that this variability decreased with the older children, which suggests that they were developing an increasing control over exchange patterns and the interactional demands of response production. We can note, however, the importance of considering discourse constraints on interturn pause length, as means taken across a variety of exchange types may obscure the variability which only becomes apparent in a more fine-grained analysis.

Let us look now at overlaps. Recall that it is necessary to distinguish between cases where more than one speaker talks at the same time, as in interruptions, and predictable overlaps which occur at turn transition relevant points, in which the listener reasonably predicts turn completion and overlap occurs because the speaker continues. It is this second type with which we are concerned here, as such overlaps support the view that conversationalists display precision timing in their management of turn transitions.

Garvey and Berninger (1981) found that overlaps were rare in their data, and when they did occur were terminated quickly. They suggest that young children may not rely so much on a projection of possible turn completion as on cues such as terminal intonation patterns as well as a brief interval of silence following their partner's speech as a means of deciding that it is their turn to talk. Jamison (1981) has analysed overlaps in the data from Siobhan and Heather. She found that overlaps increased with age and also occurred more regularly at turn transition relevant points. In other words, as the children grew older, they seemed to be developing the ability to anticipate possible completion points.

To illustrate the extent to which children exhibit precision timing in their turn-taking, we can look at some examples of self-initiated other-repairs. These usually occur when the current speaker is unable to complete the ongoing turn and either explicitly or implicitly invites the listener to complete the turn. All the cases in the current data involved implicit invitations, where the current speaker paused before the turn's possible completion point. For example:

(1)   Siobhan: sure we can leave these things in the (0.8)
      Heather: car
      Siobhan: car
               and just take our bags

      (Siobhan 4;9, Heather 5;1)   (IV:9:401–4)

Here Siobhan pauses before the point of possible completion of her turn and Heather supplies a possible completion. In one case overlapped turns resulted because the current speaker continued after the pause simultaneously with the next speaker's repair utterance:

(2)   Siobhan: I got no lun-
              I . I got
      Heather: she's got she's got no bag this time . now

      (Siobhan 3;8, Heather 4;0)   (I:4:536–8)

In (2) the listener offered a candidate turn completion following a disfluency such as a hesitation in the current turn. The general principle of aiming for a fluent production seems to override the principle that a current speaker should be allowed to continue until the turn's first possible completion point. Such other-repairs can, of course, be rejected, as in the following example:

(3)   Heather: pretend that's a . pottie for the . bathroom
                  you can have you can have um=
      Siobhan: =potties in=
      Heather: =toilets in the bathroom

      (Heather 5;5, Siobhan 5;1)   (V:13:308–11)

Heather's turn exhibits several disfluencies: hesitations, a repetition and a filled pause. Siobhan offers a possible completion but this is in turn rejected by Heather.

   In other cases, overlap resulted because the current speaker continued to talk beyond a possible completion point while the next speaker started up with a possible continuation:

(4)   Heather: yea but not with your mummy
      Siobhan: no cos she
      Heather: she doesn't live in there

      (Heather 4;0, Siobhan 3;8)   (I:4:57–9)

In this example Siobhan has reached her first point of possible completion with *no*, which marks agreement with Heather's prior turn. She goes on to justify her *no*, but Heather starts up at the same time with her own continuation. Similarly with the following example, in which Siobhan completes a grammatical clause and continues with a projected co-ordinated clause. Heather starts up at the completion of the first clause:

(5)   Siobhan: so we'd better put . that in there right and put that
      Heather: this in there
                put that in there

      (Siobhan 5;1, Heather 5;5)   (V:13:648–51)

We can note that Heather's timing is precise. In the first part of her turn, she supplies the object *this* following Siobhan's verb *put*. She then reconstitutes the whole of the predicate in the next part of her turn.

Finally, there were several examples in the data which illustrate how overlap could result from the children observing the principle of avoiding gap. The following is a typical example:

(6) Heather: I'd better take it all back
        (0.6)
        <u>cos</u> I'm going to get all the things
    Siobhan: <u>but-</u>

(Heather 5;5, Siobhan 5;1)   (V:13:399–401)

There is a gap of 0.6 seconds following the completion of Heather's turn. Both children start up and on this occasion Siobhan stops, thus allowing Heather to maintain the turn.

We are now in a position to draw certain conclusions from these examples about the children's linguistic and interactional competence. We can see that the children display an ability to monitor the turn in progress, not only for its projected completion but also for its projected content. They are able to supply a candidate completion when the current speaker becomes disfluent and seems unable to complete the turn smoothly. We saw how this often involved precise timing, as in (5), where an object noun phrase was produced at precisely the correct point to follow the other speaker's verb. Some of the other examples are even more striking in this respect. In (1), for example, Heather is able to supply the noun *car* to fit appropriately into the slot following *in the* in Siobhan's prior utterance. This is evidence of her grammatical ability to select an appropriate grammatical item, her semantic ability to select a meaningful item, her pragmatic ability to select the item which is appropriate to the situational context, and her interactional ability to time her contribution so that it occurs at precisely the correct place. Example (3) is interesting in that the syntax of the first turn is kept intact across three turns.

If we examine the turn following an occurrence of overlap, we can see that the children often display a sensitivity towards the potential impairment of the content of the turn by the overlap. In (5) we saw how Heather reconstituted the whole predicate in her next turn, adding the verb from Siobhan's turn to the object and prepositional phrase of her own. Similarly, if we look at the self-repetition in (2) of *she's got*, we can see that on the first occasion the words overlapped with Siobhan's turn. Heather's repetition may be evidence that she is aware of the possible impairment of this part of her turn owing to the overlap and of her attempt to follow the principle of producing well-formed grammatical clauses by recycling the overlapped subject and verb (Schegloff 1973).

Finally, as we have seen, these examples show how the children orient to the turn-taking system by timing their turn beginnings with precision (Jefferson 1973) and by relinquishing the floor in the case of overlap in order to maintain the basic turn-taking principle of 'one speaker at a time' (Sacks et al. 1974).

Requests for clarification

Requests for clarification are a type of conversational repair mechanism in which the listener diagnoses a problem and requests clarification, and the speaker of the repairable utterance carries out the repair. They are to be distinguished from other-corrections, to which we will be turning shortly, as in these the listener not only diagnoses the problem but also carries out the repair. The simplest type of clarification request involves the repetition of all or part of an utterance which the listener has either not heard or not understood. There are, however, several other types and it will be helpful to outline these briefly, as they are important developmentally. The different categories of clarification request and some examples (based on Garvey 1977b; 1979) are as follows:

1 *Non-specific request for repetition*
A: do you like his big brother?
B: what?
A: do you like his big brother?

2 *Specific request for repetition*
A: do you like his big brother?
B: his what?
A: his big brother

3 *Specific request for confirmation*
A: do you like his big brother?
B: his big brother?
A: yes

4 *Specific request for specification*
A: do you like his big brother?
B: which one?
A: the one with the curly hair?

5 *Potential request for elaboration*
A: I saw his friend
B: when?
A: this morning

6 *Potential request for confirmation*
A: I saw his friend
B: this morning?
A: yes

The first four types are particularly important for developmental studies. Types 1 and 2 differ in that, although they both request repetition, type 2 requests repetition only of a specific part of the prior utterance. While the response to a type 1 request is undifferentiated and involves only simple repetition, type 2 requests require their recipient to isolate the appropriate item (in the above example, the object noun phrase). Tyep 3, request for confirmation, requires a *yes/no* answer and as such places minimal linguistic demands on its recipient. Type 4 is especially interesting, as it occurs in the environment of insufficient information, when, for example, the speaker has made false assumptions about what the listener knows. In the example quoted, the speaker assumes that the listener knows which brother is being referred to. An inability to correctly assess the listener's knowledge displays communicative egocentrism, which we would expect in the utterances of very young children. The clarification request poses problems for both participants. The listener has to specify which aspect of the utterance is unsatisfactory, while the speaker has to supply the appropriate requested specification. Thus the ability to make and respond to specific requests for specification displays a considerable degree of interactional and linguistic competence.

Types 5 and 6 are analytically problematic, as they focus on an element which is missing from the surface form of the prior utterance but which is 'potentially available' (Garvey 1977b:71). The cited examples should be fairly clear, though obviously there could be problems in delimiting what is potentially available in an utterance. Garvey suggests that the potential case arguments of a verb are candidates. Thus for the verb *give*, which has the potential case arguments agent, object and beneficiary, only agent and object might be specified in an utterance and the query could focus on the beneficiary. For example:

(7)   A: I'm giving a present
       B: to whom?

In the analysis which follows, potential requests for elaboration will include requests such as *where, when* and *why*. These are distinguished sequentially from WH-questions as they occur in relation to a prior utterance in which the particular element being queried has not been specified.

Clarification requests in the developmental literature

There have been various studies of clarification requests in the developmental literature, focusing on different aspects such as their production and comprehension by children, their forms and functions, their occurrence in adult–child as well as child–child talk and their potential effect on language development.

Garvey (1977b) studied 48 children in dyadic peer interaction, the ages of the children ranging from 2;10 to 5;7. In the analysis of her observational data, she examined children's responses to clarification requests, distinguishing between expected responses, other relevant responses, and unsatisfactory or null responses. Her results indicated that children generally responded to requests for clarification with either the expected or some other relevant response. Older children made fewer null responses to non-specific requests for repetition. As far as the use of each clarification request type was concerned, it was seen that non-specific requests for repetition were more frequent than other types. The results did not permit an analysis of development from non-specific to more specific types.

Garvey also points out how the analysis of clarification request sequences can provide useful information about children's language abilities. As well as the discourse knowledge required for the successful accomplishment of such a sequence (which I shall discuss more fully later in relation to my own data), she also shows how a comparison of two utterances by one child within a sequence – that is, the repairable utterance and the response to the request for clarification – can reflect the child's ability to segment surface strings and to produce semantically, functionally or formally equivalent phrases. On the phonological level, children often marked their second utterances with a reduction in tempo, more careful articulation, increase in volume, widening of pitch range or use of contrastive stress. Grammatically, their second utterance displayed either a reduction of the prior by repeating only the essential propositional content, or an expansion of the prior, by adding further relevant material. Finally, on the speech act level, they substituted different forms of related speech acts, for example, direct for indirect requests.

Other investigators have studied younger children's comprehension of clarification requests. Gallaher (1981) found that children aged 1;11–30 responded appropriately, especially to requests for confirmation. Johnson (1979), investigating children's use of clarification requests in children aged 1;6–3;0, found that specific requests for confirmation emerged first, at age 1;6, but accounted for only 1 per cent of the children's utterances. In addition, few were convincing examples. They often appeared to be echoes of the mother's prior utterance, taking the form of single words with rising intonation. Non-specific requests for repetition, realized by *hm?*, emerged by 2;2. There seemed to be a development from the use of general to more specific types, with a small number of specific requests for specification and potential requests for elaboration being produced by the older children. Johnson's study dealt with the use of clarification requests by children in interaction with their mothers. She found that the requests were less successful than in Garvey's study (overall 66 per cent expected response received as opposed to over 80 per cent in Garvey's study), and suggests that children take clarification requests at face value and respond accordingly, whereas mothers responded in other ways. For example, non-specific requests for repetition by the child received only 28 per cent responses which were repetitions of the repairable. Mothers tended to provide other responses such as other types of clarification using analogy or demonstration. For example (Johnson 1979:7):

(8) J: dolly
     Mother: the dollies . . . they're called puppets
     J: hm?
     Mother: they're puppets
     J: hm?
     Mother: see, you put your hand in . . .
     J: hm?
     Mother: remember, we've got the owl at home?
     J: hm?
     Mother: hello Jane
     J: (laughs)

This raises the whole question of the coding of requests for clarification. It is evident from this example that J's mother is not treating J's *hm?* as a non-specific request for repetition. Johnson also provides evidence that the children themselves did not always treat *hm?* as if it required repetition, as they often continued directly after *hm?* with a second clarification request or some other verbal or non-verbal response to the mother's prior utterance. For example (Johnson 1979:6):

(9) Mother: D'you have any tea?
     J: hm?
              I'm not going to buy some

Similar problems are discussed by Langford (1981) who provides evidence that mothers' forms such as *what?* and *pardon?* are often treated by their children not as indications of a failure to hear a preceding utterance but as opportunities to monitor for a source of trouble. The most convincing evidence for this argument is that the children often reformulated their utterances rather than simply repeating them. For example (Langford 1981:165–6):

(10) Child: Is Derek a nice boy?
     Mother: Pardon?
     Child: Is Derek a bad boy?

Here the child seems to have taken the mother's clarification request not at its face value as a request for repetition on the grounds of intelligibility but as evaluating part of its propositional content. We can note in passing that the intonation of *pardon* could be a relevant variable here.

Corsaro (1977), in a study of clarification requests used by adults to three children aged 2;8–2;10, 2;10–3;0 and 5;0–5;2, describes the forms and functions of clarification requests taking into account their interactive significance in adult–child talk. The functions are interesting because, as well as showing that they have the expected functions of requesting clarification of preceding utterances which had not been clearly heard or understood, Corsaro also provides evidence for the functions of marking or 'filling in' a turn in the interaction (marker of acknowledgement) and of signalling surprise at a preceding utterance. Indeed, with the younger children, he found that the most frequent function was to mark acknowledgement, using the form of simple repetition of the preceding utterance. For example:

(11) B: I'm gonna buy some sneakers
     Father: gonna buy some sneakers?
     B: yeah

To the older child, the most frequent function was to mark surprise. Corsaro attempts to explain this use of clarification requests to mark acknowledgement by examining the social context of adult–child speech. He suggests that adults suspend the basic *interpretive procedures* (Cicourel 1973) used in talk to other adults when they talk to young children. These refer to the *reciprocity of perspectives*, whereby social actors normally assume that they interpret the world in a similar fashion, the *et cetera assumption*, whereby vagueness and ambiguity is allowed to pass on the assumption of this common understanding, and the *retrospective–prospective sense of occurrence*, whereby interpretation of utterances is often postponed in the expectation that meanings will become clear as talk proceeds. In interaction with children, adults suspend these procedures and request clarification immediately. The absence of *back-channel behaviours* (Duncan 1972) in adult–child interaction, which have the function of marking acknowledgement of a prior utterance, is also suggested as a reason for adults' use of clarification requests as acknowledgement markers, as these are a more explicit means of getting the child to signal acknowledgement of the adults' preceding utterance. Corsaro also suggests that adults' use of clarification requests has an effect on children's developing communicative competence by exposing children to the necessity of providing background cues and showing them the existence as well as the solution of communicative problems. Stokes (1977) also points to the educative use of clarification requests, suggesting that they motivate children towards a development of their knowledge of language by forcing them to test and evaluate their current hypotheses about the form and use of their language. Like Langford, Stokes notes that children often respond to their mothers' clarification requests not with simple repetitions but with corrections and elaborations. Their corrections showed an effort to test alternative rules for linguistic forms:

(12) Child: oh, she ate me
            somebody else wants to be ates
     Adult: what?
     Child: eaten

The fact that the children also changed from a correct to an incorrect form was further evidence that clarification requests occasioned experiments with alternative linguistic rules. For example:

(13) Child: I'm gonna let one dry out
     Adult: huh?
     Child: I'm gonna let one . . .
            I'm gonna let one dries out
     Adult: oh

So, in drawing together the main points from the preceding overview of research into clarification requests in child language, we see that children use and respond to clarification requests from an early age, perhaps as early as 1;6, and that that there is a development from general to more specific types. Difficulties have been experienced with ascribing functions to the linguistic forms which realize these requests and it seems, on the basis of the evidence discussed, that it is not clear that forms such as *what?* or simple repetitions of the preceding utterance are invariably requests for clarification at all. Indeed, it seems that, although they may superficially have this function, they are often used to further other interactional aims such as marking acknowledgement of children's turns which are otherwise difficult to respond to in any substantive way, marking surprise or as a delaying or 'putting off' tactic (see discussion in chapter 5). One interesting point is their effect on the development of children's linguistic and communicative competence, in that they force children to monitor their language both for the forms they use and the ways in which they use these forms.

Clarification requests in the data

We turn now to the use of clarification requests by the children in my sample. Clarification requests were infrequent in relation to the children's utterances, ranging from about 1 per cent to 5 per cent. The use of clarification requests peaked in session III and then declined. Various explanations are possible. While we might assume that children become more able to make clarification requests as they grow older, it is also possible that at the same time this effect is cancelled out by their increasing awareness of *recipient design*. Thus clarification requests would actually decrease as the children became more skilled at avoiding breakdown in the first place. The children used the full range of clarification types, although non-specific requests for repetition were predominant. There was little evidence in this limited sample of a development from non-specific to more specific request types, though as both children displayed a range of all types in session I, it is possible that any such development preceded the period of investigation.

As far as responses to clarification requests are concerned, the children generally provided the expected or some other appropriate response and by session V were responding appropriately to all clarification requests. Some of the inappropriate responses will be analysed in greater detail in the following as they reveal interesting points about the children's conversational abilities.

Structure of clarification request sequences
It is revealing to examine the structure of clarification request sequences. As Garvey writes, 'the well-formed query sequence exemplifies a finely engineered and co-operatively achieved production.' We will look at the children's clarification request sequences to see whether they were well formed and how the children achieved these structures as a co-operative production. Before doing this, we need to explain what structures are involved. If we distinguish broadly between the type of utterance which can stand in the first slot in such a sequence, we have the following structures:

1 (a) Request for information
   (b) Clarification request
   (c) Clarification
  (d) Response to (a)
2 (a) Request for action
   (b) Clarification request
   (c) Clarification
  (d) Response to (a)
3 (a) Informative (statement)
   (b) Clarification request
   (c) Clarification
  (d) (Acknowledgement) initiate new sequence

At a further level of delicacy, types 1 and 2 are distinguished by the types of response in part (d); in type 1 the expected response is a linguistic reply, whereas in type 2 it is a non-verbal act. However, as we saw in chapter 5, other responses are possible to requests for action, if the addressee wishes to indicate non-compliance. This possibility as well as the possibility of recursion, where, for example, requests for clarification are repeated and part (d) is thus delayed, would have to be built into a more detailed model of these structures. Type 3 structures allow for the possibility that responses to informatives can be optional, though this again depends on whether we make more delicate distinctions between types of informative. Following the clarification, a new sequence can be initiated with the response to the preceding parts left implicit.

Type 3 requests were by far the most frequent, representing almost 80 per cent of the total. Of these, roughly 10 per cent ill formed. Similar results were found for ill formedness in the other types. This suggests that the children had acquired the ability to jointly construct this type of discourse sequence. Furthermore, the number of ill formed sequences decreased in the later sessions.

We can now examine the ill formed sequences to see how they were ill formed and what they reveal about the children's conversational abilities. Taking type 1 sequences first, that is, those queries following requests for information, we find that two sequences were ill formed. The first was example (14):

(14) 1 Heather: some day when I come here can I have a bath with Siobhan? (addressed to author)
  2 Siobhan: uh?
  3 Author: umhmm
    (6.0) (Siobhan looks at Heather)
  4 Siobhan: what?
  5 Heather: a bath

(Siobhan 3;8, Heather 4;0)   (I:1:104–8)

This sequence doesn't fit our proposed structure in that the clarification request (line 2) is not made by the recipient of the request for information (line 1). The request for information and its response (line 3) could have constituted a well-formed exchange or adjacency pair, but the intrusion of the clarification request poses problems. Siobhan does not receive a response to her first clarification request and following a gap of 6 seconds she reinitiates it and also directs her gaze at Heather. From this point onwards the sequence follows the proposed structure. So, although this sequence is ill formed according to the strict application of our criteria, Siobhan performs conversational 'work' in order to bring about a successful outcome. That is, she recognizes that Heather has not responded, reinitiates the query and directs her gaze in order to further support the query and to indicate to Heather that she is its intended recipient.

The second type 1 sequence is similar:

(15) 1 Heather: then why do you not look for them?
      2 Siobhan: what?
      3 Heather: then why do you not look for them?
                   (5.0)
      4 Heather: Siobhan
                   (1.0)
      5 Heather: Siobhan (raises volume, leans over to face Siobhan)
      6 Siobhan: I'm too busy to talk

(Heather 4;10, Siobhan 4;6)   (III:7:6–11)

In this case the sequence has proceeded satisfactorily until the slot for the part (d) is reached, the response to the initial request for information. Following a gap of 5 seconds, Heather reinitiates the request by use of a vocative and repeats after a further gap of 1 second, raising her voice and leaning over to face Siobhan. These strategies achieve a response, albeit not the response which Heather expects. Here again we see that, although the sequence is ill formed, one of the children brings considerable conversational skill to bear in order to try to resolve the breakdown.

The one instance of an ill formed type 2 sequence was a follows:

(16) (Siobhan wants to look through video camera)
      1 Siobhan: Daddy I want to do one
      2 Author: one what?
                   (2.4)
      3 Author: well have a look then

(Siobhan 5;5)   (VI:15:194–6)

Here part (c) is missing, so that we have the following structure:

(a) Request for action (line 1)
(b) Clarification request (line 2)
(c)
(d) Response to request for action (line 3).

What is missing is the response to the query *one what?* However, this is not a straightforward sequence. It is obvious from the fact that the author responds to the request for action that the query itself was not intended as a request for clarification. Its function may have been simply as a delaying tactic to put Siobhan off the idea of wanting to play with the camera. In addition, Siobhan's non-verbal activity of approaching the author and trying to grasp the camera was a clear indication of her intent, rendering the embedded clarification sequence unnecessary.

There were 11 instances of ill formed type 3 sequences, representing 11.5 per cent of this type. Six of these occurred in session I. However, three of these were failures to respond to clarification requests by the copresent adult (the author), and there was evidence of the child attempting to cope with this failure to respond by continuing the sequence. For example:

(17) Siobhan: I don't want to go to Heather's house daddy
    Author: alright we'll go back to our house
            (1.0)
    Heather: what?
            (2.0)
            and then I'll stay at her house

   (Siobhan 3;8, Heather 4;0)   (I:5:41–4)

Other cases of ill formed type 3 sequences involved failure to respond in part (c), that is, to provide the response to the clarification request. In all of these cases, the child who made the clarification request was either able to answer herself, didn't wait for an answer, or continued with a new or related topic. Talk was not addressed to securing a response. Given that the children evidenced in other examples that they were conversationally equipped to pursue responses (see (14), (15) and discussion of reinitiations in chapter 4), then we can be fairly confident in concluding that in these cases a clarification was not of prime concern. The following examples support this claim:

(18) Siobhan: I know his name
    Heather: who?
    Siobhan: I do
    Heather: I know
            Michael
            isn't it? (answers herself)

   (Siobhan 3;8, Heather 4;0)   (I:1:327–32)

(19) Heather: I'm starting to bleed
    Siobhan: what?
    Heather: I'm start-
    Siobhan: <u>now could I</u> be the baby (doesn't wait for response, but
            initiates new topic, causing overlap: note that Heather begins
            response)

   (Heather 5;1, Siobhan 4;9)   (IV:8:471–4)

(20) Siobhan: you're not having mine (sweets)
    Heather: no?
            (7.0)
            only got three left

   (Siobhan 5;1, Heather 5;5)   (V:14:328–30)

Here, after a gap of 7 seconds, Heather continues the conversation by initiating a related topic.

Finally, two cases were unclear. In the first the children were diverted while travelling in the car and in the second, also in the car, it was not clear whether a minimal non-verbal response had been made, as no video recording was available.

To bring together the discussion in this section, we have seen that, even where clarification sequences were ill formed in terms of the structures we proposed as accounting adequately for most examples, the children seemed to be aware of these structures by pursuing the noticeably absent responses. In those cases where this did not happen, it was arguable that they were not expressly concerned with eliciting a response anyway.

Sequential ordering of clarification requests

There are some sequences in which more than one clarification request is used. The question arises of whether these occur in any recognizable order. Schegloff et al. (1977:369 footnote 15) claim that the ordering of clarification requests in a sequence is based on their relative strength to locate a repairable item, and cite two pieces of evidence in support. Firstly, they find that weaker forms can be interrupted in mid-production and replaced by stronger forms. Secondly, they find that, where more than one clarification request is used, they are used in an order of increasing strength. Adapting their request types (which have to be inferred on the basis of a few examples), we have the following proposed ordering:

1 Non-specific request for repetition	(NRR)	weak
2 Specific request for repetition	(SRR)	
3 Specific request for specification	(SRS)	
4 Potential request for elaboration	(PRE)	
5 Specific request for confirmation	(SRC)	
6 *you mean* + specific request for confirmation	(+SRC)	strong

This claim is empirically verifiable. In the data for Siobhan and Heather, there were 17 instances of clarification request sequences containing more than one clarification request. Of these, all but three conformed with the proposed ordering. We can further discount two of these counter-examples by allowing for the possibility of recursion in a sequence, for example:

(21) 1	Heather:	why is there gates here?	Request information
2	Author:	so that a lot of people can't get in that aren't allowed in	Response
3	Siobhan:	why?	PRE
4	Heather:	why are they not allowed in?	PRE
5	Author:	you're only allowed in if you work in there	Clarification

```
 6  Heather:  what?                                        NRR
 7  Author:   you're only allowed in if you work
                in there                                 Clarification
```

(Heather 4;0, Siobhan 3;8)   (I:5:49–55)

Here we have NRR following PRE. If, however, we allow for the possibility
of the need to have a clarification repeated, as in lines 5–7, then this
ordering is permissible. It would certainly seem to be intuitively satisfactory,
in that (21) does not strike us as an ill formed sequence.

The third example suggests that there are some problems with the
ordering of SRC (specific requests for confirmation), which seem to be less
restricted sequentially. Again, this seems to be intuitively reasonable, as we
might expect that a speaker could request confirmation about a preceding
utterance and then go on to request further specification or elaboration
about particular elements. Let us look at this example:

```
(22)  1  Heather:  guess what I was doing for Emma . um Siobhan's teacher
      2              I was helping her                     Repairable
      3  Siobhan:  so was I
      4  Author:     were you?                             SRC
      5              what to do?                           PRE
      6  Heather:  you weren't
      7  Siobhan:  I was
      8  Heather:  what?
      9  Author:   what to do?
     10  Heather:  help her tidy up                        Clarification
     11  Author:   ah yes
                   (3)
     12  Siobhan:  I was
```

(Heather 5;1, Siobhan 4;9)   (IV:10:19–30)

This is a complex sequence, as other material is embedded within it – for
example, Siobhan's line 3 and its rejection by Heather's line 6 followed by
Siobhan's rejection in line 7 and a request for repetition by Heather in line 8.
Ignoring these items, we can see that the author's SRC precedes his PRE.
The SRC does not receive a response, suggesting that it had a conversational
'turn-filling' function here. However, a response would have been possible
before the PRE, so we must allow for the possible occurrence of this
ordering.

To summarize, the data has presented some confirmation for the strength
hypothesis for the ordering of clarification requests in a sequence. Two
additional points were made following examination of apparent counter-
examples. Firstly, there is a need to allow for recursion in the system to

permit requests for clarification of preceding clarifications. Secondly, it seems that SRC (and probably *you mean* + SRC) are less restricted in their placement and can occur freely within a sequence. It is, however, possible that further constraints on these rules would emerge from examination of a wider range of data. What is interesting is that the children have acquired this ability to order their clarification requests non-randomly.

Clarification requests: general remarks
In this section I would like to present some further points which arose from an examination of the clarification requests of Siobhan and Heather. Firstly, I would like to examine the relationship between a child's repairable utterance and its subsequent clarification. We have seen that such a comparison can reveal various aspects of a child's linguistic and communicative competence. Children can perform various operations in order to clarify their utterances. Sometimes this involves further specification or elaboration. For example:

(23) Siobhan: I see . shells on that lorry
     Heather: what lorry?
     Siobhan: that one that's blue

(I:4:203–5)

(24) Siobhan: don't put your shoes on my seat
     Heather: why?
     Siobhan: cos
               cos um you might you might make it all dirty

(Siobhan 3;8, Heather 4;0)   (I:5:389–92)

In (23) Siobhan has to specify which lorry she is referring to. This involves here use of a restrictive relative clause as well as substituting the pronoun form *one* for the noun *lorry*. In (24) she has to search for the reason for her prior request for action. This search is problematic as we can see from her hesitations. In both cases the child is able to perform a satisfactory specification or elaboration. It is possible that exposure to such sequences has beneficial effects on a child's language development by forcing the child to be aware of the need to make utterances specific enough for particular listeners. Thus it is possible that a child might learn from such episodes to design utterances with such necessary specification or elaboration in mind.

It is also interesting to examine those clarifications which were responses to requests for repetition. We often find that the clarification is more than a simple repetition as the child can expand, change or reduce the utterance in various ways. For example, in (25):

(25) Siobhan: sure I got a basket and you haven't got a basket
     Heather: I have
     Siobhan: what?
     Heather: I have
             (1.0)
             I have got a basket
             I've got a basket in the house . so
     Siobhan: well sure I got a basket here . with my lunch

(Siobhan 3;8, Heather 4;0)   (I:4:285–91)

Here, after repeating *I have*, Heather expands by adding the ellipted *got a basket*, then continues by adding the adverbial phrase *in the house*, specifying location. As in many other cases, what occurs here is not just a simple clarification of a mishearing. Rather Heather's utterances can also be seen as a rejection of Siobhan's claim *you haven't got a basket* (note Heather's *so* which challenges Siobhan to respond to her rejection).

Other examples involved changes of various sorts in the clarifying utterance. Some of these changes were grammatical. For example:

(26) Heather: do you like his big brother?
     Siobhan: what?
     Heather: do you like his big br- her big brother?

(Heather 5;9, Siobhan 5;5)   (VI:16:36–8)

Here Heather changes her clarification in mid-production to substitute *her* for *his*, with this modification being possibly occasioned by the clarification request and the request itself being possibly the result of Siobhan's inability to locate the referent of *his*. Other examples involved grammatical changes such as a change from declarative + tag to interrogative form, while in another example the polarity of the utterance was reversed in the clarification. Finally, repetitions could also involve reductions of items not necessary for the propositional content being expressed. For example:

(27) Heather: I didn't
     Siobhan: yes
     Heather: I didn't
             sure I've got it on me there
     Siobhan: what?
     Heather: I've got it on me there

(Heather 5;1, Siobhan 4;9)   (IV:9:318–23)

Here Heather omits the *sure* in the repetition of her repairable utterance. *Sure* is a connective in Ulster English which occurs before a justification in the domain of a prior reversed polarity utterance (for example, here Siobhan's *yes* in contrast to Heather's *I didn't*). This connective is then ommitted in the repetition. Similarly, other connectives and additional items (for example, *I think*) were omitted in clarifications.

The second point concerns the extent to which clarification requests yield self-repairs, bearing in mind the alternative term *other-initiated self-repair* as well as the claim that there is a preference for self-repair in that even other-initiated repairs yield self-repair (Schegloff et al. 1977). Out of 143 clarification requests, only 10 (about 7 per cent) did not yield self-repair. Some of these cases were discussed earlier, where we saw that some sequences did not involve real requests for clarification and the speaker of the request was able to provide the response (18), wasn't interested in the clarification (19) or continued with a new topic (20). In many cases, however, the speaker of the repairable utterance was given an opportunity to self-repair, by being given either a turn to do so (18) or a gap in which to take a turn (20).

One example was interesting from the point of view of classification in that the repair was self-initiated and then other-repaired but the form of the other-repair was such that it allowed for self-repair by being a potential request for confirmation:

(28) Siobhan: do you want to buy um (0.6) um
     Heather: Raymond's (refers to confectionery shop)
     Siobhan: um um
     Heather: sweeties lollipops?   PRC
     Siobhan: no uh
     Heather: a sweetie watch?
                a sweetie watch

(Siobhan 5;5, Heather 5;9)   (VI:15:269–76)

On the first initiation of repair Heather offers the name of the shop. In the second case she suggests in PRC form what to buy. This can be rejected by Siobhan, as indeed it is. Then Heather offers a further repair to which Siobhan reacts by starting her turn while Heather is still in mid-production, anticipating what Heather was going to say. Thus, although we have here a case of self-initiated repair where it seems that the repair is made by other, the form of the repair is that of an other-initiated repair, thus allowing Siobhan the possibility of self-repair. Finally, one other-initiated repair was interesting in that it induced a self-repair while at the same time being in the form of an other-repair:

(29) Siobhan: what does twenty five makes then?
     Heather: pardon?
     Siobhan: what does twenty five makes then?

Heather: twenty fives . make?
Siobhan: twenty fives make?

.

.

.

.

Heather: I think twenty fives is a hundred

(Siobhan 5;5, Heather 5;9)   (VI:16:234–48)

Siobhan has misplaced the *s* in her first two utterances. In her clarification request, Heather at the same time provides a correction by placing the *s* correctly (note the brief pause after *fives* to highlight this location). In her next turn, Siobhan confirms and at the same time repairs according to Heather's correction.

Other-corrections

We turn now to the second type of repair which can be initiated by the listener. This type differs from clarification requests in that the repair is also carried out by the listener. For this reason, Schegloff et al. (1977) have used the term *other-initiated other-repair*. In the discussion which follows, we will prefer the more convenient label *other-correction*.

Other-corrections are placed sequentially in the turn following a repairable utterance. It is only as a consequence of the occurrence of a repair that a preceding utterance comes to be treated as repairable. That is to say, the status of an utterance as repairable is a product of the ensuing repair. To take a sample:

(30) Heather: there's some Plasticine
     Siobhan: that's not Plasticine
              it's Lego

(I:2:238–8)

Here Siobhan repairs Heather's *Plasticine* by replacing it with *Lego*. In the absence of Siobhan's repair Heather's utterance would not be seen as repairable.

It has been claimed that there is a preference in conversational data for self-initiation and self-repair (Schegloff et al. 1977). This claim is supported by the empirical observational that other-corrections are infrequent in conversation in comparison with self-repairs and, furthermore, that when they do occur, other-corrections are often modulated in form. So, for example, an other-correction might take the form *you mean X?*, where X is a possible correction. This has the effect of turning the repair into a self-repair by inviting the speaker of the repairable utterance to confirm. Other-corrections are also frequently downgraded by being presented non-seriously, for example, as jokes. This is probably a means of avoiding damage to the other's *face* (Brown and Levinson 1978). However, this preference for self-correction can be lapsed in certain contexts, as in responses to the utterances of the not-yet-competent, such as pupils in the classroom or children acquiring a first language. In fact, it is generally assumed that one of the roles of a teacher is to correct pupil error. Adults also correct their children's utterances in instructional contexts (Drew 1981).

In talk between participants of an equal status, it is usual to let errors pass if they do not obstruct communication (Cicourel 1973). One of the main functions of repairs is to deal with potential communicative breakdown. In clarification requests, for example, the recipient requests clarification precisely because the preceding utterance was problematic in some way and conversation cannot precede until the problem has been resolved. With other-corrections there is no such problem. In fact, a speaker cannot make an other-correction unless he feels sure that the preceding utterance contained a repairable item and he can provide its correction (as Siobhan does (30)). So, if a speaker of a turn following a repairable utterance can respond to that turn, he normally does so. If he feels he must correct, he normally forms the correction as a request for confirmation or an invitation to self-correct, or reduces its force in some similar way (for example, by modulations such as *I think, surely*). Taking issue with an utterance is usually perceived as marking disagreement. Consider, for example, the case of a conversational partner who continuously corrects your pronunciation or choice of words. We can even find the avoidance of other-correction in talk to foreigners to the extent that those non-native learners of a language often have to insist that native speakers correct their errors so that they can improve.

In what follows, we will examine the extent to which children correct others' utterances and whether they exhibit a preference for self-repair. We will focus on the clearest examples of other-correction in which one child corrects some aspects of the other's phonology, syntax and lexis. These are cases in which other-correction is strongly dispreferred in talk between adults of symmetrical status.

Other-corrections in the developmental literature

The ability of children to correct other's speech is generally associated with a developing awareness of language (Slobin 1978). In reviewing the literature, which consists mainly of anecdotal evidence, Clark (1978) states that, from about four years on, children become aware of the 'mistakes' of others, particularly younger siblings, and comment on these mistakes, sometimes offering corrections. She cites some examples from Weir (1962). For example:

(31) Michael: record 'top. Mine!
    Anthony: Mike only says top instead of stop

    (Michael 2;4, Anthony 5;4)

Iwamura (1980) provides a more detailed study of the correction activities of two girls in free play situations at ages 2;9 and 3;0 (and later at 3;5 and 3;8). Corrections ranged from short repair sequences involving linguistic elements to routines involving discussions of who should say what and in what order. Some of the linguistic corrections were concerned with grammaticality judgements while others were judgements of appropriateness. Corrections to pronunciation were either cases of alternative articulations, where communication was not impaired, or corrections following communicative breakdown where the breakdown was attributed to misarticulation. Corrections of syntax involved self-correction. Lexical corrections involved substitutions of lexically associated alternatives. These corrections were seen to be evidence of aspects of the children's developing linguistic systems, their mcta-linguistic ability to separate language from its communicative function as well as their understanding of the nature and structure of conversation.

Savíc (1980) found in a study of the acquisition of Serbo-Croatian by twins that the children corrected one another even before the age of three years. Corrections were lexical, phonological and morphological. In the following correction of morphology at age 2;9, the second twin stressed the second syllable, indicating the presence of a different suffix (Savić 1980:98):

(32) S: ja sam čuo de se srušio
        (I heard it collapse)
    M: da se srušilo

In contrast to the findings of Schegloff et al (1977), Savić reports that the twins often corrected in the pause while the current speaker was about to self-correct. For these children, at least, other-correction was not a dispreferred activity.

Other-corrections in the data

Linguistic other-corrections were infrequent in the data. There were only two corrections of grammar, one by each child. Corrections of lexical items were fairly evenly distributed between the children, but Heather made five corrections of Siobhan's pronunciation while Siobhan did not correct

Heather's pronunciation. Almost half the total number of corrections occurred in session I and there was some evidence that the children were less likely to correct each other's speech as they grew older. However, it would be unwise to draw any firm conclusions from such a small sample (the proportion of corrections to total utterances ranged from 0 per cent in some sessions to a maximum of 0.5 per cent).

Other-corrections of pronunciation

Most other-corrections of pronunciation occurred in session I and were corrections of Siobhan by Heather. The corrections in session IV were of a younger child who was present at one of the recordings, but who otherwise played a relatively minor role in the interaction. I shall look in some detail at two of the corrections from session I and at the corrections of the younger child in session IV.

The first example developed out of a dispute in which Heather asserted that she had some Plasticine and Siobhan demurred, saying that it was Lego:

(33) 1 Heather: there's some Plasticine
      2 Siobhan: that's not Plasticine
      3   it's Lego
                   .
                   .
                   .
      4 Siobhan: no I said it was ['lɛgo]
      5 Heather: ['lägo]
      6   ['jäło]
      7 Siobhan: no it's not
      8   it's ['lɛlo]
      9 Heather: ah you don't say it properly
     10 Siobhan: I do

(Heather 4;0, Siobhan 3;8)   (I:2:236–50)

In this example communication seems to break down. This occurs at Heather's lines 5 and 6, where she takes up Siobhan's *Lego*, repeats it and then 'corrects' to *yellow*. Siobhan rejects Heather's pronunciation of *yellow* and substitutes her own pronunciation which Heather rejects explicitly with *you don't say it properly*. It is, however, possible that in line 5 Heather was interpreting Siobhan's line 4 as an attempt to say *yellow*. We can see the similarities between each child's pronunciations of *Lego* and *yellow*, in which each child maintains the same vowel: Siobhan uses [ł] and [j] and between [g] and [ł] in Heather's lines 5 and 6.

The second example involved attempts by Siobhan to pronounce Heather's name followed by Heather's corrections:

(34) 1 Heather: wha- who does that say?
      2 Siobhan: ['häʋə]
      3 Heather: no you didn't
      4   you . you said ['hɛ·vər] ha ha
      5   say ['hɛɹər]
      6 Siobhan: ['hɛvər]
      7 Heather: ah no
      8   say ['hɛːɹər]
      9 Siobhan: ['hɛvər]
     10 Heather: no
     11   say ['hɛːɹər]

(Heather 4;0, Siobhan 3;8)   (I:4:61–71)

The main difficulty here concerns the medial [ð] which Siobhan pronounces using a labiodental [ʋ], then [v]. Heather models using an approximant [ɹ], which is, however, a possible variant in her dialect. There are, however, other differences between Siobhan's first attempt in line 2 and Heather's rendering of Siobhan's pronunciation in line 4 (different vowels and no final [r] in Siobhan's first pronunciation). Although Heather does not seem to perceive these differences, she is able to diagnose that Siobhan's medial consonant is incorrect and to offer a 'correction'.

The examples from session IV concerned the pronunciation of *pan* by the younger child as [pam]. This caused comprehension problems for Heather but not for Siobhan:

(35) Heather: [pam]
     (5;1)   what is a [pam]
                .
                .
                .
     Siobhan: it's a thing that you cook on

(Heather 5;1, Siobhan 4;9)   (IV:12:56–62)

Heather then corrects [pam] to [pan]. The subsequent discussion is interesting as, although the children have been able to correct the younger child's pronunciation, they are unable to engage in meta-linguistic discussion about the child's pronunciation:

(36) Siobhan: she she says [pram] for [pan] doesn't she?
     Heather: no she says [pam] for [pram]
     Siobhan: and she says [pram] for [pam]

                                                              (IV:12:74–6)

The correcting devices which the children used were interesting. As we saw, Heather made explicit reference to that fact that Siobhan's pronunciation was incorrect *(you don't say it properly)* in (33). She rejects with *no* in (34) as does Siobhan in her correction of the younger child. At first she uses explicit rejection (not [pam]), then she rephrases with an invitation to the younger child to self-correct or at least confirm *(that's what you mean isn't it?)*. Although this is the only example, we have an illustration of the preference for self-correction. There is some further support for this hypo-thesis in the fact that most other-corrections occurred in session I. There is, however, the additional factor that there were few subsequent opportunities for other-corrections to pronunciation, so that it is not clear whether the children develop from an earlier predisposition to correct other's pro-nunciation to a later stage where they allow or invite self-correction.

Other-corrections to grammar

There were only two other-corrections to grammar in the data and even these were problematic. I shall discuss each in turn. The first repair was to Siobhan's recitation of a nursery rhyme (only the relevant sections are cited):

(37) Siobhan: Dumpty Dumpty sat on a wall
        Dumpty Dumpty had a great fall
        all the king's horses and men
        Dumpty Dumpty couldn't get up together again
     Heather: no
        I'll do it
        Humpty Dumpty sat on a wall
        Humpty Dumpty had a great fall
        all the king's horses and all the king's men
        you said men
        you didn't say . you didn't . you didn't say king men
        all the king's horses and all the king's men
        couldn't put Humpty together again
     Siobhan: I did say king
     Heather: you didn't
     Siobhan: she said I didn't say king man so she did . Heather
     Heather: king's MEN

(Siobhan 3;8, Heather 4;0)   (I:4:126–42)

Several points emerge from this example. Firstly, we can note that here, as elsewhere, errors do not necessarily lead to correction (see Siobhan's *Dumpty Dumpty* as well as the fourth line of her rhyme). This failure to correct cannot be explained by lack of knowledge of the correct item as Heather evidences the correct items in her version of the rhyme. Secondly, we can note that 'corrections' are not necessarily correct. In isolating the error, Heather corrects to *king men*, even though in her version of the rhyme she used the correct form *king's men*. Thirdly, we can see that the correction can be disputed by its recipient and that this can be because of a failure to perceive the original error and understand the correction (see Siobhan's *I did say king* and *she said I didn't say king man*). Fourthly, there is the problem of the error. Siobhan's third line *all the king's horses and men* is grammatically correct and displays appropriate use of ellipsis. It is only incorrect in as much as this is not the form used in the rhyme. One final point of interest is the way in which the correction is accomplished. In order to make this correction, Heather has to isolate Siobhan's error *(you said men)* and then correct it *(you didn't say king men)*. She then provides a fully correct version *(all the king's horses and all the king's men)*. As we have seen, there are problems with the correctness of the corrections. However, what we have evidence of here is that Heather is able to perform the necessary steps of isolating the error and then providing a correction. This is made all the more difficult as the error is embedded within a longer piece of discourse, that is, the nursery rhyme.

The second correction to grammar was as follows:

(38) Siobhan: (referring to a toy which Heather has borrowed)
           but do you remember that you're not keeping it now?
     Heather: yea
           only . I'm only lending it for to play in the Poly playschool
     Siobhan: no I'm lending it for YOU
     Heather: no I'm lending it . FROM you

(Siobhan 4;9, Heather 5;1)   (IV:9:203–7)

The initial problem here is lexical, that is, incorrect use of *lend* instead of *borrow*. However, Siobhan's correction is grammatical in that she supplies a preposition (as well as stress on *you*). Heather's response is also a grammatical correction as she replaces *for* with an alternative preposition *from* and stresses this to indicate its function as a correction. As in the preceding example, it turns out that the correction itself is incorrect.

The low frequency of corrections to grammar accords with findings reported elsewhere that speakers focus primarily on the content of an utterance and not its form (Brown and Hanlon 1970). To some extent there is also the explanation for the child data that the children did not correct because they did not recognize the error, as, for example, in the case of over-regularized past tense forms, such as *sawed, brokened*, which occurred in the utterances of both children. However, it was also noticeable that corrections to grammar did not follow utterances addressed to the copresent adult. For example:

(39) Siobhan: Daddy I sawed the house that was broken
    Author: yes so did I

(Siobhan 3;8)   (I:4:201–2)

This would tend to support the claim that other-correction is avoided where there is no problem of communication breakdown. Errors of grammar do not usually cause breakdown in communication and so tend to pass uncorrected (Schegloff et al. 1977:380).

Other-corrections to lexical items
We have already seen some examples of corrections of lexical items. In some cases, the correction followed from disagreement realized by reversed polarity and so the correction involved replacement by an antonym; for example, *old* by *new*, *inside* by *outside*, *cold* by *hot*, *boy* by *girl*. In other cases replacement was by a more appropriate lexical item within a lexical set; for example: *Plasticine* by *Lego* (toys), *table* by *seat* (toy furniture), *stones* by *cement* (building materials). Finally, one example which didn't seem to fit the preceding types was as follows:

(40) Heather: (addressing toy dog)
               you bad bad little boy
    Siobhan: dog
    Heather: bad bad little dog

(Heather 5;1, Siobhan 4;9)   (IV:7:214–16)

Here Heather uses *boy* as an address term to a toy dog. Siobhan corrects, presumably on the basis of the literally correct label *dog*, which Heather accepts in her next utterance. Here the relationship is between potential address terms and the literal label for a referent. This example differs from most others in that the correction is not preceded by a disagreement marker but consists solely of the correction. Heather's acceptance in her next utterance indicates that she had no problems in recognizing it as a correction.

   The correction addressed to the author was interesting:

(41) Siobhan: where's the clock gone?
                    .
                    .
                    .
    Author: outside in the hall
    Heather: that isn't outside
               that's inside
               you mean outside in the hall?

(Siobhan 4;6, Heather 4;10)   (III:7:84–96)

Here, in addition to correcting *outside* to *inside* Heather continues by using a more modulated repair form which provides an opportunity for self-repair. This form is more typical of adult interaction (Schegloff et al. 1977), displaying a preference for self-correction. Its placement following prior other-corrections is however a reversal of the sequential ordering which Schegloff et al. claim is more frequent.

Self-repairs

One of the themes which has been stressed throughout the preceding two sections is that there is a preference for self-repair in conversational data. One aspect of this preference concerns the forms which are used to realize other-corrections. A second aspect is their lower frequency in relation to self-repairs. As we can see from figure 23, self-repairs and clarification requests, which invite the speaker to self-repair, predominated in the data. Furthermore, the occurrence of other-corrections decreased with age, which suggests that the children were approximating more closely to the adult model.

	Session					
	I	II	III	IV	V	VI
Self-repair						
Siobhan	4.4	9.7	7.9	7.2	5.3	5.6
Heather	4.1	8.0	3.1	4.3	4.5	4.3
Clarification requests						
Siobhan	1.0	0.5	5.5	1.6	2.1	0.5
Heather	2.8	1.6	3.4	4.2	1.6	2.0
Other-corrections						
Siobhan	0.4	0.0	0.0	0.4	0.1	0.0
Heather	0.6	0.0	0.3	0.5	0.0	0.0

Figure 23 Occurrence of repair types as a percentage of total utterances

A further point is that the opportunity for self-repair precedes that for other repairs. According to the turn-taking principle, a speaker is allowed to reach a possible turn completion point before turn transition becomes relevant. Thus, if an error occurs within the turn, the speaker has the opportunity of carrying out the repair before the next speaker has the right to speak. For this reason, we might expect a higher frequency of self-repairs than other-corrections.

We noted in chapter 2 that self-repairs can be occasioned by a variety of factors, including speech planning and production processes, emotional state, memory lapses and other degeneracies of performance. Although there are problems in locating the source of trouble, we can look at the regularities of repair execution. In the analysis which follows, we will focus on repairs which can be described in linguistic terms, that is, cases where the speaker makes a phonological, syntactic or lexical self-correction. We will see that the children's self-repairs reveal interesting aspects of both their formal linguistic and their interactional competence.

Self-repairs in the developmental literature

Self-initiated self-repairs have received little attention in the developmental literature. One possible reason for this is that they are unconsciously edited out at the transcription stage and simply not noticed (Clark and Andersen 1979:2). Indeed, repeated listening is necessary with particular focusing on the repair phenomena in order to avoid this natural, spontaneous editing out.

Clark (1978) reviews the literature on self-repairs in relation to children's developing awareness of language. Children seem to begin to make self-repairs from about one-and-a-half to two years of age. Their earliest repairs are pronunciations of single words, where the child changes pronunciation over several repeats until the listener shows signs of comprehension (see Scollon 1979 for several examples). Slightly older children repair word endings, word order and word choices (Zakharova 1973:284; Leopold 1949, vol. 4:114).

Clark and Andersen (1979) studied the spontaneous repairs of three children aged 2;2–2;11, 2;8–3;0 and 2;11–3;7. They found that the children produced self-repairs at the rate of approximately 20 repairs per hour. Repairs were mainly phonological at first, but later there were more syntactic and lexical repairs. Slobin (1978) reports the beginning of self-corrections by his daughter at age 3;2, noting that this self-monitoring seemed to be relatively late to develop. Iwamura (1980) studied the correction activities of two girls at ages 2;9 and 3;0 and 3;5 and 3;8, classifying self-corrections as phonological, syntactic and lexical.

Clark and Andersen distinguish between repairs to the linguistic system, which are not motivated by attempts to be more intelligible, and repairs for the listener, which are motivated by the need to be understood. Repairs to the system seem to concern those items which the children are in the process of acquiring, where repairs go hand-in-hand with a growing awareness of and mastery of the system. So, for example, when children are mastering past tense forms, we would expect a closer monitoring of these forms. This does not imply that repairs lead to correction. Indeed, sometimes the repair replaces a correct item (in the adult system) with an incorrect item. For example:

(42) Child: and she ate . she eated daddy bear porridge

This is, however, evidence of the variable nature of the child's system at this stage. To take this point further, as Iwamura (1980) points out, errors provide evidence of the linguistic system and corrections substantiate this evidence by indicating what the child sees as violating the system. Similar findings are discussed by Rogers (1978), Karmiloff-Smith (1979) and Savić (1980). Rogers examined the spontaneous self-corrections of five- and six-year-olds. He found that the younger children's grammatical self-corrections mainly involved morphological rules, while those of the older children involved more complex syntactic structures. This suggests a relationship between type of self-correction and the state of the child's development of syntactic rules. Further support is provided by Savić (1980), who found that the grammatical self-corrections of children aged 1;6 to 2;6 learning Serbo-Croatian mainly involved word order rules. Similarly, Karmiloff-Smith (1979) found a high frequency in children's self-corrections of determiners around age eight when they were beginning to develop an awareness of the plurifunctional status of determiners. Finally, Clark and Andersen also examine the speech of older children (four to seven years) in role play situations and find that children also make repairs to their speech style or register according to the role they are playing, for example:

(43) A.P. (4;10): (as doctor to nurse, talking about putting medicine on the patient's arm. Starts with high voice)
let's see which one (shifts to low voice) which one is it?

Repairs to pronunciation in the data

Repairs to pronunciation were infrequent in the data. They were of two types. Firstly, there were two examples of alternative articulations of a word, where the child seemed to be aiming for a more 'correct' version. In (44), it is not clear what the target word was. Its first version was mono-syllabic, whereas the second attempt had two syllables:

(44) Heather: she has (3.2) she has three [pɛs]
['pɛnɪs]

(4;0) (I:1:32)

In the second example, the target word is *bandage*. In the first attempt the initial [b] has been replaced by [m] and the medial and final consonants seem to have been transposed. The subsequent attempts incorporate some nasalization in the medial consonant, though in the final two versions the final consonant has been devoiced (devoicing of final consonants is, however, common in Heather's dialect). So as we can see, Heather progresses towards a more 'correct' approximation to the target word:

(45) Heather: that's my ['madʒɪŋ]
         ['baŋɟɪ]
         ['baŋɟɪdʒ]
         ['baŋɟɪtʃ]
         ['baŋɟɪtʃ]

   (5;1)   (IV:10:252–6)

The second type of self-repair to pronunciation involved anticipations and repetitions where a phonetic segment from a later word was anticipated and articulated too early or a segment which had already been produced was repeated inappropriately in a later word (see Fromkin 1973 for a full discussion):

(46) Heather: cos I can't get my s- head stuck out

                                                        (IV:10:79)

(47) Siobhan: these are your favourite two fi- pictures

                                                        (III:7:519)

(48) Heather: well she s- hit me first

                                                        (IV:12:410)

Self-initiated self-repairs to grammar

Repairs to grammar were more frequent and were evenly distributed between the two children. They fell into different types, although no clear overall pattern emerged. In some cases the repairs seemed to be purely concerned with the grammatical system as such, while in other cases they seemed to be pragmatically motivated, having syntactic consequences.

The following are examples of grammatical self-repairs which seemed to be concerned solely with the grammatical system as such:

(49) Heather: wha- who does that say?

   (4;0)   (I:4:61)

(50) Heather: she's just taking her lunch box in but h-do-aren't you?

   (4;0)   (I:4:540)

(51) Siobhan: do you want more some books now . some more books?

   (4;3)   (II:6:277)

(52) Heather: where's the old witch in this . . . on this book?
               where's the old witch in this book?

    (4;7)   (II:6:367–8)

(53) Heather: well I hurt me
               I hurt myself

    (4;10)   (III:7:490–1)

(54) Siobhan: I got nothing chopped off
    Heather: so . neither did I

    (Siobhan 4;9, Heather 5;1)   (IV:8:60–1)

(55) Siobhan: and there's a the the biggest garden

    (4;9)   (IV:9:349)

(56) Heather: I thought the bin go . went outside

    (5;5)   (V:13:479)

In each case the child produces a grammatical item and then follows it with an immediate self-correction. In (49), the non-personal interrogative pronoun *what*, cut off at *wha-*, is replaced by the personal pronoun *who*, the reason being apparently because the question was attempting to elicit the name *Heather*, printed on a lunch box which Heather was pointing to as she asked the question. This is an interesting replacement as the usual form for this type of question requires the non-personal form. Heather might, however, be aware that the distinction is important in other syntactic environments and, realizing that the answer she wants to elicit is a proper noun, feels that the personal form is more appropriate.

Example (50) is an example of problems with tag forms, attentuated by the fact that the tag is readdressed, that is, the main clause reference is third person *(she)* while the tag is second person *(you)*. Here Heather is having trouble with auxiliary agreement, alternating between what would seem to be attempts at using *have* and *do* before settling on *be* (*aren't* in agreement with *be* in *she's*).

Example (51) involves a case of the ordering of premodifying items in the noun phrase. The correct structure for premodification in the noun phrase is

predeterminer; determiner; ordinal/quantifier;
open class premodifier; head

For example (Quirk et al. 1972:146):

(57) both these last two rainy days

In (51) Siobhan first produces the ordering of quantifier *(more)* followed by determiner *(some)*, then corrects to *some more.*

Example (52) is a case of the choice of appropriate preposition. Here three attempts are made. In the first case, *in* is replaced by *on*, but this is subsequently replaced by *in*. Note that the cut-off point comes before the noun *book*, the prepositional object, indicating that Heather has self-monitored items before she has actually said them. Unlike many cases, to be discussed later, the repair in the first line of (52) does not involve a recycling of a full clause structure but only of the prepositional phrase in which the repair is located. The repair in the second line does consist of a full clause, but this is probably occasioned by the fact that Heather is reinitiating her question, not just repairing her choice of preposition.

In (53) Heather corrects the pronoun *me*, replacing it with the reflexive *myself* which is required in the syntactic environment of *I hurt X/X = I.* As in many other cases, we might hypothesize that the repairable was occasioned sequentially. In this instance, the preceding utterance was

(58) Siobhan: you hurt me

The immediate response incorporates items from (58) but this is repaired because Heather realized that she has violated the rule for reflexive pronoun usage.

Example (54) is probably also sequentially occasioned. One means of expressing cohesive relations between utterances is to use a substitution device (Halliday and Hasan 1976), for example:

(59) A: I like that
     B: so do I

Heather seems to be applying this rule in (54) but then realizes that the rule also involves polarity agreement, that is, a prior negative requires a negative, and so replaces *so* by *neither.*

Example (55) is a case of syntactic relations, where the choice of a superlative form *(biggest)* requires the prior use of the definite article. Siobhan begins the noun phrase with the indefinite article *a*, which is usually required after *there*, but replaces with *the* in anticipation of the superlative form. The repetition of *the* is a further indication of 'trouble' at this precise point.

Finally, (56) is an example of choice of tense in indirect speech. The use of a reporting verb *(I thought)* in the past tense occasions back-shift of the verb in the reported clause *the bin goes outside* to the past tense (see Quirk et al. 1972:785ff. for discussion). Heather shows awareness of this rule by replacing the present tense form *go* by the past tense form *went.*

What the analysis of these examples suggests is that children display in their self-repairs an awareness of various grammatical rules. In each of the cases presented here (except for (49) and (52)) the repairable contained a grammatical error which was replaced by the correct grammatical form. The examples discussed indicate the variety of grammatical rules which have been acquired by the children. It would be interesting to make comparisons in a larger sample between the grammatical rules involved in such self-repairs and the acquisition of these rules by the children, showing whether the occurrence of grammatical self-repairs is, as suggested by Clark and Andersen (1979), related to those grammatical rules which the children are in the process of acquiring.

The second set of examples does not involve corrections of grammatical 'errors' but rather pragmatically occasioned repairs with grammatical consequences. So, for example, a repair occasioned by an attempt to be more explicit might involve substituting a noun phrase for a pronoun:

(60) Heather: and she's (1.1) this little girl's two year old

    (4;0)   (I:1:21)

(61) Siobhan: she . my friend Heather knows how to take it off herself

    (4;9)   (IV:12:360)

(62) Siobhan: just put them up . up there alright the crayons?

    (4;9)   (IV:12:376)

(63) Siobhan: I could . could I cut them out?

    (4;6)   (III:7:558)

(64) Heather: no you . do you want to put that in there?

    (5;5)   (V:13:296)

(65) Heather: you chopped your head off . you got your head chopped off

    (5;1)   (IV:8:421)

(66) Siobhan: and this is just the table that you . like that table over there

    (5;1)   (V:13:380)

Examples (60) to (62) seem to be cases of repairs for the listener, where the aim is to make an item more explicit. Each of these cases involved a pronoun which was substituted by a noun phrase consisting of, at least, determiner and noun. Example (62) is a good example of the syntax typical of conversation. In this case the noun phrase *the crayons* makes the pronoun *them* explicit, but it occurs at the end of a possible syntactic structure, in fact after the tag *alright*. This is known as 'right-dislocation', where an element which could have occurred within a clause structure has been moved to the right of the structure, leaving as a trace an appropriate pronoun form. Examples (63) and (64) involve a change of sentence type, declarative to interrogative and (probably) imperative with surface subject *you* to interrogative. These repairs are probably pragmatically motivated, as the interrogative forms fulfil the function of making the utterance more tentative and polite, by offering the addressee the choice between *yes* and *no* as a response. Example (65) is an example of a replacement of an active by a passive structure, occasioned by the need to correct propositional content; that is, the subject *you* is not the agent of the action but the affected participant. Finally, the change in (66) from a projected relative clause structure *the table that you* to a comparative structure *the table like that table over there* can be explained in various ways. It might have been occasioned by a concern with content, where Siobhan realized that the table she was talking about was not related to a table that had some connection with a table of her addressee but was like one in the room to which she could point. Another possible explanation could be that Siobhan ran into trouble with the projected relative clause structure, perhaps at the point of finding a suitable verb *(the table that you verb)* and changed to a more manageable structure. Clearer cases of this phenomenon, referred to as *repair conversion* (Schegloff 1979), will be discussed later.

The discussion in this section has been concerned with those repairs which were classified as grammatical. It is also appropriate, however, to discuss some other phenomena related to repairs which are not necessarily grammatical, where the repair reveals interesting evidence about the children's grammatical competence. One point is that the majority of repairs involving a cut-off in mid-sentence, that is, after subject-auxiliary/ verb, resulted in a recycling or restructuring which involved a full clause structure:

(67) Heather: I was going to r-
I was going to go down to your house

(4;7)   (II:6:155–6)

In cases where the trouble occurred in a subordinate clause, then usually only the subordinate clause was recycled:

(68) Siobhan: you can't do it in the car because my house isn't very em
my house isn't very far

(4;3)   (II:6:191)

(69) Heather: has that got sharp wings that can (1.0) uh that makes a noise
on the bottom

(4;0)   (I:3:22–3)

In other cases, such as (52), the recycling involved only the appropriate
constituent, for example, a prepositional phrase. These examples are further
indications of the children's grammatical systems, as the ways in which they
recycle show how they orient towards clause structure as well as an
awareness of subordinate clause and constituent structure.

A second point concerns the location of repairs. Although a repair can be
initiated anywhere within a turn (Schegloff 1979), an inspection of the child
data revealed certain regularities. For example, repairs appeared to be
concentrated either at turn beginnings or in post-verbal positions within the
clause. The following are examples of post-verbal repairs:

(70) Heather: you have the blue chairs and I have that . I have that wee
chairs don't we?

(4;0)   (I:2:62)

(71) Siobhan: and I'm going to put mine in my . my basket so I nam

(3;8)   (I:4:489)

(72) Siobhan: that's the same table as . as our one isn't it daddy?

(4;6)   (III:7:161)

(73) Heather: pretend that's a . pottie for the . bathroom

(5;5)   (V:13:308)

This distribution of repairs towards clause final position would seem to lend
tentative support to the claim that in verbal planning the speaker plans the
overall semantic content of his utterance but sometimes has trouble in
retrieving particular items (Butterworth and Beattie 1978).

A third point concerns the phenomenon of repair conversion (Schegloff
1979:273). This occurs when, for example, a word search is initiated,
usually with a filled pause *(um, uh)* but the repair solution is not a lexical
item but a reconstruction of the sentence so far, thus avoiding the need for
the missing element. In other words, a lexical repair is resolved by a
syntactic solution. Example (74) illustrates repair conversion:

(74) Heather: so your na- so your name hasn't got . um
so your

so . so you aren't a girl . you're a boy
you're called Michael

(4;0)   (I:1:318–2)

Focusing on the second repair initiated at the end of the first line, we can see that Heather is having trouble finding a suitable object noun phrase to express the idea that the addressee's name is masculine (this example also illustrates the location of repairs at post-verbal position discussed earlier). Instead of supplying this missing lexical item, Heather's solution is to restructure the idea with different syntax (lines 3 and 4). Example (75) also illustrates repair conversion:

(75) Heather: did you bring . the um
                did you bring some of this . to playschool uh things that's got
                wee things on . wee streety things

(4;0)   (I:1:229–31)

Here trouble arises again at the post-verbal position when Heather is unable to find an appropriate noun to follow the determiner *the* in the object noun phrase. Her first solution is lexical in that she substitutes the noun phrase *some of this*, but then she further specifies with the syntactic structure of noun + relative clause (*things that's got wee things on*) and further specifies *wee things* by introducing a second premodifier in the appositive noun phrase *wee streety things*. These examples are interesting in that they illustrate the child's ability to resolve what was essentially a lexical problem with a syntactic solution.

Self-initiated self-repairs to lexical items
The easiest type of lexical self-repair involved cases of replacement of one lexical item by a more appropriate one, for example:

(76) Heather: give me the wee bus
                it's going in the car wash
                in the bus wash

(4;0)   (I:1:151–3)

Here Heather replaces *car wash* by *bus wash*, realizing that the object involved is a bus and not a car. Similarly, in the following example, she has made an incorrect word choice and corrects with a more appropriate item:

(77) Heather: I never seen men with rainco- with um (1.0) umbrellas

(5;1)   (IV:8:656)

In other cases, the substitution does not involve an item which is more correct or accurate, but which expresses greater uncertainty, tentativeness or politeness:

(78) Heather: I don't want . I wouldn't have liked anybody to just take them anyhow

(5;5)   (V:14:174)

(79) Siobhan: I want . I would rather be the patient now

(5;1)   (V:14:294)

Sometimes an empty lexical item was replaced by a common noun:

(80) Heather: will I can I cut the thingies out the triangles?

(4;10)   (III:7:527)

Here Heather replaces *thingies* by *triangles*. This example also involves replacement of *will* by *can*, where the more appropriate modal verb for requesting permission is substituted for the meaning of prediction.

Otherwise, it does not seem possible to find any further regularities in lexical self-repairs. We can see how items are often replaced by other items in the same lexical set, for example, *car* by *bus* in (76), *raincoats* by *umbrellas* in (77). One example involved the replacement of *going* by *coming*, illustrating the problem children have with deictics (Clark and Garnica 1974):

(81) Siobhan: that's why it doesn't stop go- coming

(4;9)   (IV:9:8)

Lexical repairs were difficult to distinguish from repairs to propositional content, as many lexical repairs necessarily change content. For example:

(82) Heather: Father Christmas is coming today
     Siobhan: no he's=
     Heather: =tonight

(Heather 4;7, Siobhan 4;3)   (II:6:475–77)

Here *today* is replaced by the propositionally more accurate *tonight*. (Whether this self-repair was occasioned by Siobhan's *no he's* cannot be determined from this example, as Heather may have projected her self-repair already before Siobhan began her turn at talk.)

Finally, some cases were not easily distinguished from the slips on the tongue discussed under phonological self-repairs, where a segment due to occur elsewhere is misplaced. In practice, if a lexical item could be postulated for a single segment, then the repair was judged to be lexical. For example:

(83) Heather: let me s- count

(4;0)   (I:1:80)

(84) Siobhan: it doesn't matter if you d- go over the lines

(4;9)   (IV:12:301)

In (83) it can be speculated that Heather was going to say *let me see* but broke off after the *s-* of *see* and substituted *count*. Similarly, in (84), it seems that Siobhan was about to say *do* but cut off after *d-* and substituted *go*. It does not seem possible to postulate possible lexical items in the examples involving slips of the tongue. For example:

(85) Siobhan: these are your favourite two fi- pictures

(4;6)   (III:7:519)

(86) Heather: cos I can't get my s- head stuck out

(5;1)   (IV:10:79)

In (85) there does not seem to be a suitable lexical item beginning with *fi-* which could fit in the slot following *favourite two*, nor in (86) is there an item beginning with *s-* which is replaced by *head*. (Context lends further support to these claims, as in (85) Siobhan was holding up pictures and in (86) Heather was trying to put her head out of the car window, so no other lexical items seem possible here.)

Concluding remarks on self-initiated self-repairs

It will have been obvious from the examples of self-repairs discussed that most self-repairs occur within the same turn as the repairable item, before the turn reaches its point of possible completion. This is one way in which conversation provides for a preference for self-initiated self-repairs as these occur sequentially before opportunities for other-initiated repairs. Self-repairs can, however, occur in other placements. They can occur in the transition place of the turn in which the repairable utterance is located. Transition place is described as roughly 'the environment of a turn's possible completion, at which possible transition to a next speaker becomes relevant' (Schegloff et al. 1977:366 fn. 11; Sacks, Schegloff and Jefferson 1974:702–6). Example (76) illustrates this placement:

>   Heather: it's going in the car wash
>   in the bus wash

>   (4;0)   (I:1:152–3)

After *car wash* Heather has completed a potential turn unit and a possible transition to next speaker is relevant, so in this case other-initiated repair could have occurred. The final placement for self-repair is after the turn following the turn in which the repairable item is located, that is, in the speaker's next turn at talk:

(87) Heather: and you have to carry something
Siobhan: no I'm not
Heather: I mean . I said to your daddy
he has to carry something

(Heather 5;1, Siobhan 4;9)   (IV:8:644–47)

Repairs placed in this position are often marked by items such as *I mean*, aimed at remedying the misapprehension in the second turn. This is the only example of this placement in the data and it is not particularly clear, as Siobhan's turn could be seen as initiation by other of Heather's subsequent repair. A clearer case is where the other's turn does not display misapprehension but the speaker of the repairable item opts to self-repair. For example (Schegloff et al. 1977:366):

(88) Hannah: and he's going to make his own paintings
Bea: mm hm
Hannah: and . or I mean his own frames

As we saw in earlier sections, other-initiated repairs are located in different positions from self-initiated self-repairs.

One final point that emerged from the data is that the repair initiator (for example, hesitations, vowel lengthening, cut-offs) did not always immediately precede the repairable item, but could occur somewhere before it, indicating that the trouble was being anticipated before the point of its occurrence had actually been reached:

(89) Heather: so your na- so your name hasn't got . um
so your .
so . so you aren't a girl . you're a boy

(4;0)   (I:1:318–20)

As we saw earlier, the trouble in this example is with the item which ought to occur following the verb *hasn't got*. A repair is initiated at this point. However, the anticipation of repair precedes this point and occurs at the subject position with the hesitation over *your na-* and again in line 2. This anticipation would seem to indicate a level of planning further than the items which follow immediately.

Concluding remarks

In this chapter we have been examining the development of the conversational processes of turn-taking and repairs. Several points have emerged which we can summarize briefly. We have seen that young preschool children take turns in an orderly fashion in conversation and that by school age they seem to be following similar processes to adults – at least, as far as dyadic interaction is concerned. A detailed analysis of overlaps revealed that they are also able to deal competently with such problems by stopping when interrupted or by repeating overlapped portions which have been potentially impaired. Our discussion of different types of conversational repair showed that young children are able to monitor their own and other's speech and can locate, diagnose and repair conversational breakdown. The study of repairs proved fruitful as it provided useful insights into the children's linguistic and social development. On the one hand, we saw how they displayed linguistic knowledge in their repairs by manipulating grammatical, phonological and semantic items. At the same time, their sensitivity to the social factors involved in the repair of conversational breakdown, particularly in the correction of the other's speech, revealed the extent of their knowledge of the principles underlying smooth social interaction.

In this and the preceding chapters we have seen that preschool children show evidence of having developed many of the complex skills which are involved in conversational interaction. We might wonder whether they differ from adults in their conversational performance. Certainly, the emphasis in the literature is on the children's abilities rather than on their potential deficiencies. Yet many problems arise when children start to attend school and to engage in interaction of a much more diverse nature than we have been discussing so far. Although research in the area of later conversational development is scant, it will be important to consider the problems which face older children. This will be our concern in the next chapter.

8

Later conversational developmental

In contrast to the extensive literature on the development of conversation in preschool children, much of which has been discussed in the preceding chapters, little has been written as yet on development into school age and beyond. There are several possible reasons for this. One fairly obvious reason is that it is more difficult to observe conversational development in older children. On the one hand, older children are more aware that they are being observed and either become over-shy or put on a special performance for the observer. This was certainly true for the children in the present study. But another more important factor is that older children's domains of interaction extend far beyond the fairly limited and adult-dominated situations characteristic of the preschool stage. Older children run about in groups, go off riding on their bicycles, play team games and so on, and so they are often beyond the range of the observer and his recording equipment. In fact, most reported studies of older children have involved either experimental settings or classroom interaction, where the situation is more formal and controlled. A notable exception is the ethnographic work with teenage gangs, as for example in Labov (1972b). This work is, however, more restricted in its field of enquiry than the present study and usually focuses on a particular aspect of conversational interaction, generally with the aim of establishing a theoretical point. For example, Labov's study looked at the use of *sounding* or *ritual insults* by black working-class adolescents in New York, showing how these youths were extremely competent in this complex verbal activity. One of the main motivations for demonstrating this competence was to counteract the belief that these youths were verbally deficient, a belief which resulted from their failure to cope with the conventional system of schooling.

A further problem which besets research into later conversational development is that there is no model of the skilled adult conversationalist which might inform such work. With younger children we were able to trace the development of such basic conversational skills as initiating, turn-taking, repairing and selecting appropriate request forms. As yet, there is no clear account of how development proceeds after this early stage, or indeed what its end point might be. Most studies of adult conversation are fairly general (for example, the study of turn-taking by Sacks et al. 1974, which accounts for certain important and clearly recognizable aspects of casual conversation, but does not begin to take account of the wide variation that is to be found in everyday conversation, as for example in speech events such as bantering). We have little difficulty in recognizing the lack of conversational ability, in what Goffman (1957) describes as the 'faulty interactant'. It is rather more difficult, however, to make a comprehensive description of what is involved in skilled adult conversation.

Let us consider this problem briefly. It is easy enough to observe the use of the skills which we documented earlier for young children. Adults can also be observed initiating conversation by getting and directing their listener's attention. They take turns and can repair conversational breakdowns. They select appropriate forms to express politeness and indirectness in speech acts and they respond relevantly to preceding turns. As far as these aspects of conversational ability are concerned, the differences between adults and the young children we have been studying would seem to be a matter of degree. For example, adults are able to use much more indirect forms as a tactful device to conceal their intentions when the situation demands. As a result, much adult interaction appears extremely indirect and proceeds on the basis of hints, innuendos and oblique references, which depend for their appropriate interpretation on a much wider knowledge of the world than is available to the young child. One only has to consider the inability of children to unravel the temporal and logical sequence of events in a film intended for adult viewers, or to understand the humour in an adult comedy show, to recognize the extent to which competent participation in adult interaction depends on a degree of knowledge of the world which is beyond the experience of the young child.

This notion of experience poses problems, however, when we come to consider the range of interactional activities in which adults engage. Here we encounter wide variability in performance. Although we might be able to propose basic norms for adult conversational interaction involving the skills described earlier, we find wide differences between adults according to their ability to engage in specific types of conversational interaction. Some of these are the more obvious professional skills such as counselling, teaching, interviewing or chairing committees. Many aspects of such skills can be learned and there are indeed training schemes for such higher-level interaction skills (Ellis and Whittington 1981; Hargie et al. 1981). However, when we consider the types of activity which most adolescents and adults encounter – such as attending interviews, dealing with pushy salesmen or trying to initiate an encounter with a member of the opposite sex – then we find considerable differences in ability. Not only this, we find that people who are skilled in one area might often be totally incompetent in another. In other words it seems that we can characterize, to some extent, extreme interactional incompetence as manifested by those who receive remedial social skills training in specially designed mental health programmes (Trower, et al. 1978). At the other end of the scale we can enumerate the skills involved in a profession such as counselling, which generally involves special training in interaction. In between, however, we find a wide range of variation within which it does not seem possible to find a norm, except at the most general level of specification. Any study of later conversational development must take account of this problem in order to avoid the trap of assuming lack of competence when lack of experience is involved. Likewise, any remedial programme needs to consider the extent to which a skill is situationally specific or is generalizable across interactional encounters.

Notwithstanding these problems, we will attempt in this chapter to review some of the work which has been done on later conversational development. As concerns the children whose early conversational development was the topic of much of the preceding chapters of this book, only a few recordings were taken at a later age. Obviously such observations can hardly be regarded as systematic. They will, however, be discussed briefly as they show some aspects of development into the school years. Beyond this, we will consider a few studies reported in the literature of the conversational behaviour of older children and adolescents. Following this, we will look at studies of classroom interaction – an important arena of conversational interaction which frequently causes problems for young children.

Conversational development in older children

Three additional recordings were taken of Siobhan and Heather. Two of these were of free play situations, recorded in a special unit at Ulster Polytechnic at ages eight and ten years, while the third was a recording of each of the girls in interaction with an unfamiliar adult. Some of these recordings will be described briefly.

In the recording of free play at eight years, the children spent much of the time negotiating roles in pretend play, in which Siobhan was the teacher and/or mother and Heather was the pupil and/or child. This was little talk during large parts of this recording, as Siobhan wrote sums and sentences on the board for Heather to copy down. The following are some examples from the dialogue. In the first, we can see how Siobhan still uses strong forms of other-correction, although this may be due to the fact that she is playing the teacher's role in this case:

(1)   (Siobhan has been writing numbers on the board and Heather reads the
       numbers aloud)

    Heather:seven hundred and four
    Siobhan:(pointing to 104)
        that's not a
        (pointing to 204)
        that's a two
        (pointing to another 204)
        that's a two
    Heather:that's not a two
    Siobhan:(emphatically)
        that is a ONE (points to 104)
    Heather:is that a one?
    Siobhan:look
        that's a one and that's a seven (points to numbers)

Siobhan's perception of the nature of an English language lesson is interesting in the following example, where she insists that Heather does not answer the questions but should write them down and where she also insists on full sentences:

(2)   (Heather reads from board)
    Heather:what are dogs?
        what do you mean?
    Siobhan:what are dogs?
    Heather:animals
    Siobhan:yes but you write that down
        you don't tell me
        write a whole sentence, right?
    Heather:aw
    Siobhan:for goodness sake, Heather
    Heather:what?
    Siobhan:you know that you write sentences
    Heather:yes but you just said write the answer
    Siobhan:oh in sentencing

It is interesting to note a particular device which the children used to set up and negotiate pretend games. The following are examples:

(3) Siobhan:pretend I just write down what it is and then you do them

(4) Heather:pretend you just came back for a wee minute

(5) Heather:pretend those were in the shops
    Siobhan:no those weren't in the shops

It will be noticed that the children switch from present to past tense forms in these utterances beginning with *pretend*. Similar examples are *pretend I'm the mummy* and *pretend you just fell down*. A close examination of the discourse context of the use of these forms shows that they are not in free variation. Rather, the present tense seems to be used to set up a role, activity or situation which is about to be played out. The past tense, on the other hand, is used to set up a situation in the past which has current relevance for the next role play. So, for example, Siobhan's returning in (4) is to be related to what Heather plans to do next; the form in (5), which refers to clothes they are about to put on, is an attempt to set up a situation of trying on clothes in the shop (rather than, for example, the literal meaning that the clothes were, but are no longer, in the shops); and the form *pretend you just fell down* sets up a situation where mother can tend the child, an ambulance can arrive, and so on. (A smilar usage of past tense in games of pretend has been reported by Lodge 1979.)

One final point is the way in which the children convey the switching of roles para-linguistically, as can be seen in (6). Previous to this, the children had been arguing about the location of the pretend play area in the room. Siobhan first addressed the pretend children as teacher and then, with much lower pitch, addressed Heather as herself:

(6) Siobhan:I'm just going out to the play area and you know where the play area is

The session with an unfamiliar adult formed part of a study of the use of cohesion by Siobhan and Heather at age eight years.[1] The girls were asked to carry out the following tasks:

1 Tell two stories which were represented by a series of pictures (these were the 'Bus story' from the Renfrew Action Picture Tasks and the 'Football story' used by Hawkins 1973).
2 Give the adult instructions on how to play two games, one a board game with marbles and the other a card game. This task was carried out under two conditions – an absent condition, under which the game being described was in a far corner of the room, and a present condition, under which the game was placed in front of the child and the adult.

The main items to be investigated were the children's use of anaphoric and exophoric reference and of conjunctions. In the two stories it was found that the children used mainly anaphoric reference (Siobhan 78 per cent, Heather 68 per cent). Their usage of exophoric reference was not necessarily inappropriate as the pictures were placed between the adult and themselves and so they could make appropriate reference to items by pointing and using exophoric devices such as pronouns and the definite article. As far as conjunctions were concerned, the most commonly used where *and* and *then*, although Heather also used *so* and *because*. In addition, Siobhan used the discourse devices *well* and *now*.

The instruction tasks were designed to take account of the appropriate use of reference in present and absent conditions. It was expected that, if the children were aware of the appropriate use of reference devices, they would use more exophoric reference in the present condition, where items could be identified by pointing and the use of pronouns. This was indeed the case. For example, in one of the instruction tasks Siobhan made four times as many exophoric references in the present as in the absent condition. More generally, it was found that a greater range of cohesive devices, such as conjunction, substitution and ellipsis, was used in the instructional as compared with the narrative tasks, which suggests that the former required a greater degree of explicitness from the children. There is also the important methodological point that the children's ability to use these devices was only demonstrated adequately in the instructional tasks, which were perhaps pitched more accurately at their level of competence. The narrative tasks may have been too easy and may therefore not have elicited such a full range of cohesive devices, thus under-representing the children's abilities in this area. This conclusion is also supported by the finding that there were more repairs and disfluencies in the instructional tasks, which suggests that these were more difficult for the children and required a higher degree of verbal planning.

The football picture story, as well as a series of pictures about a fishing episode, was used to elicit narratives from children aged five, seven, nine and eleven years by McClements (1976). Among the variables which were studied was the children's use of conjunctions. McClements found a general development through the age groups as follows:

Five-year-olds
Conjunctions still being acquired.
Often disregarded sequential and logical constraints.
Main conjunction used was *and*, followed by *and then*.

Seven-year-olds
Wider range of conjunctions used, including *when, until, so . . . that*.
Higher percentage of correct usage.

Nine-year-olds
Development towards wider and more well-formed usage appeared to be halted.
Little elaboration of stories beyond basis outline of picture.

Eleven-year-olds
Wide range of conjunctions used *and, and then* used only by two out of eight children.

The general picture, as we can see, is from little and incorrect usage towards a wider range of conjunctions used correctly. *And* is used commonly by the youngest children, but infrequently by those children who have acquired other options. The exception to this picture is the nine-year-old group. This is explained by McClements in terms of the attitudes of this group to the task. The boys in particular were unruly and mocked the others' efforts, so that there was little encouragement to elaborate the pictures. This in turn had a detrimental effect on the children's performance. However, while this result and the explanation might be viewed as exhibiting a weakness in the design of the study, it is possible to look at it in a rather different way as a clear case of the role of situational factors in the execution of an experiment. Such factors are often overlooked or discounted, yet they clearly affected the results in this case. As we will see in chapter 10, one of the contributions of discourse analysis has been to the closer examination of such 'contaminating' factors in tests and experiments designed to assess children's language abilities.

Similar results were found in a large-scale cross-sectional study of the acquisition of adverbial conjuncts and disjuncts by six-, eight-, ten- and twelve-year-old children (Scott 1983). The most commonly used conjuncts were *then, so, now* and *anyway* (in decreasing frequency). Development consisted of a considerable increase in usage of conjuncts as well as a wider range of items uscd (for example, the use of *and* decreased as other related conjuncts were used). There was little usage, even in the oldest group, of attitudinal disjuncts such as *in fact, obviously* and *actually*.

We can conclude this section by mentioning briefly some work on discourse skills of older children. In a study of the development of the ability to argue persuasively in children, Clark and Delia (1976) presented children in grades two to nine with hypothetical situations which required persuasive skills. One example was that the child had found a puppy and had to go the nearest house and ask the woman who lived there if she would keep it. The children's requests were coded according to the form of the request and the use of request supports. For example, the following were some of the categories used:

Form of request
1 Statement of desire or request.
2 Request phrased to forestall counter-arguments.
3 Request phrased to acknowledge the wishes of the recipient of the request.

Request support
1 Demonstrate need for request.
2 Deal with counter-arguments.
3 Discuss advantages to recipient of request.

As an example of how a child might support a request by dealing with counter-arguments, we find the following:

(7)   it doesn't cost much to feed a dog if you buy big bags of food

There was considerable variability across children, although the general finding was that the older children used more higher-level strategies, which reflected a more sophisticated ability to assess the other's viewpoint. Such findings relate to the discussion of request strategies in chapter 5, and the general design of this experiment could provide a useful model for training programmes in the development of social skills such as persuasion.

A second line of research is associated with a project directed in Edinburgh by Gillian Brown into the communicative skills of Scottish children, ages 14 to 16 years, in secondary schools (Anderson et al. 1982). Brown and colleagues used tasks similar to those employed in studies of referential communication, such as describing, giving instructions, making comparisons, telling stories and so on. A methodology was developed for the objective scoring of the children's performances (Yule and Smith 1981). The main outcome from this research which is of interest in the present context is that the performance of fairly mature and competent speakers, i.e. adolescent schoolchildren, could be improved if the task forced them explicitly to focus on their hearer's needs or if they had previously taken the hearer's role. This is an important finding, since previously the performance of younger children on such tasks was assumed to be affected by their egocentrism. If egocentrism is discounted for adolescents (and adults), as the general theory would predict (Piaget 1959), then other factors must come into play. The same factors could equally be involved in the performance of younger children. Additionally, there is the important finding that communication skills can be taught. This supports findings from other research studies (Asher and Wigfield 1981; Patterson and Kister 1981; Robinson 1981). Finally, the methodology and the development of a more objective scoring scheme than has normally been used in such studies has implications for the design and implementation of training schemes involving the teaching of social and life skills in communicative settings (see chapter 10).

Conversational interaction at school

Going to school is, for many young children, a new experience which can be fraught with problems. There is a transition from the more intimate relationships to which the child has been accustomed at home to the more impersonal relationships in the larger community of the classroom. Whereas learning may have been totally informal and pleasurable at home, it now becomes the explicit focus of attention at school. Obviously many children, particularly those who have previously attended nursery or playschool, make this transition easily. Some children, however, fail to meet the expectations set by the educational system, sometimes in spite of indications of ability in various domains outside the classroom, including verbal skills. The question that we might be led to ask is whether there is, for some children, a discontinuity between the type of conversational interaction experienced at home and that of the school, such that these children find it difficult to meet the linguistic demands of the school and so become 'educational failures'. There is already a massive literature on the issue of verbal deprivation at the levels of language such as syntax, semantics and phonology (see, for example, Edwards 1979). The main outcome of this research is that there is little or no evidence to suggest that children are deficient in the basic elements of language as a consequence of their home backgrounds; that there are differences for some children between the accents and dialects of the home and those of the school; that those children whose home language is closer to standard English may have less difficulty in the development of literacy; and that some children may be disadvantaged at school not because of their language but because of their teachers' attitudes to their language (Trudgill 1975; Stubbs 1976).

Many of these issues are still unresolved and this is not the place to pursue them further. Instead, we will look at a question which has developed out of this research and which bears on the main theme of this book – whether there are differences in experience of language at the level of conversational interaction between the home and school which make participation in the classroom more difficult for some children. In other words, is there a discontinuity between the style and structure of conversation of the home and the classroom? We will look first at some studies which suggest that there is little discontinuity and then at studies which highlight the differences. However, as we will see, it is not sufficient to demonstrate that there are differences. We also need to show that these differences are the cause of difficulty. In order to do this, we will need to look more closely at the nature of classroom interaction, particularly in the early school years, to see whether any differences which we have found between home and school interaction can be shown to result in actual problems for some children.

Talk at home and at school: some similarities

It will be recalled from our outline of conversational structure in chapter 2 that one of the most common exchange types which occurs in classrooms is the three-part exchange in which the teacher elicits a response from a pupil and then evaluates the response before moving on to the next exchange. The following is a typical example:

(8) Teacher: what is the opposite of 'polite'?   Initiation
     Pupil: 'impolite'   Response
     Teacher: that's right   Follow-up

This type of exchange has often been described an as IRF exchange.

A second point which we can note about much of classroom talk, which is also illustrated in this example, is that teachers ask questions to which they themselves know the answers. The function of such questions, often referred to as test, display or pseudo-questions (see chapter 1), is not to request information but to test the knowledge of the addressee. Because the teacher already knows the answer, s/he is able to evaluate the pupil's response and correct it or, alternatively, ask further questions which may lead the pupil to the correct answer.

The question we might now ask is whether this type of interaction is a new experience for children when they begin school and whether it causes them problems. One study, which has made a detailed comparison of talk at home and at school, as part of the Bristol Language Development Programme, would argue against the theory of discontinuity (MacLure and French 1981). An analysis of the sequential structuring of conversation at home and at school revealed similar structures. For example, children experienced three-part exchanges at home, they were asked questions to which the questioning adult already knew the answer, and they could either be corrected or led to a correct answer if their response was wrong in the first instance. At this level then, at least, there is no evidence of discontinuity. We will return shortly to some of the differences which these authors have pointed out. In the meantime, however, we might note that this study does not look at individual cases, for example by analysing in retrospect the interaction at home of those children who were performing poorly at school to see whether their experience of talk at home was different from what was expected at school.

An interesting study by Willes (1981) looked at the ways in which children learn to take part in classroom interaction by investigating whether the children could predict the next event in a simulated classroom sequence. Willes found that the children in her study learned quickly without explicit instruction, a result which suggests that, at this level, participation in classroom interaction is not a problem for young children. It should be noted, however, that Willes found differences in performance between children and that some pupils failed to perceive classroom interaction as orderly and predictable. One possibility, which was not pursued further in this study, is that these children experienced problems in their performance at school.

Finally, with reference to IRF exchanges, it can be argued that it is not the case that children have little experience of such exchanges at home. Rather it seems that a style of interaction which emphasizes the asymmetry of status between the participants, and in which the child is expected to produce minimal responses which maintain the perspective of the initiator of the exchange, is not conducive in the long run to the development of the type of communication commensurate with educational success (Wells 1981b). Here the argument has gone full circle. At first it was argued that children found classroom interaction problematic because they had little experience of IRF exchanges and pseudo-questions at home. Now it seems that a style of home interaction which consists predominantly of these discourse features is less beneficial to the child. In order to pursue this problem further, we will have to look at the interactional demands of IRF exchanges and pseudo-questions and ask how they might be seen as a more restricting type of interactional style. In order to do this we will need to look at some of the ways in which talk at home and at school differ from one another.

Talk at home and at school: some differences

There are differences both in frequency and distribution of discourse features in talk at home and at school. Requests for clarification, which, as we saw in chapter 7, are used commonly by young children, are infrequently used by children in classrooms. This is perhaps because of the way turn-taking is distributed in the classroom. Children have to bid, often by raising their hand, in order to get a turn in the classroom, and by the time they get their turn the opportunity may have passed to make their clarification request directly contingent on a repairable utterance. In this case, they may have to utilize more sophisticated devices for re-establishing a previous discourse topic, devices which may be beyond their current competence (Christian and Tripp 1978).

The organization of classroom turn-taking, determined by the two main aims of the teacher to pursue a pedagogic curriculum and to manage interaction in a large group, results in a more limited set of conversational options available to the child at school in comparison with the situation at home. For example, most questions, particularly requests for display, are asked by the teacher, the child does not have the right to correct the teacher's utterances, and the teacher talks generally much more than all the children combined (as much as two-thirds of the time, according to many accounts) (Maclure and French 1981).

How do these differences relate to educational achievement? One way of approaching this question is to consider the nature of the linguistic demands which children are expected to meet at school and to assess the ways in which their experiences of talk at home and at school equip them to meet these demands. One important aspect of the use of language at school involves the child's ability to reflect on present and past experiences, to predict and consider alternative possibilities, and to project into the feelings of others (Tough 1981). Yet another aspect, which is particularly important when it comes to writing, is the ability to use language which is disembedded from its context, which is explicit and does not rely unduly on the reader's background knowledge for its coherence – language which is sustained and sequential. This style of language differs from much of casual conversation which is more context bound and often less sustained topically (Blank 1982).

Let us look at the ways in which children's experience of talk at home may or may not prepare them for this special use of language at school. We will draw on the work of the Bristol language development programme, part of which was concerned with an analysis of talk at home and at school, making comparisons between the styles of interaction experienced by a group of children in both settings and relating these to the children's performance at school (Wells 1978, 1981b; Wells and Montgomery 1981).

Following an analysis of some examples of talk at home, Wells (1978) suggests some features of the type of conversational interaction which he believes leads to an effective use of language by children. These are as follows:

1 A warm responsiveness to the child's interests and a recognition of the child as an autonomous individual with valid purposes and ways of seeing things.
2 Negotiation of meaning and purpose in the joint construction of an intersubjective reality.
3 An invitation to the child to consider the immediate present in a wider framework of intention and consequence, feelings and principles.

The essential feature of this style of conversational interaction is that it is *supportive*. The adult acknowledges the child's contributions and encourages the child to continue and to select topics, and so the child has the opportunity to produce linguistically more mature utterances on a topic of interest. This style is contrasted with a *leading* style of interaction, in which the adult asks display questions and the child makes minimal responses within the perspective set by the adult. In this case the child's options are severely reduced and the conversation is devoid of the *joint construction of meaning* which is considered essential for the development of effective communicative ability. To cite Wells again (1981b:150):

> In the classroom environment, where intentions have to be explained and actions justified, and where each child is expected to share his news with teacher and fellow pupils, it is a disadvantage indeed not to have learnt to play one's part in dialogue, but to be restricted instead to the unilateral expression of one's own individual point of view.

So far, the relationship between a child's experiences of particular styles of conversational interaction and subsequent achievement at school is hypothetical. The claim is that children who experience more of the supportive style will be more able to deal with the demands of the school which we described earlier – the use of language to predict and project, to negotiate meanings, and to produce sustained discourse which is disembedded, where appropriate, from its context. Comparisons between children whose home experience of interaction varied along the dimensions described, suggests that the quality of adult–child interaction does indeed have a bearing on educational achievement. More specifically, those children who experienced a supportive style of interaction were more advanced linguistically on entry to school, and, after two years at school, were more advanced in their reading attainment (Wells and Raban 1978).

However, the picture is not entirely clear, as there is also evidence from the Bristol studies to suggest that some children's performance at school is deflated when we compare it with their display of ability in conversational interaction at home. We can cite from a small case study of one child, Rosie, in talk at home and at school. The following is an extract from a dialogue between Rosie and her teacher (Wells and Montgomery 1981:212–15):

(9) (A group of children, including Rosie, are making calendars from old Christmas cards. The teacher is attempting to interact with Rosie)
Teacher: what are those things

           .
           do you know what they're called?
Rosie: (shakes head)
Teacher: what do you think he uses them for?
Rosie: (takes the card and examines it)
Teacher: it's very nice
           after play we'll put some ribbons at the top

           .
           .

           what's- what are those?
           what do you think he uses them for?
Rosie: go down
Teacher: go down
           yes you're right
           go on
           what's the rest of it?
           you have a little think and I'll er get the little calendar for you

           .
           .
           .

           he uses those to go down
           is it a hill or a mountain?
Rosie: a hill

Teacher: a hill
       yes
       and what's on the hill
Rosie: ice
Teacher: yes ice
       they're called skis

In this extract, in which we have omitted much of the original for the sake of clarity of exposition, we can see that the teacher is having great difficulty in eliciting talk from Rosie on what might be considered a fairly simple topic. Our impression, which is confirmed by several similar examples, might be that Rosie is severely deficient in her conversational ability. However, an extract recorded at home (Wells and Montgomery 1981:210–12) shows that she is able to use language to communicate a variety of functions, such as reporting on completed events, negotiating future activity and considering the consequences of a hypothetical course of action. Her performance is also better in a second school extract cited and discussed in the same article. The crucial variable which affects Rosie's performance seems to be the extent to which the topic of the talk is familiar and interesting to her and to which her co-conversationalist accepts her perspective and incorporates it into the talk. In other words, Rosie performs reasonably well when the adult's conversational style is supportive but appears almost communicatively incompetent when dealing with unfamiliar topics where she has to take the adult's perspective. It could, of course, be argued that communicative ability is reflected in the ability to use language effectively in a wide range of situations, some of which may be new and unexpected. It may also be the case, however, that some children need more assistance in making the bridge between the language of the home and the more disembedded and unfamiliar language of the school curriculum, and that particular teaching strategies are required in order to facilitate the learning of these children. We will return to the implications of this point when we discuss teaching and remedial strategies in chapter 10. In the meantime we can note the importance of a careful analysis of individual differences when we consider educational problems and the inadequacy of global assessments of verbal deficiency, particularly when attempts are made to relate this to social class origin (see Wells 1977 for further discussion of this topic).

On becoming a competent member of the classroom community

We have looked at some of the problems which children encounter when they start school, particularly where the use of language at school places unfamiliar demands on children. We can now turn to a study of the ways in which children become competent participants in classrooms, as an indication of the processes which underlie this development. For this we will describe a detailed ethnographic study of a first-grade classroom, studied over the course of a year. In isolating what is involved in competent classroom participation, we will hope to pinpoint some of the areas in which some children may experience problems.

The following is based on a study by Mehan (1979), who looked at teacher–pupil interaction in a first-grade classroom. Mehan claimed that success in school involved the integration of two types of ability: academic knowledge and interactional skills. He then went on to show how children achieved this integration over the course of their first year at school.

The development of children's ability to integrate academic knowledge (content) with interactional skills (form) resulted from an experience of classroom interaction with a teacher. The appropriate behaviour is usually to bid by hand-raising and then to reply directly with a relevant response. Mehan showed that children could display either content without form or form without content and that instances of each had particular interactional significance. In the first case, content without form, a pupil would typically call out an answer without having been allocated the floor. Irrespective of whether the answer was correct or not, this behaviour was usually evaluated negatively by the teacher, with the result that the pupils soon learned the appropriate ways in which they could display their knowledge. The converse case, form without content, occurred when pupils gained the floor appropriately but were unable to answer, thus losing their opportunity to express their knowledge and consequently appearing inattentive or unexpressive.

We have seen that pupils are restricted in their right to initiate topics in classrooms. Mehan, however, shows that there are subtle ways in which children can contribute their own topics in lessons and that they improve on their ability to do so over the course of their first year at school. The first essential is to recognize the appropriate point in the flow of talk for the introduction of a new topic or for an attempt to gain the floor. As we have seen, much of classroom interaction consists of three part exchanges of the structure IRF. Looking at these in terms of speaker, the sequence is teacher–pupil–teacher. This exchange can then be followed by a similar IRF exchange, and indeed a sequence of such exchanges is common. The appropriate point for a pupil to attempt to gain the floor is thus at the completion of such an exchange, or, more subtly, at the end of a series of exchanges on a single topic. In the earlier part of the first year of Mehan's study the children often attempted to gain the floor during the course of an exchange. As the year progressed, however, they became more skilled at recognizing these breaks in the flow of discourse and so were more able to contribute their own information.

A second aspect of the initiation of topics by pupils concerns the nature of the contribution. It was found that unless the pupils contributed something new which had some bearing on the overall theme of the lesson, they received a minimal response from the teacher who then proceeded with her own lesson plan. During the year Mehan found that there was an increase in the quantity of pupil contributions and that these also increased in quality. As a result, there were fewer cases of teacher sanctions, fewer pupil contributions ignored by the teacher and more pupil topics incorporated into the lessons.

A detailed analysis such as this can tell us how pupils learn to become competent participants in classrooms by integrating their academic knowledge with the use of appropriate classroom interactional skills. We can also see how this development is guided by the teacher's reactions to the pupils' behaviours. Undesirable behaviours are evaluated negatively and so discouraged. More importantly, as far as this teacher was concerned, the pupils were shown implicitly that their contributions could be accepted and incorporated into the lesson as long as they were related to the theme of the lesson and contributed something new. Obviously there is considerable skill and flexibility required from a teacher to postpone the immediate demands of the curriculum and move off in the direction taken by the pupils. The consequence of the skilful application of this flexibility is that the pupils can learn to judge what information is relevant and interesting at a given point in time in the overall discourse and how to introduce such information with the minimum of disruption to the ongoing interaction. We can assume that the ability to make such judgements and to accomplish such interactional tasks underlies much of the smooth management of interaction between competent adult conversationalists.

Communication in small-group discussions

Whereas children have fewer rights for initiating talk in classrooms, they have a greater opportunity in small-group discussion to offer opinions, engage in exploratory talk and initiate new topics. In this section we will review a study of the talk of 13-year-olds in small-group discussions involving tasks set by their teachers (Barnes and Todd 1978). One of the most positive aspects of this study was the surprise and delight which the teachers showed when they listened to the recordings of their pupils' discussions. It seems that the children's discussions exceeded the quality of their usual classroom contributions and that they were exhibiting skills which their teachers had not expected them to have. The following is an example of such talk, accompanied by the authors' comments, taken from a discussion about the problems of providing national parks for outdoor pursuits and tourism while at the same time preserving the natural landscape and protecting farming (Barnes and Todd 1978:24–5):

(10) Alan:	do you think this is a good idea for big national parks? I think it is a, an excellent idea because, erm, people like us have the erm, countryside around us, but other people in the, erm, centre of Leeds are less fortunate and do not have erm, centre- countryside that they can go out into within easy reach	Initiates discussion by raising an issue not set on the task card. Answers his own questions and sets up a context for the ensuing discussions of the set questions
Bill:	yeah	Provides encouragement
Alan:	without being polluted and erm, chimney stacks all over the place	Makes the antithesis more explicit
Pauline:	this is all right as long as there in't gonna be too many buildings around the place, 'cos it's gonna spoil it completely I think. It's all right for a few like cafes or, er, camping sites, a few camping sites. That's all right, but nothing else	Qualifies Alan's contributions, thus turning the discussion towards the set questions. She reinforces part of what Alan said, but suggests that limits need to be drawn
Alan:	I think this is one of the best ideas of the erm, national parks because they erm do not, don't allow buildings to be built without permissions and planning special, you know, so it blends in with the countryside and not stuck out like a sore thumb	Accepts the qualification which leads to his extending the concept of the national parks to include the regulation of building
Jeanette:	yeah, but it just depends on what the ground's like, dun't it?	Qualifies that part of Alan's statement that refers to blending with the countryside

As the authors point out, the children in this and many of the other passages cited in the book are not simply reproducing previously digested knowledge but are actually shaping and rearranging their knowledge as they talk, trying out new ideas, combinations and implications. The hesitant nature of the talk is seen as a positive feature and described as *exploratory talk*, in which children can collaboratively and without the pressure of being assessed work towards an expression of their shared meanings. In the view of the authors, meanings are not predetermined but develop during the course of talk. Various speech acts are produced which occur rarely if at all in open classroom discussion. These include the following: initiating discussion of a new topic, qualifying another's contribution, providing examples, using evidence to challenge an assertion. The implications of this work for the development of projects on oracy in schools are beyond doubt.

Discourse analysis and second-language acquisition

There is a growing interest within second-language acquisition research into the ways in which adult and child second-language learners learn a language as a result of participating in conversations with native speakers of the language. Data on such conversations is sparse and any analysis has to be regarded as extremely tentative as it depends heavily on the analytic methods and categories of discourse analysis, which is, as we have seen, still a rapidly developing area of research. By its very nature this work has also been concerned with the conversational characteristics of interactions between first- and second-language learners and so can yield some comparisons with the topics discussed throughout this book. We will look briefly at the main characteristics of conversations between first- and second-language learners and then go on to examine some of the ways in which participation in such conversations might be seen as contributing to the acquisition of the formal properties of a second language.

Analyses of conversations between child second-language learners and child native speakers of the target language have suggested that the same sorts of conversational skills are developed as those which have been described in detail throughout this book (Hatch 1978a; Peck 1978). These include attention-getting, attention-directing, the playful use of language, and the use of repetition to take a conversational turn and make a relevant contribution when unable to say anything more substantial in the language. Hatch cites the following example from Wagner-Gough's data of a five-year-old Persian-speaking child, Homer, in conversation with an English-speaking peer (NS):

(11) NS: come here
Homer: no come here (=I won't come)
NS: don't do that
Homer: okay, don't do that (=I won't do that)
NS: where are you going?
Homer: where are you going is house

We can see the similarities with Keenan's (1974) twin data where repetition and substitution were used as a simple means of making a conversational contribution. In a similar vein Peck (1978) observes that such routines give the second-language learner an opportunity to produce grammatically acceptable sentences by filling in with only one or two new words, and she hypothesizes that the regular practice which child–child discourse affords in such routines may contribute to the second-language learner's acquisition of syntax.

Hatch (1978b) has also looked at the conversational devices used by adult second-language learners. She found that learners had particular difficulties in establishing discourse topics, as topics in adult–adult conversation, as opposed to those in child–child or child–adult conversation, are not usually tied to present objects or ongoing activities. Hatch also looked at the discourse strategies used by native speakers in conversations with second-language learners. She found that native speakers used a variety of repair strategies as a means of establishing discourse topics with second-language learners. They also tended to restate the learner's speech in a summary form, possibly with the function of checking and confirming understanding. Other researchers have also supported the view that native speakers rarely *correct* the speech of second-language learners. Gaskill (1980) examined the incidence of other-corrections in native speaker/non-native speaker conversation and found that other-corrections were infrequent or else modulated, as in the data for first-language speakers discussed by Schegloff et al. (1977) (see chapter 7). Corrections usually occurred in the environment of a *search format*, where a speaker who was experiencing trouble would indirectly invite correction, as in the following example:

(12) Hassan: it's dependent um . . . . (1.5) with distance
       (0.8)
     Debbie: uhhuh it depends on the distance
     Hassan: yah

We can see how the native speaker, Debbie, allows Hassan to continue beyond the first repairable item (the incorrect construction *it's dependent*), beyond the word search (indicated by vowel lengthening on *um* and the pause), right to the end of the turn where there is a gap which allows for a self-repair by Hassan before Debbie starts up. Even so, Debbie's *uhhuh* indicates that her turn is being constructed to serve the function of displaying agreement or understanding before she offers a correction. The intonation patterns in Debbie's turn are not available, but it would have been interesting to see whether she places the nucleus on the repaired items (for example *on*), as we might expect if she were a teacher correcting a pupil, rather than on the more natural placement on the syllable *dis* (see also Hughes 1983).

Second-language learners are also able to use repair devices and deal with trouble sources even in the absence of much formal language competence, as Schwartz (1980) has shown in a detailed analysis of several extended examples of conversations between second-language learners. Speakers negotiated and conferred with each other in order to achieve understanding, using word searches and soliciting assistance from their listeners as well as using other-initiated repairs. These examples show just how much communication can be achieved by elementary speakers of the language. The implications of this point will be taken up in chapter 10 when we look at some aspects of language teaching methodology which derive from a more functional and communicative perspective.

How might participation in conversation contribute to second-language learning rather than the development of conversational skills? The answer to this question depends crucially on how we view the relationship between discourse and language acquisition. This is a complex topic which will be discussed more fully in chapter 10. For the present we can review some of the suggestions that have been proposed by second-language researchers. As far as child second-language learners are concerned, similarities with the discourse patterns described by Scollon (1979) (see chapter 1) have been pointed out. These involve the use of *vertical constructions*, where two items are related sequentially in a dialogue. The two items may either be spoken by the same person or may be spoken by each participant in the dialogue. The main characteristic is that the items are not linked intonationally, but that there is some sort of semantic link. To recall some of the examples from Scollon's data:

(13) (Brenda lifts her foot and holds it over the tape recorder, pretending to step on it)
      Brenda: tape
               step

(14) Brenda: hiding
      Ron: hiding
              what's hiding?
      Brenda: balloon

Scollon proposes that Brenda is linking *tape* and *step* in (13) and *balloon* and *hiding* in (14), even though the words are produced singly, each with its own intonation contour. He suggests that this vertical construction precedes the *horizontal construction* in which the relations are expressed syntactically within the same utterance, as in:

(15) Brenda: Brenda
              see that

Here the syntactic structure verb + object has been expressed horizontally, while the subject is related vertically. Scollon would see the next stage as being the horizontal expression of the three-term structure subject–verb–object. In other words, his claim is that syntax emerges out of discourse. For second-language learners similar patterns have been observed (Hatch 1978a; Peck 1978). The following is an example cited by Hatch from Huang's data of a five-year-old Taiwanese child, Paul:

(16) Paul: this boat
     NS: mmhmm boat
     Paul: this my boat

Here Paul moves from a structure subject–complement to one in which the complement phrase structure is expanded (determiner + noun), which can be represented as in figure 24. Of course, much more detailed research is necessary if we are to further substantiate the ways in which discourse can contribute to the acquisition of structure in a second language.

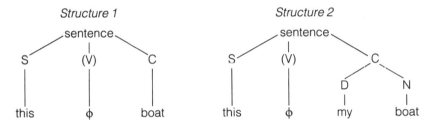

Figure 24 Structure of example (16), chapter 8

A further way in which discourse analysis is used in the explanation of second-language learning is in the investigation of the nature of input to second-language learners. Comparisons have been made between the differential contributions of child and adult partners for child second-language learners. Hatch (1978a) shows that adult partners usually use a lot of questions asking for identification and elaboration within a fairly restricted set of syntactic structures constrained by the requirements of maintaining conversational relevance and engaging in shared activities. These questions, which involve structural patterns such as *where is, what is, what is – doing*, have been related to the early acquisition by child second-language learners of the copula and auxiliary *be* as well as inflections such as *-ing*. In child–child discourse, on the other hand, the emphasis is less on the exchange of informational content and more on language play, in which repetition and sound play afford copious opportunities for practising substitutions of basic phonological and syntactic patterns (Peck 1978). Much further work is required in this area, involving the collection, transcription and analysis of second-language data. We can see from this brief review, however, how discourse analysis has contributed to our understanding of the processes of second-language learning. Some further implications, particularly in relation to language teaching, will be taken up in chapter 10.

Cultural variation

It might be objected that much of our present account of the development of conversational ability in children is representative of Western white middle-class culture. We might expect that many of the aspects of conversational ability which we have been describing would be generalizable across cultures. It is important, however, to consider some sources of cultural variation. Space does not permit a fuller account, so we will restrict ourselves to a few examples which warrant particular attention, as the variation can give rise to serious communicative misunderstandings and breakdown. In what follows, we will interpret the term *culture* widely as referring to differences on a large scale between different societies as, for example, between British and Indian speakers of English, as well as differences according to ethnic and social class background as, for example, between black and white speakers of English or between working-class and middle-class speakers.

Some of the most important culturally based differences relate to communicative norms and expectations. In Western societies there is a conversational principle that questions demand an immediate response. This principle is not universal, as Philips (1976) has shown in a study of some American Indian cultures where questions may be answered after a delay of as much as a day. It is also assumed that participants feel a need to talk and will find gaps and long stretches of silence embarrassing. This is certainly the case for many speakers from Western societies. In other communities, however, silence is valued. Basso (1972), for example, showed that Apache Indians would choose silence in situations which were perceived as unpredictable or ambiguous, such as encounters with strangers, courtship or family reunion after a long separation. In these situations, Western speakers would try to fill the silence with talk, as the silence would be perceived as embarrassing or threatening. Indeed, there are special conversational *fillers* and topics available for just such occasions. We can anticipate that cultural differences in expectations about the role of silence could give rise to misunderstandings. This is in fact the case, as we can see from reports of teachers' reactions to the silent Indian child (Philips 1972) or to the unresponsive black child in educational test situations (Labov 1969). On closer examination we can also find differences regarding norms for speaking and silence within Western society, for example between the French, who encourage their children to be silent when there are guests for dinner, and Russians, who encourage their children to speak (Coulthard 1977). Milroy (1980) also found a difference between middle-class and working-class norms in one city, Belfast.

Several aspects of non-verbal behaviour are also subject to cultural variation. Watson and Graves (1966) contrasted the proximity norms of American and Arab students, finding that Arab students would stand and sit more closely than their American counterparts and were more likely to touch each other and talk loudly. Such behaviour would probably be interpreted as either too intimate or as overbearing and hostile by Americans. In contrast, the Warm Springs Indians described by Philips (1976) used much less body motion during talk than Americans as well as less mutual gaze. Instead, they used more eye and eyebrow movement.

As far as norms for speaking are concerned, we can find differences in the degree of directness considered desirable in a community. House (1979) found that Germans tended to use more direct forms of speech acts in situations requiring a protest or a reproach than their English counterparts. This contrasts with Philips's (1976) account of the speech act forms used by the Warm Springs Indians who tended towards extreme indirectness. For example, when issuing an invitation, the Warms Spring Indians would use an implicit form such as simply passing on the information that an event was to take place. This could give rise to misunderstandings, as speakers from Western cultures would expect a more explicit invitation and would often complain that Indians never invited them to their homes. As far as the use of questions is concerned, Saville-Troike (1982) reports that, whereas questions are encouraged in English-speaking children as a means of re-questing information or permission, they are discouraged for Navajo children and more indirect forms are used. Again, we could anticipate problems in a society where the key to advancement is through the appropriate use of questions as a means of acquiring knowledge.

Much of our information about cultural differences in conversational expectations is scanty and anecdotal. Some of the most detailed work on miscommunication arising from cultural differences has been carried out by Gumperz (1982a, b; Gumperz and Tannen 1979; Gumperz et al. 1979). We will look at some of this work briefly in order to show how a detailed and careful analysis of conversational interaction can shed light on the nature and source of some cases of communicative breakdown.

Miscommunication can range from fairly trivial and easily repairable cases of misunderstanding between participants sharing the same general cultural background, such as husband and wife or professional colleagues, to cases of serious breakdown of communication between people from different ethnic groups. The basic method which Gumperz employed was to tape record examples of miscommunication and then to question the participants extensively about their respective intents and interpretations. In this way, considerable light could be shed on the way in which miscommunication was attributable to differences in communicative systems and strategies. An example of miscommunication involving different systems of intonation is seen in the following:

(17) Black child: I don't wanna read (with raised pitch on I and a drawn-out fall-rise on read)

When questioned, white informants interpreted the child's utterance as a refusal to read, while black informants, on the other hand, saw it as eliciting further encouragement to read (Gumperz and Tannen 1979:318–19). We can see how such examples might give rise to a serious misinterpretation of intent which is not easily remedied without an appreciation of the differences between the respective prosodic systems.

It is at the level of prosodic and para-linguistic cues that Gumperz feels that the most serious cases of miscommunication occur. These cues are a means of conveying interpersonal intentions and attitudes as well as regulating the flow of conversation. Although often described as surface features of conversation, they are automatic and conventional within a given cultural group and so taken for granted. A failure to recognize cultural differences in the usage of these cues can often lead to communicative breakdown and perceptions of antagonism or aggression. These points can be illustrated by citing some work Gumperz carried out on communication between British and Asian Indian speakers of English in a variety of crucial situations such as job interviews and teacher–parent consultations (Gumperz et al. 1979). The Asian speakers usually had a good command of English and had reached a high level of professional attainment in their own country before emigrating to Britain. Yet these speakers frequently experienced difficulties when communicating with British officials. Often the Asians were unaware of the extent to which they were being misunderstood and they would make inaccurate interpretations of what British people had said to them. The British speakers, on the other hand, often perceived the Asians as rude, surly, unemotional, irrelevant and discursive.

Two types of conversational skill have a bearing on the types of miscommunication analysed by Gumperz:

1 Differences in ways of structuring information
2 Differences in ways of speaking.

As far as the structuring of information is concerned, English uses prosody to break the flow of speech into tone groups, marks new information within the tone group by means of nucleus placement, and conveys a variety of attitudinal and discourse information by means of the pitch direction of the nuclear tone. A rising tone, for example, can convey (among other things) that the message is incomplete and that the speaker has more to say (Crystal 1975). In Indian languages, on the other hand, the flow of information is conveyed by means of grammatical devices and prosodic cues are also used differently. Pitch level, for example, is used to signal emphasis.

Let us consider now the implications of these differences for a conversation between a British and an Asian Indian speaker of English, both of whom are unaware of these surface features of each other's speech. An inappropriate use of prosody by the Indian speaker will result in his speech being perceived either as flat and unemotional or else as unduly excited. The use of inappropriate tones can also cause confusion. Consider the following example:

(18) A (British speaker): this is not the case
     B (Asian Indian):   no (with low falling tone)

As far as speakers of British English are concerned, the use of low falling tone on *no* would convey agreement and, if the Asian speaker's subsequent talk contradicted this interpretation, confusion and perhaps annoyance would ensue. In order to convey disagreement the Asian speaker would have to have used high falling tone.

Problems also occur with a failure to structure the information according to the conventions of English. Indian speakers often begin a response with background information in order to avoid too direct a response. In addition, the background information is given increased stress while for the newer information the Indian speaker shifts to a lower pitch and amplitude. The result of this difference in ways of structuring information is that British speakers of English often perceive Indian speakers as being irrelevant, and they cease to attend, or interrupt, at precisely the point where the Indian speaker is beginning to reach his new information. This is perceived in turn by the Indian speaker as rudeness and an unwillingness to consider his point of view.

Differences in ways of speaking also involve prosodic cues, in this case as a means of conveying the speaker's attitudes. We can illustrate a cross-cultural problem with the following example:

(19) (Indian speaker at a bank counter)
    Indian speaker: I want to deposit some MONEY (nucleus on money,
                        rise-fall tone; loud)

A British speaker, on the other hand, would place the nucleus on *deposit*, as this is the item of new information in this utterance, while the voice would be lowered on *money* because this information would be obvious from the situation. The use of an inappropriate tone as well as its inappropriate placement would result in the Indian speaker being perceived as stating the obvious in an aggressive or pushy manner. Thus the wrong attitude would be conveyed by the usage of a set of apparently trivial speech cues. The effect of such breakdowns in communication can be cumulative and can reinforce feelings of mistrust and hostility between members of different cultural groups. Obviously a detailed and careful analysis of such problems is necessary before steps can be taken to alleviate such problems.

In this chapter we have looked at the development of conversational ability into the school years and beyond. We have touched on some problems that arise in encounters between members of different ethnic, cultural or social class groups. While our account is necessarily brief, it suggests some problems which face the child on the road to the conversational ability of a mature adult member of society. Others are less fortunate and make less progress along this road. We move on now to consider the difficulties of those whose conversational ability is disordered and for whom normal conversational interaction is problematic.

9

Disorders of conversation

So far we have been concerned with the development of conversational ability in children. However, as we mentioned in chapter 1, the term *ability* can also imply its converse – *disability*. We turn now to the question of conversational disability. Are there children (or adults) who exhibit disorders in the areas which we have been describing? Are these disorders general or is conversational disability characterized by problems in specific areas of conversation, such as initiating new topics? Is it possible to classify conversational disorders using the types of linguistic profile which are now appearing for the analysis of syntactic, prosodic, phonological and semantic disorders (Crystal 1982)? These are some of the questions which will be considered in this chapter. We will begin with a general review of the literature on pragmatic and conversational disorders, and follow with a case study of a child whose deficiencies appear to be predominantly in the domain of conversation. Much of the chapter will be exploratory owing to the current state of the field in which the analysis of conversation is an emerging area. It is hoped, however, that it will be possible to clarify some of the more relevant issues and to develop an approach which can direct further research in this area.

Disorders of conversation: a review of the literature

It will be obvious from even a cursory glance at the contents of language pathology journals that researchers are increasingly reporting findings of investigations into disorders which lie outside the traditional areas of speech and language. These articles often include in their titles terms such as *communicative function, discourse devices, pragmatic deficits* and *requesting strategies.* Two main problems characterize research in this rapidly developing field. The first concerns a proliferation of technical terms which are often poorly defined and which vary from one investigator to another. The second concerns the premises on which most of this research is based –

that is, that research usually involves a comparative analysis of the conversational abilities of normal-speaking and language-disordered children. As we shall see, this approach assumes that conversational ability is derivative of language disorders and excludes the theoretical possibility of conversational disorders which are independent of and unrelated to language disorders. Let us look more closely at each of these problems.

The problem of technical terminology pervades any scientific enquiry. It is particularly acute, however, in the area of conversation because conversation, as we saw in chapter 1, is a relatively new area of enquiry. Moreover, research in conversation is carried out from a variety of different perspectives which reflect the contrasting (and often confusing) theoretical concerns of the contributing disciplines. Thus conversation is studied by linguists, sociologists, psychologists, anthropologists, educationalists and others, who usually fail to take account of each other's work. As far as investigations of conversational disorders are concerned, there is often confusion as to the relationship between pragmatics and other levels of language, while the nature of conversation is frequently misunderstood. One of the main purposes of the present book is to clarify some of these issues.

As a representative example of problems of terminology in the current literature, let us look briefly at the ways in which the term *request* is used. This term features regularly in the titles of articles. However, when we investigate more closely, we often find confusing definitions. Sometimes the term is used to refer to requests for action *(directives)*. Often it also includes requests for information and sometimes it can be interpreted even more widely to include requests for repetition and clarification. As we have seen in the preceding chapters, these various types of requests have different functions and distributional properties and need to be kept separate in analysis.

The following definition of *commands* is typical of the terminological confusion which pervades the literature (Bedrosian and Prutting 1978:84):

> *Commands:* commands were defined as statements in the imperative
> mood expressed by the infinite form of the verb as a
> request for action.

Here we find confusion of different levels of analysis. We have the functional category *command* and the grammatical category *imperative mood*. The definition implies a direct relationship between the two, so that all commands are realized by imperatives and all imperatives realize commands. As we saw in chapters 2 and 5, this is clearly not the case. A confusion of terminology of this nature must lead the reader to suspect the system of classification on which such research is based and to question any conclusions reached in the research. Other problems arise in the definition. For example, the term *request for action* is used in conjunction with the term *command*. Are we to take it that these terms are being used synonymously in this context. In this case this is probably the most reasonable assumption. It should, however, be noted that other authors do not treat these two terms as synonyms. For example, commands are often treated as a particular subcategory of requests for action. Finally, we have the use of the term *statement*. Statements are often taken to be a separate functional category from requests for action. This would not seem to be the case here. Rather, it seems that the term is being used loosely in the sense of *utterance*. Similar examples could be presented from the literature. However, we have seen sufficient to convince ourselves of the necessity of caution in current research on conversational disability and of the need to examine definitions, classification systems and, above all, conclusions reached on the basis of these, with the utmost care.

Let us look now at the second problem, which concerns the assumptions underlying the design of research into conversational disability. Theoretically, there are several possible research designs. The one which is most frequently used involves comparisons between an experimental group of language-disordered subjects and a control group of normal-speaking subjects. Language disorder is usually taken to mean a delay of at least one year, involving expressive or receptive language abilities (or both), although frequently the precise nature of the language disorder is not made explicit. For example, it is rarely that we find more specific reference to phonological, syntactic or other disorders. The research then proceeds to compare the groups on a set of conversational features such as the frequency and distribution of speech acts. A typical example of such a design is a study by Rom and Bliss (1981) which compared the speech act usage of three groups of subjects: 20 language-impaired children with a mean MLU of 2.91 and a mean age of 4.29, 20 younger normal-speaking children with MLU of 3.09 and age 2.79, and a third group of 20 older normal-speaking children with MLU of 5.48 and age 4.28. Thus the language-impaired group was matched with the younger group for MLU and with the older group for age. This permitted an investigation of the hypothesis that the language-impaired group would be similar to the younger group in the frequency and distribution of speech act usage, thus exhibiting delay in this area. Generally speaking, this hypothesis was confirmed. One difference which did emerge, however, was that the language-impaired group used the speech act *answering* more frequently than either group. The authors suggest that this was because more questions were asked of the language-impaired group as they were more likely to be misunderstood. We can see that this implies that a sequential analysis of the data would be more revealing in this respect than a simple classification of individual speech acts in isolation. A further problem concerns the degree of contextual variation in the usage of particular speech acts. This issue was addressed in an investigation by Bedrosian and Prutting (1978) which considered the communicative performance of mentally retarded adults in four conversational settings: with a clinician, with peers, parents/guardian, and a young child. The results showed a wide range of variation in interactional behaviour across these settings, which indicates a weakness in those studies which fail to take contextual variation into account (see chapter 10 for further discussion).

We can see from this brief account that this type of study is useful as it provides a comparison between groups of subjects identified as language impaired and normal speaking. The importance of controlled studies of this nature cannot be overemphasized. The point which I wish to make, however, is that a restriction of research to this design prejudges the issues and potentially excludes the investigation of a wider range of conversational disorders. This research is based on the hypothesis that language disorders predict conversational problems. Indeed, this hypothesis is often made quite explicit (Musselwhite et al. 1980). The implication is that subjects with language disorders will also exhibit disorders in conversational ability. This gives rise to two problems. Firstly, there is a need to specify more clearly the relationship between the types of disorder. For example, are the language disorders the cause of the conversational disorders (or vice versa) or are they simply related? Given that they are related in some way, what is the precise nature of this relationship? These issues could be investigated in more thorough research which proceeds on the basis of the hypothesis of this relationship between the types of disorder. Indeed, the results of some studies would suggest that linguistic and pragmatic impairment are not necessarily related. In some cases, for example in the use of initiations and responses in mother–child interaction, language-impaired children have performed less well than normal-speaking children at the same language stage (Conti 1982; Conti and Friel-Patti 1983, 1984). Such children have also been found to be less likely to request clarification of inadequate messages, despite being able to produce the language forms necessary for such requests (Donahue et al. 1980). Conversely, it has been reported in several studies of referential communication tasks that language-impaired children's performance is superior to their peers matched for MLU. This finding has been explained in terms of the greater social and cognitive skills of language-impaired children in comparison with young children who have similar language skills, suggesting an independence of language form from language use (Fey and Leonard 1983).

The second problem is, however, more serious, as a restriction to this type of research design precludes the investigation of other possibilities – for example, of subjects whose language development is normal but who exhibit deficiencies in the use of language (as, for example, in the study by Blank et al. 1979, described in chapter 1). For this reason, a second type of research design is recommended which attempts to present a profile of conversational disability irrespective of whether the subject exhibits language disorders or not. Let us look at a typical example of such a study.

Greenlee (1981) presents a case study of the discourse features of an eight-year-old boy diagnosed with an organic brain disorder (tuberous sclerosis) and childhood psychosis. Frequent communicative failures in interaction with this child indicated deviant patterns in his use of language, although in other respects his language was similar in its stage of development to children of comparable mental age. The following were some of the features which Greenlee identified as unusual:

1 The use of *what's that – an* X sequences (e.g. *what's that – a chair*), in which the child both asked and answered the question. Although such sequences occur with very young children (Atkinson 1979; Ochs et al. 1979), they are most unusual in children of this age and at this stage of language development.
2 Combinations of portions of his conversational partners' utterances in his own utterances.
3 Self-directed statements in the middle of a conversation.
4 Problems in pronoun reference.
5 Difficulties in establishing discourse topics.
6 An inability to deal successfully with communicative breakdowns.

As Greenlee points out, this child presents a cluster of features which occur rarely or only at very early stages in normally developing children. It is this combination of unusual features which accounts for the child's deviant patterns of language use.

Such a study has the advantage that it attempts to present a complete profile of the subject's conversational abilities, while at the same time making comparisons with normal development, where possible. This is a valuable approach as it enables us to identify and assess the conversational abilities of a subject independently of other issues. One practical problem is that such cases will be rarely encountered by clinicians who restrict their attention to patients diagnosed as having speech and language disorders. Alternatively, the clinician might have no strategy for dealing with such cases as they fall outside the traditional patterns of speech and language disorders and so tend to be referred elsewhere. It is important to emphasize that language is involved, although at the level of the use of language rather than at the level of structure.

The final approach which we will consider is to proceed from a clinical diagnosis and then investigate the range of linguistic and conversational disabilities which this group of patients presents. Autistic children are characterized more by deficiencies in their use of language for communicative purposes than by their knowledge of language structure, although there are often delays in areas such as syntax, due partly to cognitive retardation. Generally, however, the most striking disability is in the use of language (Fay W. and Schuler 1980; Fay D. and Mermelstein 1982). We will refer to the communicative problems of autistic children in more detail later. For the present we can note that the following are common characteristics: an inability to adapt topics to the listener and setting, to accommodate to the reciprocal nature of conversation and to continue conversation, and a tendency to ask inappropriate questions (Hurtig et al. 1982).

The value of this approach is that it facilitates explanation of the disorder in terms of a clinically diagnosed syndrome. The main problem is that it prevents the comparison of similar disorders across a range of clinically distinct aetiologies. In the present state of our knowledge it is perhaps more helpful to attempt a linguistic definition of the disorders which can later be correlated with external factors. This approach is similar to that adopted in the LARSP profiles of grammatical disability (Crystal et al. 1976; Crystal and Fletcher 1979). Accordingly, we will now look at disorders of conversation described in the literature on the basis of the descriptive categories developed in the preceding chapters of this book.

Initiations

Initiations are utterances which predict or expect a response. Initiating utterances ensure that the conversation will continue for at least one more turn. As such, they are an important mechanism for the maintenance of conversation. There are two crucial aspects of initiating utterances: attention-getting and attention-drawing. Attention-getting is a reliable indication of communicative intent, while attention-drawing relies on various aspects of communicative ability such as the cognitive ability to assess the listener's state of knowledge accurately and design the utterance accordingly, as well as linguistic devices appropriate to the realization of speaker's intentions. Let us look at these aspects of initiations as reported in the literature on conversational disorders.

Generally attention-getting does not feature in the literature. We might assume that attention-getting devices are fairly basic and are acquired very early by children. This is certainly true for normally developing children, as we saw in chapter 4. Furthermore, we can assume that children have some intention to communicate, even before they have developed language. For this reason, we might not expect attention-getting to be a particular problem. Indeed, in the one case where attention-getting is explicitly mentioned (Greenlee 1981), it is pointed out that, in contrast to other discourse features, the child displayed the ability to get the listener's attention by the use of strategies such as summons–answer routines. One further possibility, of course, is that researchers have overlooked this aspect of conversation. It would be useful therefore if profiles of conversational disability were to include attention-getting as a potential area of difficulty, differentiating clearly between the various verbal and non-verbal devices which were described in chapter 4. One major exception to the pattern described here is to be found in the literature on autistic children, where it is often reported that these children fail to use devices such as establishing eye contact, vocatives and attention-getting words such as *hey* (Fay and Schuler 1980). This would be consistent with the view that autistic children lack communicative intent, although there is still a need for more detailed analyses in this area.

Most of the literature on disorders relating to attention-drawing also comes from studies of autistic children. Some typical problems are as follows:

1 A failure to introduce new topics with devices such as *by the way, remember* (Fay and Schuler 1980)
2 An inability to distinguish old and new information with a resultant usage of odd intonation patterns and a misuse of anaphoric pronouns, definite articles and relative pronouns (Baltaxe 1977)
3 A tendency to over-specify discourse referents with the result that speech is often redundant – that is, the child tells the listener more than he needs or wants to know (Fay and Schuler 1980).

Greenlee (1981) also notes that her subject had problems in establishing discourse referents. Where these disorders are to be distinguished from cases of developmental delay can be seen from the fact that language structure had already developed in these children. For example, they were able to use and understand definite articles, anaphoric pronouns and relative pronouns, but they were using them inappropriately in conversational contexts. This contrasts with the situation of very young children whose problems in establishing discourse topics are partly due to their underdeveloped syntactic systems (see chapter 4).

Looking at initiations in general, it has been reported that autistic subjects tend to initiate less frequently than other disordered subjects such as dysphasics. This is again consistent with the view that autistics lack communicative intent. However, frequency is not always the only problem. There are also cases of the inappropriate use of initiations. Baltaxe (1977) reports a tendency in adolescent autistics to ask the same question over and over again, despite receiving an answer. In a study by Hurtig et al. (1982) it was found that the autistic subjects' use of questions was excessive in frequency and that they tended to use questions inappropriately. Questions appeared to be used as a means of initiating conversation but not as a means of requesting information. In this case the subjects seemed to realize that questions obligate a response and so are a useful device for initiating conversation, but were unable to select appropriate topical material. This suggests that, in this case at least, the autistic children had some communicative intent but lacked the ability to participate appropriately in conversation. They also recognized the discourse expectations of their partners' responses and were more likely to respond to utterances which were more elaborated than a minimal response or to those responses which contained a question. These categories are similar to the categories R/(I) and R/I which we described in chapter 6. The overall picture is confusing and indicates the need for more detailed analyses using a comprehensive framework of analysis. In this way it would be possible to make more subtle distinctions between the various types of conversational ability involved and to take into account stages of development and degrees of disorder.

The same remarks apply to the few observations which have been made about reinitiations. Fay and Schuler (1980) note that, in general, autistic children are rarely able to rephrase requests to take into account their listener's needs. They do, however, report an ability to rephrase initiations at a more elementary level, by adding, for example, *I* or *please* to requests of the form *want* X and by using devices such as increasing volume, raising pitch, whining or throwing a tantrum if the rephrasing strategy failed. The picture with language-disordered children is unclear. Hoar (1977) reports that language-impaired children are less likely to rephrase reinitiations and that syntactic rearrangements were only to be found in older language-impaired children. This implies, as we might expect, a relationship between ability to rephrase and level of syntactic development. A similar pattern was found in a study by van Kleeck and Frankel (1981), although here it was found that even the lowest-level children observed (MLU 1.8) were able to perform substitution operations effectively in their reinitiations. More detailed studies are required which will take into account the levels of complexity involved in different types of reinitiation and the ways in which these are related to their realizations in syntax.

Requests for action

As we saw from chapter 5, the ability to comprehend and produce requests for action involves a range of complex skills, such as the ability to infer the speaker's intent in the case of indirect requests, or to take the listener's status and wishes into account in formulating a request with the appropriate degree of politeness. We will look at two studies which have investigated these issues with language-disordered children.

Prinz (1982) looked at the comprehension and production of requests by normal and language-disordered children. The sample consisted of 15 normal-speaking children (aged three to five years) and 15 language-disordered children (aged five to seven years). The investigation involved both naturalistic observation and an experimental session which included passive judgements of politeness and a comprehension task. As far as the naturalistic observation was concerned, no differences were found between the groups as to the number of direct and indirect requests used. Both groups produced more indirect than direct requests. The normal-speaking children were, however, more successful in the task which involved judgements of politeness. The ability seemed to develop in the normal-speaking children between three and four years and in the language-disordered children between five and six years – a clear pattern of delay. There were few differences on the comprehension task. A more detailed analysis of the request forms produced by the children in the naturalistic setting revealed that the request forms of the disordered children were less syntactically and phonologically complete. They used fewer linguistic devices for expressing politeness, although simpler modifications such as *please* were employed. The general conclusion to be drawn from this study is that some language-disordered children exhibit a pragmatic deficit in the production, comprehension and modification of requests. What is not clear, however, is whether their deficiency is related specifically to their delayed development in the areas of syntax and phonology or whether it derives from deficiencies at the level of social-cognitive development which would result in an inability to perceive differences in listener attributes and to formulate and modify their requests accordingly.

These issues were investigated in a study of Donahue (1981) which looked at the requesting strategies of learning-disabled children. The subjects were grade 2, 3 and 4 children who had been diagnosed as having difficulty in both language and social development. It was hypothesized that these children would lack the social knowledge necessary to perceive social distinctions between listeners when making requests and to appreciate the implications of these distinctions. On the linguistic level it was hypothesized that they lacked an adequate linguistic repertoire of request forms. The investigation was designed to enable a separate consideration of these variables. The forms and level of politeness of requests were analysed as well as their level of persuasiveness – based on additional utterances used to support or justify the request. It was found that the children had an adequate linguistic repertoire of requests and were not deficient in the use of politeness strategies. The main deficiencies were at the level of social understanding. The children seemed unable to appreciate the implications of listener attributes for socially appropriate speech. Low-power listeners often elicited more polite requests than high-power listeners, appeals were generally unsophisticated and not specifically tailored to their listener's characteristics. Thus in this study the children's disability was not related to their level of linguistic development but to their degree of social understanding. The implications are that the area of conversation which concerns the use of speech acts such as requests is an extremely complex one which involves linguistic and social knowledge, and that research into conversational disability which investigates only those children previously diagnosed as language disordered or delayed runs the risk of ignoring the pragmatic deficiencies of those children whose language is otherwise intact.

We can further illustrate this point by noting the problems presented by high-functioning adolescent and adult autistics (i.e. whose language and communication are normal or near normal) in respect of politeness and appropriacy. Autistics tend to speak too loudly in public places (Ricks and Wing 1975) and are unable to differentiate polite and casual forms of address (Baltaxe and Simmons 1977). These problems are illustrated vividly in the following extract in which a high-functioning adult autistic describes his difficulties with the appropriate use of language (Dewey and Everard 1975):

> I do not know what subjects to talk about with different people. I have commented that certain girls are sexy, because I have heard guys say this about girls. Once I told a bank teller to her face that she was sexy, and that was probably not the right thing to say. But I heard guys talking dirty to each other and I told them this was not right, and they got angry with me. I have learned that it is normal for guys to talk this way with each other, but I still do not think it is normal to do it around girls. Yet, sometimes I do hear guys say fresh things to girls and the girls don't get mad at them. But they do with me.

Clearly there is nothing wrong with this subject's language as such. The problems lie in his inability to select appropriate topics in relation to social (and possibly personal) attributes of his listeners as well as the setting in which the conversation takes place. Any attempt to specify clear guidelines for behaviour in this situation will reveal the complexity of the issues involved. At the same time, the contrast between the difficulties experienced by this patient and the apparent ease with which others handle such situations indicates that such problems are real and inhibitive of smooth conversational interaction. While the problems are not strictly linguistic, an element of language usage is involved. Probably the most useful approach to the analysis of such issues would draw on the work of linguists in conjunction with analysts of socially skilled interaction.

The construction of dialogue

Following a successful initiation of a topic, the continuation of a dialogue depends on the ability of the speakers to respond appropriately to each other's turn and to elicit or provide for the possibility of further talk. The nature of a response depends on a variety of contextual factors such as the aims of the speaker, the speech situation and the nature of the topic. Generally, however, we can assume that a minimal response, while satisfying the requirements of its preceding eliciting utterance, does not carry the conversation any further, in contrast to an utterance which responds and simultaneously predicts a further response.

Failure to respond to preceding initiations or the use of inappropriate or unrelated responses is commonly reported in the literature. Greenlee (1981) noted that 40 per cent of questions to her subject, an eight-year-old psychotic boy, received no response, while 25 per cent received inappropriate or unrelated responses. The following is a typical sequence:

(1)   1 Adult: did you go camping in the woods?
    2 Child: camping in the woods? (shouts)
    3 Adult: yeah, did you ever do that?
    4 Child: yeah, he ever do that

.
.
.

    5 Adult: when are you going home?
    6 Child: um- he IS going home

The child's utterance 2 can possibly be analysed as a request for confirmation, although we might note the inappropriate over-loudness which often characterizes the speech of autistic and psychotic children and which might, given further evidence, suggest a level of inappropriacy and non-contingency in the response. Utterances 4 and 6 are complicated by the child's problems in pronoun reference. Here *he* is being used for first person reference *(I)*, but inconsistencies in the child's usage elsewhere created difficulties of interpretation for his conversational partners; for example, *he* was sometimes used appropriately for third-person reference. Without further background knowledge we cannot ascertain whether utterance 4 was appropriate in terms of the accuracy of its content. Utterance 6 is clearly deviant as it fails to respond appropriately to the *when* question with a statement of time and instead asserts what was already presupposed in the question – that is, that he was going home.

Inappropriate responses were also noted in a study which compared the request–response sequences of normal and language-disordered children (Brinton and Fujiki 1982). The disordered children (aged 5;6 to 6;0), produced significantly more unrelated responses than their normal-speaking peers. As far as yes/no questions were concerned, the responses were usually structurally intact but the content was contrary to fact, which suggests that the children recognized that a response was required but were unable to provide the specific information requested. In other words, they were able to operate at the lower levels of conversational interaction in that they took turns appropriately and recognized the discourse expectations of the partner's utterances. Their difficulties were at a higher level which involved the processing and organization of information.

An even lower level of response characterizes the speech of autistic children. This is where the child repeats the other's preceding utterance rather than makes a response. There are many degrees of this phenomenon, known as *echolalia*, which involve both structural and functional definitions (Baker et al. 1976). For our present purposes, we can look at immediate and mitigated echolalia. In immediate echolalia, the child either reproduces the preceding utterance 'exactly' or reduces it in some way. In mitigated echolalia the child alters the utterance he is repeating in some way, usually by adding some new material. We can note the vagueness of these definitions, a problem which pervades much of the literature on echolalia. Let us move on, however, to consider some structural and functional properties of echolalic utterances in the context of our review of disorders in the construction of dialogue.

It is often claimed that echolalic utterances have the discourse function of affirmation by repetition. That is, the child acknowledges and affirms the preceding utterance by repeating it. In this case we can see similarities with the early devices used by normal-speaking children to acknowledge and affirm (Keenan 1975) (see chapter 6). It has, however, also been suggested that echolalia rarely occurs in conjunction with message comprehension or that, at least, some stimuli appear to be appropriately processed while others are not (Fay 1969). Here we can see the need for a rigorous sequential analysis of the exchanges in which echolalic utterances occur. The association of echolalia with comprehension problems was supported by a study in which the incidence of echolalia could be related to the type of preceding utterance. Specifically, yes/no questions were more likely to be followed by echoes than WH-questions, and these in turn were more likely to produce echoes than utterances which only required completion of an item (e.g. *this is a*) (Paccia and Curcio 1982). These findings were explained on the basis of decreasing processing requirements. In any case, it is possible to argue that even exact echoes have a potential discourse function as a device for maintaining social interaction. Some evidence for this function can be found in cases where the child seems to expect some acknowledgement of his echolalic utterance and becomes upset if this is not forthcoming (Prizant and Duchan 1981).

The discussion so far suggests that a more detailed analysis of structural aspects of echoes is necessary if we are to arrive at interpretations as to their discourse function and if we are to differentiate lower from higher levels of functioning. Paccia and Curcio (1982) noted that about half of the echoes produced by their subjects involved the use of contrastive intonation contours, which suggests a more advanced responding strategy. They also found that echoes which were restructured semantically or syntactically (mitigated echolalia) were often accompanied by prosodic modification. This also raises, of course, the whole problem of the classification of echoes as 'exact'. In a similar vein, Prizant and Duchan (1981) demonstrated that echoes can have a variety of functions ranging from the lowest level of turn-taking through labelling and affirmation by repetition to requesting (as, for example, in the exchange *what do you want? – what do you want a sweetie?*). The implications of this work are that it is important to look at the patterns of usage of echoes by individual children and to examine the structural and functional characteristics of echoes carefully in order to ascertain their developmental status.

We noted earlier some similarities between the use of echolalic utterances by autistic children and the discourse devices used by normal-speaking children. We can recall from chapter 6 that Keenan (1975) reported a development from the use of full or partial repetitions in responses to the use of substitution processes. This development was related to the child's increasing competency in syntax and semantics, for example in the use of anaphoric pronouns and definite articles. A similar pattern of development was found in a study of three children with delay in receptive and expressive language skills (van Kleeck and Frankel 1981). The children were all able to produce substitutions, but the two lower-level children (in terms of MLU) produced more repetitions than substitutions, a trend which was reversed for the more advanced child. This study lends some support to the hypothesis that language delay predicts delays in conversational development and that the order of development is similar for normal-speaking and language-delayed children.

Moving on now to the devices used to construct continuous sequences of dialogue, we find that this area is relatively unexplored. Fey and Leonard (1983) review a number of studies which suggest that children with specific language impairment exhibit deficiencies in conversational participation. These children are generally unresponsive to their mothers, thus discouraging their mother's attempts at initiating interaction (see, for example, Wulbert et al. 1975). They often make excessive use of back-channel behaviours, indicating a willingness to participate in conversation but, at the same time, using a device which avoids the need to initiate topics or expand responses. What is not clear from these studies, however, is whether this lack of conversational assertiveness is peculiar to particular contexts, whether it characterizes all or only some language-impaired children, and whether, and to what extent, it is related to comprehension deficits. More fine-grained studies are needed in order to further investigate these issues.

As far as autistic children are concerned, it has been observed that they experience difficulties in speaking on topic, tend to talk *ad nausem* about things of interest only to themselves, and produce pseudo-dialogues in which they leave no room for their conversational partners to ask questions and make responses (Ricks and Wing 1975). There is also the observation which we noted earlier that autistic children show some awareness of the discourse expectations of their partner's conversational contributions and are more likely to continue following utterances which function as R/I and R/(I) rather than those which are minimal responses, R (Hurtig et al. 1982). Clearly, however, there is a need for much more extensive research in this area, taking into account structural, functional and sequential properties of utterances.

Repairs

Little has been written about conversational repairs in language-disordered children. General observations suggest a lack of awareness of the need to repair conversational breakdowns as well as an inability to use repair devices successfully. Brinton and Fujiki (1982) found that their language-impaired subjects produced fewer requests for clarification than their normal-speaking peers, while the child studied by Greenlee (1981) responded appropriately to only two out of a total of 27 requests for clarification. Gallaher and Darnton (1978) analysed the responses to requests for clarification of 12 children whose language was delayed by at least one year below their chronological age. The results were compared with an earlier study of normal-speaking children (Gallaher 1977), in which it was found that the older subjects in the sample used more complex responses involving the elaboration, reduction or substitution of grammatical constituents. While the language-delayed children displayed a sensitivity to the conversational demands of breakdowns by revising their utterances, they used less sophisticated devices and the differences between the age groups were not significant. Moreover, the responses of these children were less elaborate than would be predicted by their acquired level of grammatical ability. This suggests not only that the language-impaired children were delayed in relation to the normal-speaking sample, but also that their conversational abilities were qualitively different, in that they were less sophisticated and failed to utilize the grammatical knowledge which the children had at their disposal. In other words, conversational ability is distinct from and not predicted by linguistic ability. We will return to a discussion of the implications of this presently.

We took care to emphasize the different types of clarification request in chapter 7. The need to make these distinctions and to take account of contextual features such as variation in conversational partner has been demonstrated in a study of the responses of three boys with severe speech disorders to requests for clarification (McCartney 1981). The children were video recorded in conversations with three partners: their mother, another child, and a previously unacquainted adult. More requests for clarification were addressed to the least intelligible child, as we might expect. Mothers used more requests for confirmation, which depend on an ability to understand the repairable utterance, while the other conversational partners used more requests for repetition. One important conclusion from this study which has implications for remediation procedures was that different types of clarification request made different demands on the children's linguistic knowledge. Requests for specification required them to review their utterances for deficiencies at a communicative level, while requests for confirmation provided them with a model at the linguistic level and sometimes occasioned responses with phonetic modifications. For example:

(2) Mother: what's he called?
    Child: sheriff ['tɛwɪ]
    Mother: sheriff?
    Child: yea, the sheriff ['ʃɛwɪ]

Thus children's use of and response to clarification requests can provide us with important information concerning both their conversational and their linguistic ability, while the use of clarification requests in natural and experimentally controlled conditions can occasion modifications from the child which might promote development towards the adult linguistic system.

As yet there appears to have been no investigations of other types of repair in the literature on language and conversational disorders. We can, however, suggest the potential usefulness of research in this area. Other-corrections would be an important index of children's ability to perceive errors in the speech of others and to propose alternatives. Self-repairs would show the extent to which children are aware of their own errors as well as their ability to monitor their own speech and modify it appropriately. The analysis of turn-taking would establish more reliable norms for response latencies by measuring the length of gap between turns as well as investigating the extent to which children can process ongoing speech and predict potential points of turn completion. We presented a detailed account of the development of these conversational processes in chapter 7. More empirical investigations are now required into the development of these processes in the speech of children with disorders of language and conversation.

Conversational incompetence: a case study

The following case study is of a boy whose language problems appear to be primarily in the area of discourse. The study is presented in some detail in order to show how an analysis of the child's conversations, along the lines described in this book, might shed some light on the nature of his disorder and lead to some suggestions for a course of treatment. The child is a ten-year-old boy who is in full daytime attendance at a language unit and who has received speech therapy for several years. His phonology and syntax are reasonable enough not to warrant special treatment. As far as semantics is concerned, he shows signs of occasional problems with spatial and temporal expressions as well as deictic verbs. His suprasegmental phonology is abnormal: he uses an unvarying intonational pattern, usually with a rise in pitch and intensity on the final syllable of his utterance. He also lacks existential voice quality, so that, taken together, the suprasegmental features of his production make his speech sound 'flat and unemotional'. His major problems, however, are in the area of conversational interaction, where his use of language has been described by educational psychologists, speech therapists and teachers as 'bizarre and confused', 'stilted and formal'.

The data for the present study is as follows:

1   Four samples of natural conversation in an informal interview situation, either with his speech therapist or with the author. The sessions were video recorded.
2   A series of referential communication tasks in which the child was required to describe pictures containing symbols such as squares and numbers to a listener who had to draw identical pictures on the basis of the descriptions. In a second task the child had to describe a series of sequentially related pictures so that the listener could identify each of the pictures from an identical set arranged in random order.
3   A series of description tasks which included recognizing and describing an anomalous picture (for example, a bicycle with square wheels); telling a story based on a series of pictures (for example, a child getting up, dressing, having breakfast, going to school, and so on); and discussing a picture which depicted a problem situation and outlining potential solutions (for example, a child locked out of the house and unable to find his key).

The data was transcribed and subjected to a preliminary analysis using the checklist for conversational development which was presented in chapter 2. The results can be summarized as follows:

Turn-taking This was not a problem; the child took turns allocated to him, did not interrupt, and generally responded without undue gaps. Most of the time the gaps between the end of his interlocutor's turn and the beginning of his own turn were less than 1 second and many responses were latched directly on to the preceding turn.
Responses Responses were nearly always appropriate, apart from some

difficulties with *how* questions. Most responses were to questions rather than other speech acts. Responses were usually minimal; in other words, the child did not continue with additional content which might have helped sustain the dialogue. This could, of course, be attributed partly to the asymmetrical relationships in the dialogues discussed here, although the child's speech therapist and teachers remarked that he was particularly unforthcoming in this respect in comparison with other children and that he engaged very little in any interaction with his peers.

Initiations The conversations afforded the child little opportunity to initiate exchanges, as the control was mainly in the hands of the adult participant. Nevertheless, he was able to ask questions appropriately and to use verbal and non-verbal devices to direct attention to the referents of his talk, apart from the occasional 'egocentric' reference to persons unknown to his interlocutor. *Then* was the predominant connector used when narrating. The main deficiency, to which we will return in greater detail, was his failure to use ellipsis and to use appropriate misplacement prefaces when changing the topic or re-establishing an old topic.

Requests for action The ability to use appropriate request forms and politeness markers was not tested in the interviews and did not emerge in the natural course of the interaction.

Repairs The child was able to respond to simple requests for repetition, confirmation and specification, but did not produce any such requests. Again, this could be merely a sampling problem. No other-corrections were produced and self-repairs were normal disfluencies and hesitations characteristic of spontaneous speech.

The general impression from this brief summary is that the child can cope reasonably well at the interactional level, apart from a tendency to re-dundancy in his failure to use ellipsis and a general failure to produce continuing utterances (R/Is). A closer analysis of the content of his utterances, however, revealed deficiencies which quickly become apparent to anyone who engages in a prolonged conversation with the child. Often he contradicts what he has previously said, with the result that details of his personal life and experiences often appear totally confused, giving the impression of a series of blurred images. He showed deficits in his understanding of every-day behaviour in terms of what might be expected from a child of his age. At the same time, he paid great attention to details of times and dates beyond the vague references that typify casual conversation. As we will see, his problems seem to be mainly in his inability to organize his knowledge and experiences, and to present these appropriately to a conversational partner. His abnormal discourse is symptomatic of this deficiency and it is only by means of a detailed analysis of his discourse that a greater appreciation of his disorder is possible. This will be illustrated by examining first the interactional aspects of his conversations followed by the transactional. It will be seen that he shows an inability to integrate these two basic components in his conversations.

Interactional problems

It has already been mentioned that the child seemed unable to provide more than the minimally required response, but that his responses were usually appropriate. Some responses were, however, odd. The following is a typical example:

(3)   Adult: now do you want to see if you can play some games with me?
      Child: yes
      Adult: they're very easy games um (1.0)
      Child: they are indeed
      Adult: well we'll see

The adult hesitates in the course of his explanation with a filled pause followed by a gap of 1 second. At this point, the child fills the gap. This is itself an appropriate behaviour typical of a skilled conversationalist. However, the content of his turn is inappropriate, as he could not possibly know yet that the games were easy. It seems as if he felt the obligation to take a turn and he selected a form which agreed on a superficial discourse level with the preceding turn, but which was inappropriate at the level of content.

Although the child failed to produce more than the minimally expected response in terms of content, he often provided responses which exceeded what is maximally expected in terms of form and his utterances were noticeable for their repetitiveness and redundancy. It has already been noted that he often failed to use ellipsis appropriately. In one of the sessions the investigator attempted to minimize this tendency by starting up at the point where the child's utterance was potentially complete, thus forcing him to ellipt. This was often successful, although the following example shows how the child seemed to be almost obliged to provide a complete sentence:

(4)   Adult: do you play with P?
      Child: yes I do=
      Adult: =umhmm=
      Child: =play with him
      Adult: after school?
      Child: yes
      Adult: umhmm
      Child: I play with him after school

The adult inserts *umhmm* following *I do* and these turns follow with no perceptible gap. However, the child continues to restore the remainder of the sentence which the adult was attempting to leave ellipted. The remainder of the example illustrates a related feature, where the child repeats the content of his own preceding utterances at a point where he might have been expected to add new content. It seemed that he recognized the social obligation to continue his turn but had nothing that he was able or willing to contribute. The following is a particularly striking example during the course of a narrative in which he was describing a hotel:

(5) Child: it's got twenty windows in it
      Adult: um
      Child: it has rooms . it has . it has a lift
      Adult: um
      Child: in it
          (2.0)
          has a lift in it
          (1.2)
          lift in it
      Adult: how long did you stay there for?

Once the child has mentioned the lift, he is unable to continue, although he proceeds with gradually reduced repetitions of his previous utterances. The situation is saved by the adult who initiates a new topic. We will return to the implications of these examples shortly.

Transactional problems

In the course of conversations with the child he often contradicted what he had just said, so that it was difficult to gain an accurate picture of such routine events as his journey from home to school, his out-of-school activities, and simple details about members of his family and his friends. As much of this information is not easily verifiable, the communication and description tasks were introduced as the child's ability to handle information could be more accurately assessed. Space does not permit a full account of these tasks, so the results will be summarized briefly.

In the communication tasks, the child sometimes failed to take his listener's perspective sufficiently into account and underspecified his information. He was, however, able to amend his instructions following feedback from the listener. In the description task, which involved telling an everyday story about a child based on a series of pictures, he failed to see the sequential links in the story, although he was able to describe each picture accurately. His most striking error was to change the sex of the child from a boy at the beginning of the story to a girl later on. In the task depicting the problem situation of a child standing outside his house, with the contents of his pockets emptied on the ground, he failed to make the expected inference that the child in the picture had lost his key, although he was able to produce other possible explanations – for example, that the child was looking for money to pay for his dinner. A similar inability to remark on the more salient aspects of a picture is illustrated in the following example which involved a picture of a boy whose clothes were covered in mud. This example also illustrates the child's obsession with exact time:

(6) Child: this is a boy going to school
     Adult: umhmm
     Child: he's going to school
     Adult: can you notice anything special about him?
     Child: he's going to school at nine o'clock . it's it could be nine o'clock
           when he comes to school
     Adult: uhhuh
     Child: it could be nine o'clock
     Adult: yes
     Child: or it could be about nine thirty
     Adult: okay
     Child: he could be out of the bus
     Adult: but do you notice anything special about him=
     Child: =yes=
     Adult: in this picture
           what?
     Child: that's his schoolbag
     Adult: uhhuh
     Child: his schoolbag
           that's his blue trousers
           I think that's muck in it
     Adult: yes that's what I was thinking
     Child: that's muck
     Adult: do you notice he's all mucky
     Child: yes because he was playing about with football

The child arrives at the expected response after considerable prompting and even proposes a possible explanation. On the way, he describes the less salient aspects of the picture, with some imagination but also much repetitiveness.

One final example will show how the child is unable to remedy cases of communicative breakdown. He was discussing a forthcoming sports day at school with his speech therapist:

(7) Adult: which race would you like to be in?
     Child: I like to be in X (a town several miles from the school) in the
           sports day
     Adult: in X?

Child: yes
Adult: what do you mean?
Child: I mean something
Adult: is there a sports day in X?
Child: there is not, there is a sports day in Y (at the school)
Adult: then what's X got to do with it?
Child: nothing
Adult: then why did you mention it?
Child: indeed I did mention it
Adult: why did you mention it?
Child: I don't know

General remarks

The preceding examples support the general conclusion that the child's conversations are 'confused and bizarre' as well as 'stilted and formal'. He appears to have deficiencies in some of the interactional skills which have been described throughout this book, but more particularly in his organization and presentation of large-scale knowledge configurations. This becomes apparent in his inability to describe temporal and causal relations between events and to make simple inferences which depend on a basic knowledge of the world. Future work could be directed towards practice in these areas, in which he would be introduced to a wider range of experiences and a comprehensive discussion of events, feelings and ideas through a series of carefully selected stories and pictures. He would also need practice in assessing the extent of his listener's knowledge and distinguishing his own from other's knowledge. This could be managed through simple roleplay in which he had to project into the minds and feelings of others. As he appeared responsive to explicit prompts, his attention could be drawn to particular breakdowns in communication and he could be guided towards an understanding of their causes.

It is interesting that this child uses 'coping strategies' which are typical of children with receptive language disorders or with hearing loss, although the underlying cause in this child's case is different. The basic strategy is to attempt to fulfil conversational obligations to the satisfaction of the interlocutor. At a superficial level this means fulfilling the minimal requirements of taking turns and making the minimally appropriate response. These requirements appear to override the additional obligation regarding the content of the talk. The conversational strategy adopted by the present child can be seen as a set of ordered requirements, as follows:

1 If the demands of informativeness and accuracy cannot be easily fulfilled, then give any answer which is potentially appropriate, even if you know that it is not actually appropriate.

2 If no such answer can be given, then fulfil the requirements of taking your turn by using a non-elliptical response and/or a stereotypic acknowledgement.
3 If more is required, then repeat your own preceding utterance.
4 If all else fails, then retreat by saying *don't know* or by changing the topic.

These points emerge from several of the examples cited earlier. In (3) the adult pauses in the course of an explanation and the child starts up to fill the gap. This is an appropriate behaviour as far as turn-taking is concerned, but is inappropriate in terms of content requirements. Example (4) shows the avoidance of ellipsis and the repetition of his own utterance as a means of taking a turn when he has nothing new to add, while (7) shows how he proceeds through the whole series of response strategies.

In conclusion, it might be helpful to outline some of the advantages of the present analysis. As little is known about disorders of conversation, it seems that case studies will offer the most useful approach. It is important to attempt to study the child's performance in detail in order to arrive at a fuller understanding of his deficiencies. Simply applying a diagnostic label such as *autism* or *retardation* would be unhelpful in such a case, even though certain features show similarities with clinically recognized syndromes. Similarly, it would be insufficient to score the child's performance on a set of tasks or to quantify his language usage in terms of the range of speech acts used or similar measures. The detailed analysis of the data which has been presented here has shown that there is a need to distinguish between the child's basic deficiencies, which are predominantly in his organization and presentation of knowledge, and the strategies he uses to cope with these deficiences. In other words, in this case it is not so much a matter of a conversational disability *per se*, but a disability (probably best described in terms of higher-level cognitive structures) which manifests itself in the child's discourse. The nature of the deficiencies can only be appreciated, however, following a detailed sequential analysis of the discourse, along the lines outlined here.

Concluding remarks

In this chapter we have reviewed the literature on pragmatic and discourse development. Obviously this is a new area of research which is still very much in its infancy. We have also pointed to some weaknesses in this research. In particular, there is the criticism that pragmatic disorders are treated as a correlate of language impairment at other levels of linguistic analysis. At any rate, the design of many studies makes such assumptions, which, as we have seen, beg the question we ought to be asking – that is, what precisely might be the relationship between development of pragmatic abilities and of language abilities at other levels. For this reason, case studies, such as the one presented here, will continue to provide an important corrective to the tendency to categorize and generalize prematurely. Indeed, we may well find that pragmatic disability is not a unitary phenomenon anyway. Rather, it may be the case that different types of disability are involved and consequently different remediation programmes. We can cite two recent proposals along these lines. Fey and Leonard (1983) propose three levels of pragmatic disability:

1 A general pragmatic impairment, in which the subject is unresponsive in social interaction and unwilling or unable to engage in conversation
2 Responsive but non-assertive conversational behaviour, marked by a high use of back-channel behaviours and possibly reflecting impairments in comprehension and the use of syntactic structures
3 A general conversational and speech act repertoire similar to other children at the same level of language but restricted because of deficiencies in specific linguistic forms.

Rather a different set of categories is proposed by Prutting and Kirchner (1983). They distinguish between pragmatic disabilities which reflect social, cognitive and linguistic deficiencies respectively:

1 *Social* A lack of sensitivity to the social context and rules of conversation
2 *Cognitive* An inability to establish and maintain discourse topics, and to identify and establish discourse referents
3 *Linguistic* A lack of linguistic forms to enable cohesive ties between utterances to be marked (for example; anaphoric pronouns and ellipsis).

Obviously much more research is needed to establish whether these are valid categories or not. Their value is that they provide a basis for further research. Nevertheless, we have still a long way to go before we can confidently propose profiles of conversational disability similar to those now in current use in syntax and other areas of language.

10

Implications and applications

As discourse analysis is a relatively new area of study, perhaps the best way to begin a review of implications and applications is to highlight the contributions which discourse analysis has made to investigations of language development. This can then lead on to some proposals concerning directions which further research might take.

Two major applications of discourse analysis have been apparent throughout this book. The first has been concerned with the development of discourse and conversational abilities in children. This can be, as the present book has attempted to show, an area of study in its own right. By specifying what skills are required to engage in conversational interaction, we have been able to trace in outline, with some detailed exemplification, the development of these skills from early infancy through the preschool years to early adolescence. The work of researchers like Gumperz, described at the end of chapter 8, shows how this approach can also be useful in assessing the problems of second-language learners in interethnic communication.

The second aspect, which we will want to look at in greater detail in the present chapter, is concerned with the way in which a close analysis of interaction can reveal otherwise unexpected aspects. Discourse analysis involves a detailed description of the language used in an encounter, the non-verbal behaviour of the participants, their shared and background assumptions, and the nature of the situational context or setting. As well as shedding light on the conversational skills of the participants, such a description can highlight aspects of the language used, the strategies employed by the participants to further their respective interactional ends, and the constraining effects of the situation on participants' performance. Let us exemplify these points in greater detail.

Two areas in which participants' strategies have been shown to be important are in studies of language comprehension and in assessments of school performance. As far as studies of children's language comprehension are concerned, the earlier tradition attempted to distinguish between the following factors which are involved in the processing of linguistic items and to focus on the first only (Dale 1976:119):

1 Knowledge of words and syntactic structure
2 The linguistic context
3 The non-linguistic context
4 General knowledge of the world.

More recently it has come to be accepted that it is difficult, if not impossible, to separate the other three aspects from strictly linguistic aspects of comprehension, and that, in any case, even if such attempts were successful they would tell us little about the ways in which children try to make sense of what is said to them in the 'real' world. For this reason, researchers have begun to look more closely at the context of comprehension studies. The following brief review illustrates some of the issues raised by this approach, based on a summary of a review article entitled 'Comprehension in context' by Bridges (1982).

One of the first criticisms of traditional studies which emerges in this new approach is that results were often distorted by the methodology of grouping data, that is, analysing how groups of children (for example, three-year-olds as compared with four-year-olds) respond *on average* to sets of linguistic stimuli, such as sentences in the passive voice. As Bridges points out, such an approach can average away two or more different response strategies. Indeed, in one study by Sinclair and Bronckart (1972) it was found that at least six different response strategies were being used by children at one stage. The very existence of these different strategies would have been lost if the results had been expressed as percentage scores for the group as a whole. In other words, a more careful and detailed analysis of the performance of each child can yield different results in comparison with the traditional method of grouping the data and obtaining average scores. Furthermore, the existence of different response strategies and biases, which affect the results in crucial ways, is often obscured by the more traditional methodology. So the new approach provides support for a methodology which requires a detailed analysis of each case in order to ascertain which strategies are being employed.

The next question which we might wish to ask is: what types of response strategy do children use in comprehension tasks? Bridges (1982) divides these into four basic types in her review of the comprehension literature, and a brief summary of each of these will serve to illustrate the contribution which discourse analysis has made to this field.

The first set of strategies can be described as *primitive approaches*. These are restricted generally to children under three years and include *intransitive* responses, where the child fails to make one object act upon the other in a stimulus of the type *make the car hit the lorry* (i.e. simply takes one object and moves it about or acts out an event in which neither object is the recipient of the action). A second type of primitive response is where the child acts as agent in the action; for example, the child carries out the nominated action on one of the objects rather than making one object act upon the other.

The other response strategies can be described briefly. They are *event probability*, *spatial arrangement* and *order of mention*. The effect of the plausibility of an event described by a sentence on the child's response is most apparent in bizarre sentences such as *the fence jumps over the horse*, which can only be enacted appropriately if the child is aware of the implications of the syntactic ordering of the elements subject–verb–object on the meaning relations expressed and does not allow these to be over-ridden by common-sense knowledge, for example in this case that horses jump fences but fences do not jump horses. Disregarding the potential methodological criticisms that such test items might invite, it is nevertheless the case that younger preschool children respond according to event probability rather than on the basis of word order information. Spatial arrangements refers to a strategy where the child consistently moves first the object which is already in their hand or is nearest and makes it agent of the action on the other object, again irrespective of the syntax of the stimulus sentence. Finally, order of mention describes a strategy in which the first-named object is treated as the agent of the action, a strategy which results in incorrect responses in passive sentences such as *the horse is chased by the cow*, as the child will make the horse the agent and the cow the recipient of the chasing. In sum, it looks from these more detailed analyses of children's response strategies that different children respond at different ages in a variety of ways to comprehension tasks. Obviously only this type of analysis can reveal which response strategy a child is using at any given time. A failure to attend to such contaminating variables will render the results of any comprehension task open to question.

We can move on now to a second way in which close attention to children's strategies has revealed unexpected findings – that is, in the assessment of children's school performance in standardized intelligence and achievement tests. The following summary is based on some detailed ethnographic analyses by Mehan (1973) of how such tests are often conducted. Mehan points out that the basic assumption which underlies such formal tests is that correct answers are the result of correct search procedures by the child, while incorrect answers are the result of faulty reasoning, lack of ability or lack of knowledge. However, in some cases the child may be using a perfectly valid line of reasoning, but one which is different from that of the tester. Mehan describes an example of a test administered to children aged four to six years in which pictures of children were shown with their heads concealed and the question was asked *which is the tallest child?* The expected answer was *don't know*, as the crucial evidence was missing in the picture. Some children, however, chose the child with the biggest feet, showing that they knew that the test required comparison and reasoning that some sort of positive answer was expected by the tester. It was only by questioning these children as to the reasons behind their responses that it was possible to show that their superficially incorrect responses were in fact based on sound reasoning, even though they did not share the tester's criteria. A test which did not seek out the child's reasons for their responses would simply have scored these responses as incorrect. Obviously a large number of such instances would have a grossly detrimental effect on a subject's score which would then fail to represent the subject's actual reasoning abilities.

This aspect of Mehan's work bears some similarities to accounts of children's response strategies in comprehension tests. A further aspect which Mehan examines is the behaviour of the tester in assessment procedures. In standardized tests it is assumed that the administration of the test is identical for each child. For example, the following instructions were given to different children (Mehan 1973:251):

1 look at that picture and find a
2 y'see all the things in that picture
3 now you look at those pictures
4 I want you to look at that picture and tell me what you see by looking at the picture
5 what those?
6 okay, now I want to find the right ones

In some cases the differences between the instructions may be considered to be minimal. However, in some cases the child is being told to look and find the correct pictures, while in others the child is simply being told to look. Moreover, in no case is there any indication of what might constitute a correct response.

Evaluation of responses is often problematic as well. Mehan found that children's reactions often included instances of the correct response. For example, they might touch two pictures in succession, one of which was the correct one. Was this to be taken as a correct response? In fact, what was found was that scoring was often arbitrary and that testers, rather than assessing objectively, were actively engaged in the process of interpreting aspects of the children's behaviour as instances of potential answers. Once again, the cumulative effect of such a process could have a biasing effect on a child's overall score. Indeed, the logical conclusion from this type of analysis is that tables of scores are unsatisfactory as they obscure the child's understanding of the materials and task, do not capture the child's reasoning abilities, and fail to show the negotiated, context-bound measurement decisions which the tester makes while scoring the child's answers as 'correct' or 'incorrect' (Mehan 1973:247).

The constraining effects of the context on performance

A detailed description and comparison of discourse contexts can also show how the nature of the setting can have an effect on a subject's performance. Perhaps the most dramatic illustration of this is to be found in Labov's paper 'The logic of non-standard English' (1969), in which the performance of a child is compared across several situations. In the first, a school interview with a friendly white interviewer, the child, a black boy, provides mainly monosyllabic responses, which could give rise to an assessment of severe verbal deficit. Labov showed that this behaviour was not necessarily a result of the ineptitude of the interviewer but rather of the more general sociolinguistic factors which control speech. Accordingly, various changes were made in the social situation, such as making the interview less formal by bringing along the child's best friend, allowing taboo words and topics, and reducing the height imbalance between the interviewer and the children by getting the interviewer to sit on the floor beside the children.

Gallaher (1983) has reviewed a number of studies which investigate the effects of context on children's language use, including variations in communicative partner and physical setting. It has generally been reported that children produce longer utterances in interactions with their mothers at home than with a clinician in a clinic. However, there are wide individual differences between children and, in several studies, children actually performed better in the clinical setting. As far as the effects of physical setting are concerned, the type and number of toys can influence children's communicative behaviour (see also Conti 1982). As the effects for any individual child cannot be predicted a priori, Gallaher recommends the use of a preassessment schedule by means of which the clinician can ascertain factors affecting each child's performance, such as usual communicative partners, preferred play activities and marked variations due to change in partner and activity. (See Gallaher 1983 for further details.) Such information would guide clinicians in obtaining a representative sample of a child's communicative behaviour, give that contexts cannot be standardized across children but must instead be prescribed for each child on the basis of his or her own pattern of language use variability.

This work has implications for the analysis of interaction between speech therapists and patients and for the development of remediation programmes – the area which Crystal (1981) has described as *linguistic management*. Some of the more general aspects of this area have been discussed in an article by Seibert and Oller (1981), entitled 'Linguistic pragmatics and language intervention strategies'. The authors criticize the traditional use of the behaviourist learning theory/reinforcement paradigm in speech therapy, particularly in relation to the problem of the generalization of training effects. Therapy is of little use if the patient can respond appropriately in the clinic but fails abysmally outside. Accordingly, the authors propose that assessment procedures should incorporate various pragmatic functions which would reflect the uses to which the patient would normally put language in settings outside the clinic. The ecological validity of much therapist-patient interaction is questioned and various proposals are put forward. These include directing therapy more at interaction with others such as parents and peers rather than working entirely within one-to-one therapy situations, looking critically at the use of test questions, which usually violate rules of sincerity and naturalness, and tailoring the environment to a greater extent to the patient's needs and interests, for example by encouraging and responding to the patient's initiations.

There have been few studies of the nature of clinician–patient interaction. One study by Prutting et al. (1978) examined the proportion of communicative acts produced in a large sample of clinician–child discourse, the types of communicative acts used and their distribution, and the distribution of the rights of topic initiation. It was found that clinicians produced 65 per cent of the talk as opposed to 35 per cent by the children. The most commonly produced speech acts were requests by the speech therapists and responses by the children. Generally the requests were questions to which the therapist knew the answer – that is, test or display questions. As far as the initiation of topics was concerned, it was found that clinicians tended to follow a plan of action which had been devised beforehand and that they only responded to questions from the child which were relevant to the task at hand. Similar results were found in studies of the interpersonal skills of speech pathology students (Volz et al. 1978; Klevans et al. 1981). In these studies it was found that speech therapy students, who were recorded in training sessions with child patients, tended to ask numerous questions, mainly of the closed type, which elicited minimal information and put high constraints on the type of response possible. These students were compared with students in human service curricula who produced a greater number of *continuing* responses, that is, utterances which encouraged their interlocutor to continue with their talk.

What are the implications of these studies for the training of speech therapy students? Prutting et al. (1978) suggest that children have little opportunity in therapist–patient interaction to practise the syntactic patterns which occur in requests, questions and statements, as their turns are mainly confined to responses. A further point is that the children do not have the opportunity to practise the range of speech acts which they would expect to use in their everyday interactions outside the clinic. In addition, there is the question whether the children are able to generalize from the clinical setting to other settings. In fact, it seems that there is the danger that therapist–patient interaction produces the paradoxical situation in which an attempt is made to elicit spontaneous language but the very techniques used inhibit the use of such language (Hubbell 1977). That is, clinicians use techniques such as prompts, limitations, questions, reinforcement – all of which are commands to talk – which clearly do not have the effect of producing spontaneous talk. We can illustrate this point by analysing some samples of therapist–child interaction. The following is a typical example:

(1) Therapist: let's have a look at some pictures
                 what's this one about?   I
    Patient: milk   R
    Therapist: what time is it at school?   I
    Patient: break-time   R
    Therapist: and what are the children doing?   I
    Patient: drinking milk   R
    Therapist: that's right   F
                 why are there some empty bottles in the crate?   I
    Patient: drink all   R
    Therapist: that's right   F
                 those children have drunk it all up

As we can see, this discourse is made up of exchanges of the structure IR and IRF, in which the therapist has control and the patient supplies the minimally expected response. In some cases the answer is already known to the therapist, while in others the patient has some latitude to construct his response from a range of reasonable alternatives, as in the initiation *why are there some empty bottles in the crate?* However, if we consider the distribution of the moves I and R, we find that I is predominantly taken by the therapist and R by the patient. In fact, in the ten-minute sample from which this extract is taken, there were only two cases where the patient initiated. In the first case he added to the response predicted by the therapist's preceding initiation:

(2) Therapist: what's the teacher showing the children?   I
    Patient: flower   R
    Therapist: and what are the children doing?   I
    Patient: looking at it   R
    Therapist: it's like your nature class isn't it?   I
    Patient: nature table   R
                 I got a nature table   cont (I)
    Therapist: what have you got on your nature table?   R/I
    Patient: a lot of things   R
    Therapist: what's the wee boy doing here?   I
    Patient: writing   R

Here we have a slight deviation from the pattern of IR and IRF exchanges as the patient continues his turn with information which provides for the possibility of further talk. However, we can see that the therapist is, as it were, locked into the predominant discourse pattern. She responds implicitly to the patient's move by incorporating it topically into her next initiation and then moves on to another topic in the next exchange.

The second case of an initiation by the patient receives no response at all. The therapist takes out a book about a farm and the patients comments:

(3)	Patient:	I got that story at home	I
	Therapist:	have you been on a farm	I
	Patient:	(nods)	R
	Therapist:	what did you see?	I
	Patient:	cows and tractors	R

Let us now consider the implications of our analysis of such patterns of interaction. Firstly, we can note the contrast with casual conversation where the privileges of discourse initiation are distributed more symmetrically and exchanges are linked by the use of moves which respond while simultaneously initiating a further response. If the aim of the interaction is to train the patient to be able to participate in normal, everyday conversation, then this type of experience will be of little use. We must bear in mind, however, that the aims of the dominant participant in such interactions, whether it be a teacher, doctor, interviewer or speech therapist, may be quite specific. For example, the aim may be to test a pupil's knowledge, to diagnose an illness, to gather information or to elicit samples of language. These aims may be fulfilled by the types of discourse structure which we have been illustrating. What is important to consider is that such exchanges constrain the options available to the lower-status participant so that his responses are controlled by the dominant participant. This may be the explicit goal of the interaction, as in a Socratic type of questioning designed to lead the pupil to the discovery of new knowledge, the careful questioning by the doctor which focuses on information relevant to the diagnosis and excludes irrelevant information, or in the attempt by the speech therapist to exert control over the patient's language output by restricting it to structures and topics which the patient is known to be able to handle. The justification of these strategies is beyond the scope of the present chapter. The important point which needs to be made is that professionals who employ such interactional strategies should be aware of their limitations.

To pursue our examples from speech therapist–patient interaction. As we have seen, the patient's responses are minimal and closely related to the therapist's initiations. Such responses would be useful as an indication of the patient's ability to respond to a particular range of questions and to use elliptical syntax in these responses, but they would be less useful as a sample of language on which an analysis of the patient's syntax could be based (as was in fact the aim of this particular therapy session). As we can see, the patient produces elliptical responses which are entirely appropriate, but which do not permit an analysis of common clause patterns. For example, there are few responses in which a subject noun phrase is present, and in many the verbs are also absent. Similarly, such an interaction would be an inadequate basis for the development of conversational ability. What is required here is a type of interaction in which the patient has greater opportunity to initiate topics and to exert control over the discourse. This may be difficult within the constraints which operate in clinical practice. For this reason, some researchers have recommended techniques which depart from traditional clinical methods but which would seem to be potentially more facilitative of spontaneous talk.

For example, Hubbell (1977) suggests a more unstructured clinical strategy in which no specific attempt is made to elicit talk and the therapist waits for the child's lead and then tailors the response carefully to the child's utterance. This approach is similar to the more facilitative and supportive type of interaction which Wells (1978) suggests leads to a more effective use of language by children. Naturally the purpose of the clinical intervention is relevant to this decision. Hubbell suggests that this type of interactive style is best suited in cases of mentally retarded patients or those with functional language delay but is less suitable for those who talk adequately but whose main impairment is in an area such as phonology or syntax.

Another recommendation, which attempts to overcome the contrived nature of therapist–child interaction and the problem of generalization of training to settings outside the clinic, is that parents should be trained to interact with their language-disabled children. In other words, the parent is involved in the intervention along with the therapist. One such training program for parents is described by McDade (1981), who cites several studies to show that trained parents obtain greater responsiveness and a development of language skills in their children. The main aim of McDade's training programme was to improve interaction between parent and child. So, for example, parents were taught how to teach their child a specific task and how to remain with the task until the child achieved the correct response. Parents were also taught the use of rewarding behaviours and, more generally, were made more aware of the nature and development of their child's communicative skills. Other programmes have taught parents how to focus on objects and events which are at their child's level, how to provide opportunities for the use of particular language items such as requests, and how to respond to their children's talk (Spradlin and Siegel 1982). There is some evidence to suggest that those parents who displayed higher-quality teaching behaviours induced greater gains in their children's levels of speech skills (Weitz 1982). Research in this area is still very much in its infancy. However, enough has been said here to indicate the importance of further empirical studies into the nature of therapist–patient interaction and into the development of a wider range of therapeutic techniques and contexts which will lead to a more effective and appropriate development of the communicative skills of language-disabled patients.

Some extensions of the analysis

Throughout this book we have been looking at the development of conversational ability in children. We have moved from attempts at communication in early infancy, through the development of basic conversational skills in the preschool period, to the more complex aspects of interaction in school-aged children and adolescents. We have also considered some of the problems which arise in interethnic communication and in children with pragmatic disorders. In this section we will extend our analysis to look at some aspects of adult communication. We will deal with three main areas in which discourse analysis has made or could potentially make a useful contribution: the study of the functional communication of aphasic adults, the communicative skills of mentally retarded adults, and the approach to the analysis and teaching of interpersonal communication commonly known as social skill training. We will look at each of these areas in turn.

Functional communication in aphasic adults

Although the language problems of adult aphasics have been extensively documented (see, for example, Lesser 1978), little attention has been paid to how they use language to communicate. Two aspects are involved: on the one hand, the ability to produce utterances or non-verbal behaviours which are appropriate and effective within a communicative context irrespective of their grammatical well-formedness; and on the other, the transfer of language patterns learned in the clinic to usage in natural environments. Holland (1980) has developed a test of functional communication for aphasic adults, *communicative abilities in daily living* (CADL), which provides practice as well as an assessment procedure in this area. A set of situations is presented to the patient to be enacted in role-play simulations. The situations include exchanging important information, completing a form, using the telephone, going to the doctor and going shopping. Scores are based on the effective and appropriate use of an item rather than on its grammaticality, with two marks assigned to a 'correct' response, one mark to a partially 'correct' response and no marks to an 'incorrect' response. The following is an example from the test where the simulated situation is 'going shopping' (Holland 1980: 78–9):

(4)   Item 45: 'You need shoelaces. You can't find them. A clerk says:
      "May I help you?" What do you say?'
      (says 'yeah' and points to her own shoelaces)

This non-verbal response is scored 2, as would be verbal indication of needing shoelaces.

If the patient had merely said 'Yes' or indicated needing help but with no reference to shoelaces, as in 'I need . . . shoes', the scoring would be 1.

As we can see, the emphasis is on everyday situations which the patient would expect to encounter and the scoring is based on the effectiveness of the patient's functional communication rather than on a measure of linguistic well-formedness in phonology or syntax. A wide range of speech acts are tested. For example, the tester intentionally calls the patient by the wrong name and refers to a fictitious illness to test whether the patient can correct and request clarification respectively. Likewise, the ability to respond to an apology is tested in the following item which occurs towards the end of the test (Holland 1980):

(5)   Item 66: 'I'm sorry this all took so long.'
               'You sure could.'

Score this as 0. It is an inappropriate response for an apology. A two-point answer would be accepting it – 'It's okay' – or not accepting it – 'I am too.'

The use of the CADL in functional communication therapy for chronic aphasic adults has been reported by Aten et al. (1982). Seven male patients, age ranges 45 to 69 years with a range of post-onset of aphasia from nine to 292 months, undertook a course of group therapy which involved practice in the following situations: shopping in a grocery and variety store, giving and following directions, social greetings and exchanges, supplying personal information, reading signs and directories, and the use of gestural responses to express ideas. Significant improvement on CADL scores was found after six weeks of treatment and also six weeks post-treatment, which suggests that this type of therapy was instrumental in the improvement of the functional communicative abilities of these subjects.

As mentioned earlier, it is important to document the transfer of training to natural environments. Holland (1982) reports a study in which adult aphasics were observed in their everyday interactions in their home environments. Items scored were the ways in which the subjects asked and answered questions, made requests for clarification, changed topics, and used gestures to maintain the conversation. Subjects were classified along two dimensions – number of communicative attempts and rate of communicative failure – which resulted in the following matrix:

	Communicative attempts	Rate of communicative failure
1	high	high
2	high	low
3	low	low
4	low	high

Group 1 was found mainly in Wernicke aphasic subjects who were talkative but whose comprehension difficulties led to frequent misunderstandings. This pattern was not highly represented in the data and is more typical of demented rather than aphasic subjects. Group 2 represents subjects who are fairly successful in the area of functional communication, while group 3 represents subjects who possibly use the strategy of avoiding communication to conceal their deficiencies. Group 4 represents the most unsuccessful communicators. It is interesting to note that the whole range of aphasic types seen in the study were represented in this group, so that there was no clear association between type of aphasia and type of communicative disorder. While these classifications are obviously fairly crude, they have the merit of showing that aphasic adults can be grouped according to different communicative patterns and that these patterns are distinct from types of syndrome presented.

One further aspect of communication which Holland (1982) reports has implications for therapy. This is concerned with the strategies used by the subjects to cope with their linguistic deficiencies. For example, various strategies were used by subjects experiencing word-finding problems, such as the use of circumlocution and gestural description. Such strategies could be taught to those patients who lack them. More generally, this type of research emphasizes how language is used in natural environments and as such provides a useful basis for exploring the relationship between linguistic impairment and communicative strategies as well as showing how aphasic adults might compensate for their deficiencies in language by the use of such strategies.

The communicative abilities of mentally handicapped adults

A second area of interest is the communicative competence of mentally handicapped adults. Although the language of the mentally handicapped has often been described as extremely delayed or impaired (see, for example, the review by Rosenberg 1982), it seems that on the level of communicative interaction the mentally handicapped show an ability to communicate adequately with each other (Longhurst 1974; Bedrosian and Prutting 1978; Price-Williams and Sabsay 1979). For example, Price-Williams and Sabsay (1979) studied the conversations of nine subjects who had Down's syndrome. They found that the subjects took turns, asked questions, made appropriate responses, elicited attention and repaired utterances in cases of conversational breakdown. In short, these subjects showed all the skills which have been illustrated earlier in normally developing children. Similar findings were produced by Bedrosian and Prutting (1978), who found, however, that their mentally handicapped subjects were unable to hold a dominant position in a conversation, even in the expected case where the mentally handicapped adult was interacting with a young child.

Most studies of the communicative abilities of the mentally handicapped focus on either spontaneous conversation or the use of language in more closely controlled communicative tasks. Both these aspects were examined in a study of two mentally handicapped adults at Ulster Polytechnic.[1] The subjects lived in a residential home for the mentally handicapped. The first, R.K., is 23-years-old, with Down's syndrome. Her IQ, as measured last in 1969 with the Stanford-Binet test, is 45. The second subject, P.C., is 36-years-old and her IQ, last measured in 1974 using the Stanford-Binet test, is 37. This classifies her as 'severely handicapped'. The subjects were recorded taking part in a natural conversation and then in a communicative task involving giving and receiving instructions.

As far as the spontaneous speech sample is concerned, the subjects displayed an ability to use several basic conversational skills. For example, they took and exchanged turns regularly and efficiently and showed evidence of being able to predict possible points of completion in the other's turn. In the following example, R.K. began her turn at a potential point of completion and overlap occurred because P.C. continued with a tag:

(6) P.C.: aye, we're going out for our Christmas dinner in the centre, aren't we?
     R.K.: yes, on Thursday week

On another occasion, R.K. was able to predict the completion of P.C.'s turn and overlapped with identical content, adding a further piece of information *(and tea)* at the end:

(7) P.C.: We'd tea, we'd sandwiches and buns and cakes
     R.K.:   wiches and buns and cakes . and tea

Such overlaps, as we saw in chapter 7, are not instances of conversational incompetence but of a well-developed ability to monitor the ongoing turn and even predict its possible completion. In this respect, then, these subjects displayed an ability to communicate effectively with each other in spontaneous conversation involving familiar, everyday topics.

When we turn to the communication tasks, we find that the subjects experienced greater difficulty. In these tasks, one subject had to describe a picture to the other, who had to draw the picture on the basis of the instructions. The subjects were separated by a screen, as in many similar studies of referential communicative ability. Five simple drawings were used showing objects in different relations to one another and of different size. The objects used in the drawings were squares, circles, triangles and rectangles. A pretest was administered to ensure that the subjects were familiar with these terms. The following are some examples from the transcripts of these tasks:

(8) Picture

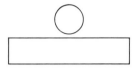

P.C.: a ball, no I mean like a ball . . . . . isn't it? A circle please, R.
R.K.: right
P.C.: like a house, R., a box

R.K. shows the following:

P.C.: R., you should have had the circle on top of the house
R.K.: circle on the top
P.C.: yea

R.K. shows the following and P.C. confirms that it is correct:

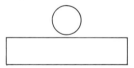

For this picture the minimal instructions would involve a description of two objects – a rectangle and a circle – as well as a statement of their positions relative to one another. At a more accurate level, the description of the rectangle would indicate that the longer sides were on the horizontal dimension. So the instructions might be something like

(9) draw a circle directly above a rectangle but not touching it

If we examine P.C.'s instructions, we find that she begins by describing two objects, a ball/circle and house/box. R.K. is able to reproduce the objects accurately on the basis of this description but, lacking instructions as to their relative positions, places the circle to the right of the box. P.C. is able to repair this without any difficulty and so R.K. produces the correct picture.

The next example proved rather more difficult. It involved a rectangle and a triangle, positioned as follows:

R.K.: a square, a taller one
P.C.: right, R. what's the next one?
R.K.: a triangle coming into the line of the square
P.C.: there you are

In this case, R.K. was giving instructions to P.C.:

(10) R.K.: a square, a taller one
  P.C.: right, R. what's the next one?
  R.K.: a triangle coming into the line of the square
  P.C.: there you are

P.C. shows the following:

R.K.: no, it should be outside coming into the line. Outside pointing to the line

P.C. shows the following:

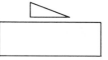

R.K.: no, pointing into the line
P.C.: is it touching the line?
R.K.: yes it is
P.C.: is that right?

P.C. shows the following:

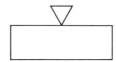

R.K.: yes it is

For this picture the minimal instructions could be something like:

(11) draw a rectangle with the short sides at the top and bottom. On the right, draw a triangle with the point just touching the long side of the rectangle

We see that R.K. uses the term *square* but adds the phrase *a taller one* to give a reasonable description of a vertical rectangle. Her instruction to draw a triangle coming into the line of the square is also reasonable, except that it does not specify which line is involved. On seeing P.C.'s first attempt, she modifies to *pointing to the line*, which still fails to produce the correct result. Her next instruction makes a further minor modification – *pointing into the line* – following which P.C. requests clarification by asking *is it touching the line?* This results in a picture which R.K. accepts as correct, although it has in fact been rotated through 90 degrees in comparison to the original.

Several points can be made on the basis of these examples. Looking first at what the subjects can do, we see that they are able to provide fairly accurate descriptions of the objects, modify their descriptions as a result of feedback, and request and give clarification. They both perform fairly well in their separate roles of speaker and listener. The main problem which the speakers encounter is that they seem unable to co-ordinate the two aspects of the instructions – the descriptions of the objects as well as their relative positions – into one coherent instruction similar to the models suggested above. Instead, their predominant strategy is to describe the pictures step by step without giving a general overview of the picture as a whole. So, at this level, it would seem that these subjects have difficulty in forming an overall impression of the task and then breaking it down into its separate parts without losing the relationships between the parts. We might anticipate similar difficulties in the narration of a complex series of events illustrating some major topic or main event. On the other hand, however, it could be argued that the speakers are aware of the limitations of their listeners and break down the information into manageable chunks. It would be interesting to make comparisons with 'normal' subjects to see how they would manage the task of breaking down the instructions while at the same time keeping track of the overall relationships between the objects.

In sum, this work presents an interesting comparison between the abilities of two mentally handicapped adults in spontaneous conversation and in a more controlled experimental communication task. The study has shown that the subjects have control of many basic conversational skills but that they encounter difficulties when the cognitive demands of the task are higher. This suggests an interaction between conversational skills and conversational content, a point raised in the case study presented in chapter 9. Further research could explore this relationship by investigating the range of strategies used by such subjects across a wide variety of interactional tasks.

Social skill training

Social skill training is concerned with the skills involved in face-to-face interaction and with how these skills might be improved. Generally this work is practical in its orientation. For example, social skill training can be used in a remedial setting with psychiatric patients, in a developmental setting with behaviourally disordered children and in training adolescents in social and life skills such as job interviews, or in specialized settings concerned with the interpersonal professions such as teaching, social work, health visiting and counselling (Ellis and Whittington 1981). The methods used in social skill training are as follows. Firstly, a series of skills relevant to the needs of the trainee are identified. For example, in the case of remedial settings this might involve some form of assertiveness training, while in the case of a health visitor skills such as questioning, reinforcement, explaining and reflection of feeling might be involved (see Hargie et al. 1981 for a detailed account of these and other skills). These skills are then taught and practised separately, usually in role play situations which are recorded on closed circuit television and then reviewed by the trainer and trainees. Later the skills are integrated and practised as a whole.

How might discourse analysis contribute to social skill training? If we look at the social skill literature, we will find that linguistics and discourse analysis have so far contributed little to this area and that the major theoretical inputs have come from social psychology in respect of the analysis of social interaction and from behaviourist psychology in respect of training techniques. The potential contribution of linguistics and discourse analysis has been outlined recently by Milroy and McTear (1983) and by Trower (1983). The following are some areas in which linguistics and discourse analysis could add a further theoretical dimension to social skill training:

Identification of skills

Social skills are seen as the components of interaction. They are identifiable units which are under the control of the individual and which can be taught (Hargie et al. 1981). Accordingly, social skill training programmes will involve setting up taxonomies of the skills which are to be taught. However, on looking at such lists of skills we find that little note is taken of the relationships between each of the items on the list. Some skills are highly particular, such as various aspects of non-verbal behaviour like eye contact and nodding. Other skills are extremely general, such as showing warmth, forming a relationship or using ideas. As well as this, there is a contrast between skills on the dimension of low versus high inference. Many of the skills described in the literature are readily observable by the trained eye. These include non-verbal behaviours, and it is one of the strengths of researchers in social skill training that the importance of non-verbal behaviour in face-to-face interaction has been identified. Other skills are of high inference. These would include the general skills mentioned earlier such as showing warmth.

Linguistics could contribute to the identification of social skills in three ways. Firstly, there is the question of the organization of taxonomies. One of the major strengths of linguistics is that it has developed a means of analysing language on several levels, with the result that questions of sound (phonology), meaning (semantics) and sentence structure (syntax) can be treated separately for the purposes of analysis. Thus a description of the pronunciation of a word would be seen as a different issue analytically from the question of how it can combine with other words to form a grammatical sentence. This is, of course, over-simplifying the complex problems involved in motivating levels of analysis and we are disregarding the interesting question of relationships and interactions between levels. However, the main point is clear: descriptive taxonomies require basic principles of organization if terminological confusion and overlapping of categories is to be avoided.

The second way in which linguistic methodology could contribute to the identification of social skills concerns the principle that descriptions of categories should be explicit and rigorous. Obviously this requirement is met in social skill training with regard to non-verbal skills. However, when we turn to more general, high-inference skills we find that little attempt is made to relate items in lists of skills to their exponents in the data. In contrast, in linguistics and in discourse analysis there are rigorous criteria for the identification of items such as nouns and verbs, and even for interactional categories such as requests (see chapter 5).

Finally, there is the problem of variability and appropriacy. To be fair, it must be said that most accounts of social skills emphasize the extent to which social skills are situation and culture specific. So, for example, while smiling might be taught as a useful social skill, some comment would be added concerning the appropriacy of the skill. However, these comments usually remain fairly general, urging the trainee, for example, to be sensitive to the characteristics of the situation and to the other persons involved in the interaction. This contrasts with the more rigorous and explicit approach adopted in sociolinguistics and pragmatics, where the components of the situation are computed and associated with the relevant exponents of the skills. Examples from the literature include the appropriate choice of address terms (see, for example, Ervin-Tripp 1972), or the reasons for asking questions in social interaction (Wilson 1980).

Description of language
To their credit, researchers in the area of social skills have placed considerable emphasis on the detailed description of non-verbal behaviour. To some extent, however, this has been at the expense of the analysis of verbal behaviour, where descriptions have by and large been analytically naïve. The areas of para-linguistics and prosody are generally recognized as being important, yet little attempt is made to use the analytic tools developed by linguists (see, for example, Crystal 1975), to describe para-language and

prosody. As a result, terms such as 'tone of voice' are used which subsume a variety of suprasegmental phenomena such as key, chunking and intonation (Milroy and McTear 1983:54). It is rare to find a detailed analysis of the language of interaction, similar to the analyses which have been presented in this book or those which are regularly produced as data bases by discourse analysts and conversation analysts. This means that many of the important aspects of language used in face-to-face interaction, such as the use of the discourse connectors *well* and *anyway*, or mitigating devices which 'soften' the force of an utterance, are overlooked. In fact, if we look at examples of language which are presented in most manuals, we find that they are invented examples, which may illustrate the particular skill in question but which fail to represent how language is used in actual interpersonal encounters to realize these skills.

Lack of a sound ethnographic base
The next point leads on from the previous ones and concerns the failure to use adequately the methods of ethnography in the identification and description of skills. Generally skills are identified on an intuitive basis or as a result of careful and insightful observation. This will often produce a set of skills which is recognized as typical by the professionals concerned. However, there is still a disparity between what, for example, a counsellor claims to be the skills of counselling and what that counsellor would actually do in a counselling encounter. In other words, there is little actual empirical support for the skills which are being trained. (The use of contrived data is further evidence of this lack of a sound ethnographic base.) Finally, there is the problem of the effectiveness of social skill training. Much research has gone into questions such as transfer of training and factors such as personality characteristics of trainees and their relationships to trainee outcomes (Ellis and Whittington 1981; Hargie and Saunders 1983). More ethnographic work is now needed on how trainees employ the skills they have been taught in real-life encounters. Here again there is a contrast with the approach adopted in linguistics, particularly in the areas of sociolinguistics and discourse analysis, where the *validity* of the data base is considered as an essential prerequisite for the motivation of descriptive categories.

Lack of an interactional perspective
Although social skills training is concerned with interpersonal communication, it tends to focus on the behaviour of one participant – the trainee – and neglects the ways in which interaction is a co-operative activity involving more than one person. Thus trainees are taught how to ask questions, explain, maintain eye contact and show warmth, but these behaviours are seen in isolation from the contribution of the other participant(s). This type of training is probably best suited for those encounters in which the trainee

will be in control of the interaction, as in teaching, interviewing and counselling, but will obviously be less suited for other contexts such as remedial settings where the relationships are more symmetrical, or indeed where the trainee is to be cast in a less dominant role. We can illustrate this problem by looking briefly at turn-taking. As we have seen (chapter 7), turn-taking is essentially a co-operative activity by means of which turns are assigned and exchanged on a co-ordinated basis by each participant. Except in highly asymmetrical settings no one participant has control over turn-taking. This applies equally to the question of the length of pauses between turns. One recommendation which is frequently made in social skill manuals is that trainees should incorporate pauses into the interaction, both before and when asking questions and after receiving responses. Pauses are seen as a means of slowing down the interaction. What is overlooked in this recommendation is that interturn pauses are a joint construction of both participants rather than the responsibility of any one participant. Furthermore, this analysis fails to recognize some of the more complex functions of pauses in interpersonal interaction, such as marking a *dispreferred response* like a refusal of a request (for other examples, see Levinson 1983:326–9).

Social skill research can also be criticized for its failure to take account of the sequential nature of interaction and the ways in which the sequential location of an utterance or behaviour have a bearing on its function and interpretation. We can illustrate this point by looking at the skill of *reinforcement*. Reinforcement as a social skill owes its origins to a stimulus–response model of behaviour developed within behaviourist psychology. As far as social skill training is concerned, one aspect of the use of reinforcement is to encourage or inhibit the use of a behaviour by the other participant. So, for example, non-verbal indications of attention such as nods, verbal acknowledgements such as *umhmm*, or more elaborate forms of reinforcement, such as reflection of the feeling or content of the other's talk, can encourage the other participant to continue. There is a wide range of experimental evidence to show that reinforcement can promote the occurrence of particular types of behaviour in the other person, such as the use of self-reference statements. What seems to be ignored, however, is the sequential location of items such as nods and *umhmms*. These are cited as the most basic exponents of the skill of reinforcement, yet no distinction is made as to whether they occur within or between turns. In the case of an interturn location, a nod or *umhmm* can have the function of a response which constitutes a turn in its own right. Further distinctions can be drawn according to prosodic characteristics. For example, *umhmm* in low key would have the function of terminating an exchange whereas *umhmm* in high key and with rising intonation would realize a request of clarification or express surprise. In any case, these forms are being used as interactional moves within exchanges as opposed to the use of the same forms, often described as back-channel behaviours (Duncan 1972), which occur during the course of a speaker's turn and indicate that the listener is attending without trying to take the floor at that point in time. However, the picture is even more subtle than this. These back-channel behaviours are often described as having the function merely of expressing interest and attention. It has also been suggested that utterances such as *umhmm, really, fancy that* can have the function of influencing the current speaker in the subsequent production of his talk in ways which differ from the function of reinforcement. For example, it seems that these utterances, spoken simultaneously with the current speaker's talk and accompanied usually by rising intonation, can lead the current speaker to modify his talk by diminishing the strength of a preceding claim or by providing additional support for it. In other words, these brief interruptions have the dual function of supporting the speaker while at the same time directing the course of the conversation without actually taking the floor (see Bublitz 1979 for further discussion). The fact that such utterances can be heard as supports facilitates their use as a means of toning down their interruptive nature. For this reason they can also be used as a means of signalling that the listener wishes to have the next turn before the point of possible completion has been reached (Oreström 1977). In other words, the focus on components of interaction in isolation from their sequential location disregards potential differences in the functions of particular forms as well as failing to take account of the dynamic nature of conversational interaction. This point can be seen most clearly when we attempt to describe a socially skilled performance, as it is clear that such a performance is more than the sum of its parts – for example, so many smiles, nods or reinforcements – and is rather a result of a complex process of negotiation involving a dynamic and ongoing assessment of the current state of play in the interaction.

In sum, as we have seen, social skill training is a useful and practical approach to the problems of interpersonal communication. It has the merits of being able to sensitize trainees to some of the complexities of interpersonal behaviour and of having developed ways of teaching the skills involved in a wide range of professional and remedial contexts. Greater attention needs to be paid to the issues of the identification of skills, the description of linguistic behaviour, the validity of the data base and the dynamic nature of face-to-face interaction. It is in these areas that linguistics, and in particular the type of discourse analysis illustrated in this book, might make its most useful contribution.

Directions for further research

The analysis of conversation has progressed considerably over the last few years, yet it is obvious that much more work needs to be done in this important and interesting area. The account of conversational development in children which has been presented in this book has shown how children's conversations can be analysed in some detail to reveal the devices they use to initiate and sustain conversation. Yet it would be fair to say that the present account has failed to provide a detailed and coherent picture of the development of conversational abilities in children similar to accounts which now exist for areas such as phonology and syntax. The emphasis has been largely on showing what children can do rather than what they cannot do. This has resulted in two major problems with the present analysis: on the one hand, it is difficult to see how children differ from adults in the conversational devices they use and, on the other, no explanations are offered as to how children pass from one stage of development to another. These are questions which future research must face. This account has sought to bring together and illustrate many of the important aspects of conversational skill. It is to be hoped that this will have prepared the way for the investigation of the important issues which have been raised here.

If research on conversational development is to be of any value, some of the problems facing discourse analysts which have been raised in passing in this book will have to be faced more seriously. These issues will be summarized briefly at this point. To begin with, there is the problem of terminological confusion and overlap. Many studies draw up taxonomies of poorly motivated categories and proceed to score the frequency of occurrence of such items with each other and with external variables such as age, sex or language level of child. Not enough is known about the nature of conversational interaction for researchers to be able to address such questions at this stage and more attention should be paid to the validity of the descriptive analysis and with providing reliable criteria for the recognition of analytic categories. In any case, it would seem that conversational interaction raises problems which do not occur in other areas of linguistic analysis. The theoretical impossibility of coding a speaker's intentions has been mentioned. Added to this is the problem of scoring conversational performance when the data is the product of the co-ordinated efforts of two (or more) participants. How, for example, are we to separate out the performance of one participant from that of the other when the contributions of each are so obviously interdependent? Finally, it should be emphasized that more attention should be paid to the sequential organization of conversation rather than to the analysis of utterances in isolation. As the conversation analysts have shown, the characteristics of a conversational turn have to be explained in relation to the sequential task in which the turn is produced. One of the shortcomings of speech act theory (and, to some extent, the Birmingham discourse analysis) is its failure to attend sufficiently to the sequential organization of conversation (see Levinson 1983, chapter 6, for a recent account of these issues).

In this book the emphasis has been on interactional aspects of conversation rather than on discourse content. An attempt has been made to isolate the abstract devices which underlie conversational interaction rather than to analyse the content of the interaction. As we have seen throughout, however, the two are interrelated. Participation in turn-taking, for example, depends on an analysis of the content of the current turn rather than on the recognition of turn-yielding cues alone. Similarly, the ability to make an appropriate response and to maintain coherence in dialogue depends on the ability to interpret the content of preceding turns. Where there is difficulty with content, as in the case study presented in chapter 9 or in the case of adult aphasics with a functional communicative disorder, there are typically implications for the interaction and, as we have seen, various strategies can be utilized to compensate for such deficiencies at the level of content. On the other hand, as we saw in chapter 3, there is a stage where very young infants have a command of basic interactional devices to regulate turn-taking and simple initiation–response exchanges even before they have developed any language with which to express these devices. Further research will need to look more closely at the relationship between interactional and trans-actional aspects of conversation.

Related to this issue is the question of how conversation relates to the more traditional levels of linguistic analysis. Much of recent work in discourse analysis has been concerned with the ways in which various intrasentential phenomena can be best explained in terms of discourse features. Examples would be lexical items such as *well* and *anyway* (see chapter 6), conjunctions such as *because*, or the choice of syntactic forms such as actives and passives (see Stubbs 1983, chapter 4 for a recent discussion of these issues). It is possible to explain the choice of a variety of syntactic forms in discourse terms. For example, the use of a subordinate clause at the start of a turn can have the function of signalling incompletion and permitting the current speaker to continue with at least one more clause before a point of possible completion is reached. Similarly, the meaning of items such as *is John there?* in telephone conversation openings would seem to be predicted by a general rule which overrides the literal meaning of the utterance in favour of the indirect meaning of a request to fetch the person named. Viewing the relationship the other way, we might also ask what the implications for the discourse might be when a particular linguistic form is selected. For example, the constraints on possible responses are different following a request realized by an imperative (e.g. *open the window*) as opposed to a request realized by an interrogative *(could you open the window?)* or a declarative *(I'd like you to open that window)*. Little work has been done as yet on the strategies associated with such choices in conversation except for accounts of politeness phenomena.

The analysis of conversational disorders is another area for further research. Here it will be important to establish whether disorders of conversation are related to disorders of areas of language such as syntax, phonology, prosody and semantics. Clearly there are cases where there is some separation between these areas. Broadly speaking, dysphasic children have deficiencies in areas such as phonology and syntax but not in conversation, and it is to these areas that intervention should be directed. Autistic children, on the other hand, are often relatively proficient in phonology and syntax but their use of language lags far behind. Similar cases are those studies presented in chapter 9 of children with discourse disorders (see the studies by Blank et al. 1979, Greenlee 1981, and the case study in chapter 9). However, there are also many cases where the exact nature of the relationship between conversation and other areas of language is unclear. The syntactic and phonological deficiencies of dysphasic children will often make their participation in conversations more difficult. There are many areas of conversational ability which depend on a prior development of ability in areas such as syntax. For example, children who have problems with the use of articles, tenses and relative clauses will have difficulty in establishing discourse referents efficiently. Similarly, the ability to choose an appropriate request form depends on having available a repertoire of syntactic forms which can be used to realize requests. On the other hand, a greater attention to discourse phenomena might enhance the treatment of language disorders. We have already discussed the restricted communicative setting of most clinical intervention and the problem of generalization of training to other environments. At a more specific level, the use of items of language, such as syntactic features like articles, tense and relative clauses, might be better motivated by introducing them within the communicative contexts where they frequently occur – for example, as a means of identifying referents which are not present in the immediate context.

One final area should be mentioned which is likely to be the focus of considerable attention in the not too distant future – the subject of man–machine communication. As computers have become more and more common in all walks of life, it has become increasingly important to develop machines which are capable of simulating natural language. Beyond the ability to parse data syntactically, computers need to be programmed to deal with the presuppositions of input sentences, to deal with inferences, to interpret coherent stretches of discourse and to produce responses which take into account their addressee's current state of knowledge. These and many other similar discourse problems are the object of intensive research in artifiical intelligence (see papers in Joshi et al. 1981). As technology advances and computers become more able to understand and produce speech, then more attention will have to be given to interactional aspects of conversation such as the co-ordination of turn-taking and the use of repair mechanisms. Research in this area will depend on a rigorous account of how such devices are used in natural language. One of the most useful ways of learning more about such devices is to study their acquisition and development by young children.

Notes

Chapter 2   The structure and process of conversation

1 This is not strictly accurate as follow-ups do relate back to preceding utterances. They are not, however, elicited in the same way as responses and so their absence is not so clearly 'noticeable'.
2 For some of the ideas presented in this and the following paragraph, as well as the general analytic framework and coding conventions used throughout, I am indebted to the analyses of child discourse developed at Bristol by Gordon Wells and colleagues (see, for example, Wells et al. 1979; Wells et al. 1981).
3 I am indebted to Margaret MacLure (personal communication) for these examples.

Chapter 4   Initiating conversational exchanges

1 Examples cited from the data are referred as follows: the first (Roman) numeral denotes the session, the second numeral denotes the recording and the third numeral(s) the lines in the transcript. So, for example, I:1:103–8 reads as: session I, recording 1, transcript lines 103–8.

Chapter 8   Later conversational development

1 This study was carried out as part of an honours project at Ulster Polytechnic by Suzanne McMullan, April 1981.

Chapter 10   Implications and applications

1 This study was carried out at Ulster Polytechnic by Joyce Rankin as part of an honours project for the degree BSc Human Communication, May 1983. Permission to use data from this project is gratefully acknowledged.

References

Allwright, R. L. (1980) Turns, topics and tasks: patterns of participation in language learning and teaching. In D. Larsen-Freeman (ed.) *Discourse analysis in second language research* Rowley: Newbury House

Andersen, E. S. (1978) Will you don't snore please? Directives in young children's role-play speech *Papers and Reports on Child Language Development* no. 15, Stanford University

Andersen, E. S. and Johnson, C. (1973) Modifications in the speech of an eight-year-old to younger children *Stanford Occasional Papers in Linguistics* no. 3, 149–60, Stanford University

Anderson, A. H., Brown, G. and Yule, G. (1982) Hearers make better speakers: hearer-effects on speaker performance in oral communication tasks *Work in Progress* no. 15, Department of Linguistics, University of Edinburgh

Argyle, M. (1975) *Bodily communication* London: Methuen

Asher, S. R. (1978) Referential communication. In G. J. Whitehurst and B. J. Zimmerman (eds) *The functions of language and cognition* New York: Academic Press

Asher, S. R. and Wigfield, A. (1981) Training referential communication skills. In W. P. Dickson (ed.) *Children's oral communication skills* New York: Academic Press

Aten, J. L., Caligiuri, M. P. and Holland, A. L. (1982) The efficacy of functional communication therapy for chronic aphasic patients *Journal of Speech and Hearing Disorders* 47, 93–6

Atkinson, M. (1979) Prerequisites for reference. In E. Ochs and B. Schieffelin (eds) *Developmental pragmatics* New York: Academic Press

Baker, L., Cantwell, D. P., Rutter, M. and Bartak, L. (1976) Language and autism. In C. R. Ritvo (ed.) *Autism* New York: Spectrum

Baltaxe, C. (1977) Pragmatic deficits in the language of autistic adolescents *Journal of Pediatric Psychology* 2, 176–80

Baltaxe, C. and Simmons, J. A. (1977) Language patterns of adolescent autistics: a comparison between English and German. In P. Mittler (ed.) *Research to practice in mental retardation. Volume II: Education and training* Baltimore University Park Press

Barker, R. G. and Wright, H. E. (1955) *Midwest and its children* New York: Harper and Row

Barnes, D. and Todd, F. (1978) *Communication and learning in small groups* London: Routledge

Basso, K. H. (1972) 'To give up on words': silence in Western Apache culture. In P. Giglioli (ed.) *Language and social context* London: Harmondsworth

Bates, E. (1975) Peer relations and the acquisition of language. In M. Lewis and L. A. Rosenblum (eds) *Friendship and peer relations* New York: Wiley

Bates, E. (1976) *Language and context: the acquisition of pragmatics* New York: Academic Press

Bates, E., Camaioni, L. and Volterra, V. (1979) The acquisition of performatives prior to speech. In E. Ochs and B. Schieffelin (eds) *Developmental pragmatics* New York: Academic Press

Bates, E. and MacWhinney, B. (1979) A functionalist approach to the acquisition of grammar. In E. Ochs and B. Schieffelin (eds) *Developmental pragmatics* New York: Academic Press

Bateson, M. C. (1975) Mother–infant exchanges: the epigenesis of conversational interaction. In D. Aaronson and R. W. Rieber (eds) *Developmental psycholinguistics and communication disorders* Annals of the New York Academy of Science 263, 101–12.

Becker, J. (1982) Children's strategic use of requests to mark and manipulate social status. In S. Kuczaj II (ed.) *Language development. Volume 2: Language, thought and culture* Hillside, New Jersey: Lawrence Erlbaum

Bedrosian, J. L. and Prutting, G. A. (1978) Communicative performance of mentally retarded adults in four conversational settings *Journal of Speech and Hearing Research* 21, 79–95

Bellinger, D. (1979) Changes in the explicitness of mothers' directives as children age *Journal of Child Language* 6, 443–58

Benoit, P. J. (1982) Formal coherence production in children's discourse *First Language* 3, 161–79

Berko-Gleason, J. (1973) Code switching in children's language. In T. E. Moore (ed.) *Cognitive development and the acquisition of language* New York: Academic Press

Berko-Gleason, J. (1977) Talking to children: some notes on feedback. In C. Snow and C. Ferguson (eds) *Talking to children: language input and acquisition* Cambridge: Cambridge University Press

Berko-Gleason, J. and Weintraub, S. (1976) The acquisition of routines in child language *Language in Society* 5, 129–36

Berninger, G. and Garvey, C. (1981) Relevant replies to questions: answers versus evasions *Journal of Psycholinguistic Research* 10(4), 403–20

Berry, M. (1981) Systemic linguistics and discourse analysis: a multi-layered approach to exchange structure. In M. Coulthard and M. Montgomery (eds) *Studies in discourse analysis* London: Routledge and Kegan Paul

Blank, M. (1982) Language and school failure: some speculations about the relationship between oral and written language. In L. Feagans and D. C. Farron (eds) *The language of children reared in poverty* New York: Academic Press

Blank, M., Gessner, M. and Esposito, A. (1979) Language without communication: a case study *Journal of Child Language* 6, 329–52

Bloom, L., Rocissano, L. and Hood, L. (1976) Adult–child discourse: developmental interaction between information processing and linguistic knowledge *Cognitive Psychology* 8, 521–52

Brady, P. T. (1968) A statistical analysis of on–off patterns in 16 conversations *Bell System Technical Journal* 47, 73–91

Brenneis, D. and Lein, L. (1977) You fruithead: a sociolinguistic approach to children's disputes. In S. Ervin-Tripp and C. Mitchell-Kernan (eds) *Child discourse* New York: Academic Press

Bridges, A. (1982) Comprehension in context. In M. Beveridge (ed.) *Children thinking through language* London: Edward Arnold

Brinton, B. and Fujiki, M. (1982) A comparison of request–response sequences in the discourse of normal and language-disordered children *Journal of Speech and Hearing Disorders* 47, 57–62

Brown, P. and Levinson, S. (1978) Universals in language usage. In E. N. Goody (ed.) *Questions and politeness* Cambridge: Cambridge University Press

Brown, R. and Gilman, A. (1970) The pronouns of power and solidarity. In R. Brown (ed.) *Psycholinguistics* New York: The Free Press

Brown, R. and Hanlon, C. (1970) Derivational complexity and order of acquisition in child language. In J. Hayes (ed.) *Cognition and the development of language* New York: Wiley

Bruner, J. (1975) The ontogenesis of speech acts *Journal of Child Language* 2(1), 1–19

Bublitz, W. (1979) Hörersignale und Gesprächssteuerung im Englischen. In G. Tschauder and E. Weigand (eds) *Akten des 14. Linguistischen Kolloquiums, Band 2* Tübingen: Max Niemeyer

Bullowa, M. (ed.) (1979) *Before speech: the beginning of interpersonal communication* Cambridge: Cambridge University Press

Burton, D. (1981) Analysing spoken discourse. In M. Coulthard and M. Montgomery (eds) *Studies in discourse analysis* London: Routledge and Kegan Paul

Butterworth, B. (ed.) (1981) *Language production* New York: Academic Press

Butterworth, B. and Beattie, G. (1978) Gesture and silence as indicators of planning in speech. In R. Campbell and P. Smith (eds) *Recent advances in the psychology of language: formal and experimental approaches* New York: Plenum Press

Cairns, H. S. and Hsu, J. R. (1978) Who, why, when and how: a developmental study *Journal of Child Language* 5, 447–88

Canale, M. and Swain, M. (1980) Theoretical bases of communicative approaches to second language teaching and testing *Applied Linguistics* 1(1), 1–47

Carter, A. (1978) From sensori-motor vocalizations to words: a case study of the evolution of attention-directing communication in the second year. In A. Lock (ed.) *Action, gesture and symbol: the emergence of language* New York: Academic Press

Christian, D. and Tripp, R. (1978) Teacher's perceptions and children's language use. In P. Griffin and R. Shuy (eds) *Children's functional language and education in the early years* Arlington, Va.: Center for Applied Linguistics

Cicourel, A. V. (1973) *Cognitive sociology* Harmondsworth: Penguin

Clark, E. V. (1978) Awareness of language: some evidence from what children say and do. In A. Sinclair, R. J. Jarvella and W. J. M. Levelt (eds) *The child's conception of language* New York: Springer

Clark, E. V. and Andersen, E. S. (1979) Spontaneous repairs: awareness in the process of acquiring language *Papers and Reports on Child Language Development* no. 16, Stanford University

Clark, E. V. and Garnica, O. (1974) Is he coming or going? On the acquisition of deictic verbs *Journal of Verbal Learning and Verbal Behaviour* 13, 559–72

Clark, R. and Delia, J. (1976) The development of functional persuasive skills in childhood and early adolescence *Child Development* 47, 1008–14

Collis, G. M. (1977) Visual co-orientation and maternal speech. In H. R. Schaffer (ed.) *Studies in mother–child interaction* New York: Academic Press

Condon, W. S. and Sander, L. W. (1974) Neonate movement is synchronized with adult speech: interactional participation and language acquisition *Science* 183, 99–101

Conti, G. (1982) *Mothers in dialogue: some discourse features of mothers with normal and language-impaired children* Unpublished doctoral dissertation, University of Texas, Dallas

Conti, G. and Friel-Patti, S. (1983) Mothers' discourse adjustments to language-impaired and non language-impaired children *Journal of Speech and Hearing Disorders* 48, 360–7

Conti, G. and Friel-Patti, S. (1984) Mother–child dialogues: a comparison of normal and language impaired children *Journal of Communication Disorders* 17, 19–35

Corsaro, W. A. (1977) The clarification request as a feature of adult-interactive styles with young children *Language in Society* 6, 183–207

Corsaro, W. A. (1979a) Sociolinguistic patterns in adult–child interaction. In E. Ochs and B. Schieffelin (eds) *Developmental pragmatics* New York: Academic Press

Corsaro, W. A. (1979b) 'We're friends, right?': children's use of access rituals in a nursery school *Language in Society* 8, 315–36

Coulthard, M. (1977) *An introduction to discourse analysis* London: Longman

Coulthard, M. and Brazil, D. (1981) Exchange structure. In M. Coulthard and M. Montgomery (eds) *Studies in discourse analysis* London: Routledge and Kegan Paul

Coulthard, M. and Montgomery, M. (eds) (1981) *Studies in discourse analysis* London: Routledge and Kegan Paul

Crosby, F. (1976) Early discourse agreement *Journal of Child Language* 3, 125–6

Crystal, D. (1974) Review of R. Brown: A first language *Journal of Child Language* 1, 289–307

Crystal, D. (1975) *The English tone of voice* London: Edward Arnold

Crystal, D. (1979) *Working with LARSP* London: Edward Arnold

Crystal, D. (1981) *Clinical linguistics* New York: Springer

Crystal, D. (1982) *Profiling linguistic disability* London: Edward Arnold

Crystal, D. and Davy, D. (1969) *Investigating English style* London: Longman

Crystal, D. and Davy, D. (1975) *Advanced conversational English* London: Longman

Crystal, D. and Fletcher, P. (1979) Profile analysis of language disability. In C. Fillmore, D. Kempler and W. S-J. Wang (eds) *Individual differences in language ability and language behaviour* New York: Academic Press

Crystal, D., Fletcher, P. and Garman, M. (1976) *The grammatical analysis of language disability* London: Edward Arnold

Daden, I. (1975) *Conversational analysis and its relevance to teaching English as a second language* Unpublished MA thesis, University of California, Los Angeles

Dale, P. S. (1976) *Language development: structure and function* New York: Holt, Rinehart and Winston

Dewey, M. and Everard, M. (1975) The autistic adult in the community *Proceedings of the National Society for Autistic Children annual conference* June, San Diego, California

Dickson, W. P. (ed.) (1981) *Children's oral communication skills* New York: Academic Press

Dittman, A. T. (1972) Developmental factors in conversational behaviour *Journal of Communication* 22, 404–23

Donahue, M. (1981) Requesting strategies of learning disabled children *Applied Psycholinguistics* 2(3), 213–34

Donahue, M., Pearl, R. and Bryan, T. (1980) Learning disabled children's conversational competence: responses to inadequate messages *Applied Psycholinguistics* 1, 387–403

Donaldson, M. (1978) *Children's minds* London: Fontana

Dore, J. (1975) Holophrases, speech acts and language universals *Journals of Child Language* 2, 1–20

Dore, J. (1977a) Children's illocutionary acts. In R. Freedle (ed.) *Discourse: comprehension and production* Hillsdale, New Jersey: Lawrence Erlbaum

Dore, J. (1977b) Oh them sheriff: a pragmatic analysis of children's responses to questions. In S. Ervin-Tripp and C. Mitchell-Kernan (eds) *Child discourse* New York: Academic Press

Drew, P. (1981) Adults' corrections of children's mistakes: a response to Wells and Montgomery. In P. French and M. MacLure (eds) *Adult–child conversation* London: Croom Helm

Duncan, S. (1972) Some signals and rules for taking speaking turns in conversation *Journal of Personality and Social Psychology* 23(2), 283–92

Duncan, S. (1973) Towards a grammar for dyadic conversation *Semiotica* 9(1), 29–46

Duncan, S. (1974) On the structure of speaker–auditor interaction during speaking turns *Language in Society* 3(2), 161–80

Edwards, J. R. (1979) *Language and disadvantage* London: Edward Arnold

Ellis, R. A. F. and Whittington, D. (1981) *A Guide to Social Skill Training* London: Croom Helm

Ervin-Tripp, S. (1970) Discourse agreement: how children answer questions. In J. R. Hayes (ed.) *Cognition and the development of language* New York: Wiley

Ervin-Tripp, S. (1972) Sociolinguistic rules of address. In J. B. Pride and J. Holmes (eds) *Sociolinguistics* Harmondsworth: Penguin

Ervin-Tripp, S. (1976) Is Sybil there? The structure of American directives *Language in Society* 5, 25–66

Ervin-Tripp, S. (1977a) From conversation to syntax *Papers and Reports on Child Language Development* no. 13, Stanford University

Ervin-Tripp, S. (1977b) Wait for me, roller-skate. In S. Ervin-Tripp and C. Mitchell-Kernan (eds) *Child discourse* New York: Academic Press

Ervin-Tripp, S. (1978) Some features of early child–adult dialogues *Language in Society* 7, 357–73

Ervin-Tripp, S. (1979) Children's verbal turn-taking. In E. Ochs and B. Schieffelin (ed) *Developmental pragmatics* New York: Academic Press

Fantz, R. D. (1965) Visual perception from birth as shown by pattern selectivity *Ann. New York Academy of Science* 188, 793–814

Fay, D. and Mermelstein, R. (1982) Language in infantile autism. In S. Rosenberg (ed.) *Handbook of applied psycholinguistics: major thrusts of research and theory* New Jersey: Lawrence Erlbaum

Fay, W. H. (1969) On the basis of autistic echolalia *Journal of Communication Disorders* 2, 38–47

Fay, W. H. and Schuler, A. L. (1980) *Emerging language in autistic children* London: Edward Arnold

Fey, M. E. and Leonard, L. B. (1983) Pragmatic skills of children with specific language impairment. In T. M. Gallaher and C. A. Prutting (eds) *Pragmatic assessment and intervention issues in language* San Diego: College-Hill Press

Field, T. (1981) Early peer relations. In P. S. Strain (ed.) *The utilization of classroom peers as behaviour change agents* New York: Plenum

Fine, J. (1978) Conversation, cohesive and thematic patterning in children's dialogue *Discourse Processes* 1, 247–66

Flavell, J. H., Botkin, P. T., Fry, C. L. Jr., Wright, J. W. and Jarvis, P. E. (1968) *The development of role-taking and communication skills in children* New York: Wiley

Foster, S. (1979) *From non-verbal to verbal communication: a study of the development of topic initiation strategies during the first two-and-a-half years* Unpublished doctoral dissertation, University of Lancaster

Fraser, B., Rintell, E. and Walters, J. (1980) An approach to conducting research on the acquisition of pragmatic competence in a second language. In D. Larsen-Freeman (ed.) *Discourse analysis in second language research* Rowley: Newbury House

Fromkin, V. (ed.) (1973) *Speech errors as linguistic evidence* The Hague: Mouton

Gallagher, T. M. (1977) Revision behaviours in the speech of normal children developing language *Journal of Speech and Hearing Research* 20, 303–18

Gallagher, T. M. (1981) Contingent query sequences within adult–child discourse *Journal of Child Language* 8, 51–62

Gallagher, T. M. (1983) Pre-assessment: A procedure for accommodating language use variability. In T. M. Gallagher and C. A. Prutting (eds) *Pragmatic assessment and intervention issues in language* San Diego: College-Hill Press

Gallagher, T. and Darnton, B. (1978) Conversational aspects of the speech of language disordered children: revision behaviours *Journal of Speech and Hearing Research* 21, 118–35

Garnica, O. (1978) Non-verbal concomitants of language input to children. In N. Waterson and C. Snow (eds) *The development of communication* New York: Wiley

Garvey, C. (1975) Requests and responses in children's speech *Journal of Child Language* 2, 41–63

Garvey, C. (1977a) Play with language and speech. In S. Ervin-Tripp and C. Mitchell-Kernan (eds) *Child discourse* New York: Academic Press

Garvey, C. (1977b) The contingent query: a dependent act in conversation. In M. Lewis and L. Rosenblum (eds) *The origins of behaviour. Volume V: Interaction, conversation, and the development of language* New York: Wiley

Garvey, C. (1979) Contingent queries and their relations in discourse. In E. Ochs and B. Schieffelin (eds) *Developmental pragmatics* New York: Academic Press

Garvey, C. and Berninger, G. (1981) Timing and turn taking in children's conversations *Discourse Processes* 4, 27–57

Garvey, C. and Hogan, R. (1973) Social speech and social interaction: egocentrism revisited *Child Development* 44, 562–8

Gaskill, W. H. (1980) Correction in native speaker–nonnative speaker conversation. In D. Larsen-Freeman (ed.) *Discourse analysis in second language research* Rowley: Newbury House

Gearhart, M. and Newman, D. (1977) Turn-taking in conversation: implications for developmental research *Quarterly Newsletter of the Institute for Comparative Human Development* 1(3)

Geller, E. F. and Wollner, S. G. (1976) A preliminary investigation of the communicative competence of three linguistically impaired children. Paper presented at the *New York State Speech and Hearing Association*, Grossinger

Gelman, R. and Shatz, M. (1977) Appropriate speech adjustments: the operation of conversational constraints on talk to two-year-olds. In M. Lewis and L. Rosenblum (eds) *Interaction, conversation, and the development of language* New York: Wiley

Glucksberg, S. and Krauss, R. M. (1967) What do people say after they learn to talk? Studies of the development of referential communication *Merill-Palmer Quarterly* 13, 309–16

Glucksberg, S. Krauss, R. M. and Higgins, T. (1975) The development of communication skills in children. In F. Horowitz (ed.) *Review of child development research* volume 4, Chicago: University of Chicago Press

Goffman, E. (1957) Alienation from interaction *Human Relations* 10, 47–60

Goodwin, C. (1981) *Conversational organization: interaction between speakers and hearers* New York: Academic Press

Gopnik, A. (1977) No, there, more and allgone: why the first words aren't about things *Nottingham Linguistic Circular* 6(2), 15–20

Greenlee, M. (1981) Learning to tell the forest from the trees: unravelling discourse features of a psychotic child *First Language* 2(5), 83–102

Grice, H. P. (1975) Logic and conversation. In P. Cole and J. L. Morgan (eds) *Syntax and semantics. Volume 3: Speech acts* New York: Academic Press

Gumperz, J. J. (1977) The conversational analysis of interethnic communication. In E. Ross (ed.) *Interethnic communication* University of Georgia Press

Gumperz, J. J. (1982a) *Discourse strategies* Cambridge: Cambridge University Press

Gumperz, J. J. (ed.) (1982b) *Language and social identity* Cambridge: Cambridge University Press

Gumperz, J. J., Jupp, T. C. and Roberts, C. (1979) *Crosstalk* Southall: National Centre for Industrial Language Training

Gumperz, J. J. and Tannen, D. (1979) Individual and social differences in language use. In C. Fillmore, D. Kempler and W. S-J Wang (eds) *Individual differences in language ability and language behaviour* New York: Academic Press

Guralnick, M. (1981) Peer influences in the development of communicative competence. In P. S. Strain (ed.) *The utilization of classroom peers as behaviour change agents* New York: Plenum Press

Halliday, M. A. K. (1975) *Learning how to mean* London: Edward Arnold

Halliday, M. A. K. (1979) The development of texture in child language. In T. Myers (ed.) *The development of conversation and discourse* Edinburgh: Edinburgh University Press

Halliday, M. A. K. and Hasan, R. (1976) *Cohesion in English* London: Longman

Hargie, O. and Saunders C. (1983) Individual differences and SST. In R. Ellis and D. Whittington (eds) *New directions in social skill training* London: Croom Helm

Hargie, O., Saunders, C. and Dickson, D. (1981) *Social skills in interpersonal communication* London: Croom Helm

Hatch, E. (1978a) Discourse analysis, speech acts, and second language acquisition. In W. C. Ritchie (ed.) *Second language acquisition research* New York: Academic Press

Hatch, E. (1978b) Discourse analysis and second language acquisition. In E. Hatch (ed.) *Second language acquisition: a book of readings* Rowley: Newbury House

Hawkins, J. (1978) *Definiteness and indefiniteness: a study in reference and grammaticality prediction* London: Croom Helm

Hawkins, P. (1973) Social class, the nominal group and reference. In B. Bernstein (ed.) *Class, codes and control* volume 2, London: Routledge

Hines, C. P. (1978) Well, ... In M. Paradis (ed.) *The fourth LACUS forum* S. Carolina: Hornbeam Press

Hoar, N. (1977) Paraphrase capabilities of language impaired children. Paper presented to *Boston University conference on language development*

Holland, A. (1980) *A measure of communicative abilities in daily living* Taloma Park: University Park Press

Holland, A. (1982) Observing functional communication of aphasic adults *Journal of Speech and Hearing Disorders* 47, 50–6

Horgan, D. (1978) How to answer questions when you've nothing to say *Journal of Child language* 5, 159–65

House, J. (1979) Interaktionsnormen in deutschen und englishen Alltagsdialogen *Linguistische Berichte* 59, 76–90

Howe, C. (1981) *Acquiring language in a conversational context* London: Academic Press

Hubbell, R. D. (1977) On facilitating spontaneous talking in young children *Journal of Speech and Hearing Disorders* 42, 216–31

Hughes, A. (1983) Second language learning and communicative language teaching. In K. Johnson and D. Porter (eds) *Perspectives in communicative language teaching* London: Academic Press

Hughes, M. (1975) *Egocentrism in pre-school children* Unpublished doctoral dissertation, University of Edinburgh

Hurtig, R., Ensrud, S. and Tomblin, J. B. (1982) The communicative function of question production in autistic children *Journal of Autism and Developmental Disorders* 12(1), 57–69

Hymes, D. (1972) On communicative competence. In J. B. Pride and J. Holmes (eds) *Sociolinguistics* Harmondsworth: Penguin

Iwamura, S. G. (1980) *The verbal games of pre-school children* London: Croom Helm

Jaffe, S. and Feldstein, S. (1970) *Rhythms of dialogue* New York: Academic Press

James, S. L. (1978) Effect of listener age and situation on the politeness of children's directives *Journal of Psycholinguistic Research* 7(4), 307–17

Jamison, K. (1981) An analysis of overlapping in children's speech *Belfast Working Papers in Language and Linguistics* 5, 122–43

Jefferson, G. (1973) A case of precision timing in ordinary conversation: overlapped tag-positioned address terms in closing sequences *Semiotica* 9(1), 47–96

Johnson, C. (1979) Contingent queries: the first chapter. Paper presented at *Language and social psychology conference*, Bristol, July

Johnson, K. and Porter, D. (eds) (1982) *Perspectives in communicative language teaching* London: Academic Press

Joshi, A., Webber, B. and Sag, I. (eds) (1981) *Elements of discourse understanding* Cambridge: Cambridge University Press

Karmiloff-Smith, A. (1979) *A functional approach to child language: a study of determiners and reference* Cambridge: Cambridge University Press

Kaye, K. (1977) Towards the origin of dialogue. In H. R. Schaffer (ed.) *Studies in mother–child interaction* New York: Academic Press

Keenan, E. O. (1974) Conversational competence in children *Journal of Child Language* 1(2), 163–83

Keenan, E. O. (1975) Evolving discourse – the next step *Papers and Reports on Child Language Development* no. 10, Stanford University

Keenan, E. O. and Klein, E. (1975) Coherency in children's discourse *Journal of Psycholinguistic Research* 4, 365–78

Keenan, E. O. and Schieffelin, B. (1976) Topic as a discourse notion: a study of topic in the conversations of children and adults. In C. Li (ed.) *Subject and topic* New York: Academic Press

Kendon, A. (1967) Some functions of gaze-direction in social interaction *Acta Psychologica* 26, 22–63

Kernan, K. (1977) Semantic and expressive elaboration in children's narratives. In S. Ervin-Tripp and C. Mitchell-Kernan (eds) *Child discourse* New York: Academic Press

Klevans, D. R., Volz, H. B. and Friedman, R. M. (1981) A comparison of experiential and observational approaches for enhancing the interpersonal communication skills of speech-language pathology students *Journal of Speech and Hearing Disorders* 46(2), 208–13

Krauss, R. M. and Glucksberg, S. (1969) The development of communication: competence as a function of age *Child Development* 40, 255–66

Labov, W. (1969) The logic of non-standard English *Georgetown Monographs on Language and Linguistics* Georgetown

Labov, W. (1972a) *Sociolinguistic patterns* University of Pennsylvania Press

Labov, W. (1972b) Rules for ritual insults. In D. Sudnow (ed.) *Studies in social interaction* New York: The Free Press

Labov, W. and Fanshel, D. (1977) *Therapeutic discourse: psychotherapy as conversation* New York: Academic Press

Lakoff, R. (1973a) The logic of politeness: or minding your p's and q's *Papers from the ninth regional meeting of the Chicago Linguistic Society* Chicago: Chicago Linguistic Society

Lakoff, R. (1973b) Questionable answers and answerable questions. In B. Kachru et al. (eds) *Papers in linguistics in honor of Henry and Renee Kahone* University of Illinois Press

Langford, D. (1981) The clarification request sequence in conversation between mothers and their children. In P. French and M. MacLure (eds) *Adult–child conversation* London: Croom Helm

Leopold, W. F. (1949) *Speech development of a bilingual child* volume 4, Evanston, Ill.: Northwestern University Press

Lesser, R. (1978) *Linguistic investigations of aphasia* London: Edward Arnold

Levin, E. and Rubin, K. (1984) Getting others to do what you want them to do: the development of children's requestive strategies. In K. E. Nelson (ed.) *Children's language* volume 4, Hillsdale, R. J.: Lawrence Erlbaum

Levinson, S. (1983) *Pragmatics* Cambridge: Cambridge University Press

Lieberman, A. F. and Garvey, C. (1977) Interpersonal pauses in preschoolers' verbal exchanges. Paper presented at *Biennial meeting of the Society for Research in Child Development* New Orleans

Lieven, E. V. M. (1978) Conversation between mothers and young children: individual differences and their possible implication for the study of language learning. In N. Waterson and C. Snow (eds) *The development of communication* New York: Wiley

Littlewood, W. (1981) *Communicative language teaching: an introduction* Cambridge: Cambridge University Press

Lloyd, P. and Beveridge, M. (1981) *Information and meaning in child communication* London: Academic Press

Lock, A. (1978) On being picked up. In A. Lock (ed.) *Action, gesture and symbol: the emergence of language* New York: Academic Press

Lodge, K. R. (1979) The use of the past tense in games of pretend *Journal of Child Language* 6, 365–9

Longhurst, T. M. (1974) Communication in retarded adolescents: sex and intelligence level *American Journal of Mental Deficiency* 78, 607–18

McCartney, E. (1981) Constructive communication failure: the response of speech disordered children to requests for clarification *British Journal of Disorders of Communication* 16(3), 147–57

McClements, R. J. (1976) Aspects of the structure of narrative speech in children aged 5, 7, 9 and 11 years *Occasional Papers in Linguistics and Language Learning* no. 2, The New University of Ulster

McDade, H. L. (1981) A parent–child interactional model for assessing and remediating language disabilities *British Journal of Disorders of Communication* 16(3), 175–83

McDermott, R. P., Gospodinoff, K. and Aron, J. (1978) Criteria for an ethnographically adequate description of activities and their contexts *Semiotica* 24, 245–75

MacLure, M. (1981) *Making sense of children's talk* Unpublished PhD dissertation, University of York

MacLure, M. and French, P. (1981) A comparison of talk at home and at school. In G. Wells (ed.) *Learning through interaction* Cambridge: Cambridge University Press

McTear, M. (1978) Repetition in child language: imitation or creation? In R. Campbell and P. Smith (eds) *Recent advances in the psychology of language: language development and mother–child interaction* New York: Plenum Press

McTear, M. (1979) Hey! I've got something to tell you: the initiation of conversational exchanges by preschool children *Journal of Pragmatics* 3(3), 321–36

Maratsos, M. P. (1973) Nonegocentric communication abilities in preschool children *Child Development* 44, 697–700

Maratsos, M. P. (1976) *The use of definite and indefinite reference in young children: an experimental study of semantic acquisition* Cambridge: Cambridge University Press

Maratsos, M. P. and Chalkley, M. (1980) The internal language of children's syntax: the ontogenesis and representation of syntactic categories. In K. E. Nelson (ed.) *Children's language* volume 2, New York: Gardner Press

Mehan, H. (1973) Assessing children's language using abilities. In J. M. Armer and A. D. Grimshaw (eds) *Methodological issues in comparative sociological research* New York: Wiley

Mehan, H. (1979) *Learning lessons: social organization in the classroom* Cambridge, MA: Harvard University Press

Milroy, L. (1980) *Language and social networks* Oxford: Basil Blackwell

Milroy, L. and McTear, M. (1983) Linguistics for social skill training. In R. Ellis and D. Whittington (eds) *New directions in social skill training* London: Croom Helm

Mishler, E. (1979) Studies in dialogue and discourse III: utterance structure and utterance function in interrogative sequences *Journal of Psycholinguistic Research* 7(4), 279–305

Mishler, E. (1979) Wou' you trade cookies with the popcorn? Talk of trades among six-year-olds. In O. Garnica and M. King (eds) *Language, children and society* Oxford: Pergamon

Mitchell-Kernan, C. and Kernan, K. T. (1977) Functional considerations in the choice of directive forms by black American children. In S. Ervin-Tripp and C. Mitchell-Kernan (eds) *Child discourse* New York: Academic Press

Mueller, E. (1972) The maintenance of verbal exchanges between young children *Child Development* 43, 930–8

Mueller, E., Bleier, M., Krakow, J., Hagedus, K. and Cournoyer, P. (1977) The development of peer verbal interaction among two-year-old boys *Child Development* 48, 284–7

Munby, J. (1978) *Communicative syllabus design* Cambridge: Cambridge University Press

Murphy, C. M. and Messer, D. J. (1977) Mothers, infants and pointing: a study of a gesture. In H. R. Schaffer (ed.) *Studies in mother–child interaction* New York: Academic Press

Musselwhite, C. R., St Louis, K. O. and Penick, P. B. (1980) A communicative interaction analysis system for language-disordered children *Journal of Communication Disorders* 13, 315–24

Nelson, K. (1973) Structure and strategy in learning to talk. *Monographs of the Society for Research in Child Development* volume 38, nos 1–2

Newcombe, N. and Zaslow, M. (1981) Do 2½-year-olds hint? A study of directive forms in the speech of 2½-year-old children to adults *Discourse Processes* 4(3), 239–52

Newson, J. (1979) The growth of shared understandings between infant and caregiver. In M. Bullowa (ed.) *Before speech: the beginning of interpersonal communication* Cambridge: Cambridge University Press

Ochs, E. (1979a) Transcription as theory. In E. Ochs and B. Schieffelin (eds) *Developmental pragmatics* New York: Academic Press

Ochs, E. (1979b) Unplanned and planned discourse. In T. Givon (ed.) *Syntax and semantics. Volume 12: Discourse and syntax* New York: Academic Press

Ochs, E., Schieffelin, B. and Platt, M. (1979) Propositions across utterances and speakers. In E. Ochs and B. Schieffelin (eds) *Developmental pragmatics* New York: Academic Press

Oreström, B. (1977) Supports in English. Report from the *Survey of Spoken English* Lund: University of Lund

Paccia, J. M. and Curcio, F. (1982) Language processing and forms of immediate echolalia in autistic children *Journal of Speech and Hearing Research* 25(1), 42–7

Patterson, C. J. and Kister, M. C. (1981) The development of listener skills for referential communication. In W. P. Dickson (ed.) *Children's oral communication skills* New York: Academic Press

Peck, S. (1977) Language play in second language acquisition. Paper presented at the *Los Angeles second language research forum* UCLA, February

Peck, S. (1978) Child–child discourse in second language acquisition. In E. Hatch (ed.) *Second language acquisition: a book of readings* Rowley: Newbury House

Peterson, C. L., Danner, E. W. and Flavell, J. H. (1972) Developmental changes in children's response to three indications of communicative failure *Child Development* 43, 1463–8

Philips, S. U. (1972) Participant structures and communicative competence: Warm Springs children in community and classroom. In C. Cazden, V. John and D. Hymes (eds) *Functions of language in the classroom* New York: Teachers College Press

Philips, S. U. (1976) Some sources of cultural variability in the regulation of talk *Language in Society* 5, 81–96

Piaget, J. (1959) *The language and thought of the child* London: Routledge and Kegan Paul

Price-Williams, D. and Sabsay, S. (1979) Communicative competence among severely retarded persons *Semiotica* 26, 35–63

Prinz, P. M. (1982) An investigation of the comprehension and production of requests in normal and language-disordered children *Journal of Communication Disorders* 15(2), 75–93

Prizant, B. M. and Duchan, J. F. (1981) The functions of immediate echolalia in autistic children *Journal of Speech and Hearing Disorders* 46, 241–9

Prutting, C. A., Bagshaw, N., Goldstein, H., Juskowitz, S. and Umen, I. (1978) Clinician–child discourse: some preliminary questions *Journal of Speech and Hearing Disorders* 43, 123–39

Prutting, C. A. and Kirchner, D. A. (1983) Applied pragmatics. In T. M. Gallagher and C. A. Prutting (eds) *Pragmatic assessment and intervention issues in language* San Diego: College-Hill Press

Quirk, R., Greenbaum, S., Leech, G. and Svartvik, J. (1972) *A grammar of contemporary English* London: Longman

Reeder, K. (1980) The emergence of illocutionary skills *Journal of Child Language* 7, 13–28

Richards, M. P. M. (1974) First steps in becoming social. In M. P. M. Richards (ed.) *The integration of a child into a social world* Cambridge: Cambridge University Press

Ricks, D. M. and Wing, L. (1975) Language, communication and the use of symbols in normal and autistic children *Journal of Autism and Child Schizophrenia* 5, 191–220

Robinson, E. J. (1981) The child's understanding of inadequate messages and communication failure: a problem of ignorance or egocentrism? In W. P. Dickson (ed.) *Children's oral communication skills* New York: Academic Press

Rogers, S. (1978) Self-initiated corrections in the speech of infant-school children *Journal of Child Language* 5, 365–71

Rom, A. and Bliss, L. S. (1981) A comparison of verbal communicative skills of language impaired and normal speaking children *Journal of Communication Disorders* 14, 133–40

Rosenberg, S. (1982) The language of the mentally retarded: developmental processes and intervention. In S. Rosenberg (ed.) *Handbook of applied psycholinguistics: major thrusts of research and theory* Hillsdale: Lawrence Erlbaum

Sachs, J. and Devin, J. (1976) Young children's use of age-appropriate speech styles in social interaction and role-playing *Journal of Child Language* 3, 81–98

Sacks, H. (1968) Lecture notes. Department of Sociology, U. C. Irvine MS

Sacks, H. and Schegloff, E. A. (1979) Two preferences in the organization of reference to persons in conversation and their interaction. In G. Psathas (ed.) *Everyday language: studies in ethnomethodology* New York: Irvington Press

Sacks, H., Schegloff, E. A. and Jefferson, G. (1974) A simplest systematics for the organization of turn-taking in conversation *Language* 50, 696–735

Savić, S. (1980) *How twins learn to talk: a study of the speech development of twins from 1 to 3* New York: Academic Press

Saville-Troike, M. (1982) *The ethnography of communication* Oxford: Basil Blackwell

Schaffer, H. R., Collis, G. M. and Parsons, G. (1977) Vocal interchange and visual regard in verbal and pre-verbal children. In H. R. Schaffer (ed.) *Studies in mother–child interaction* New York: Academic Press

Scheflen, A. (1965) *Stream and structure of communicational behaviour* Commonwealth of Pennsylvania: Eastern Pennsylvania Psychiatric Institute

Schegloff, E. A. (1968) Sequencing in conversational openings *American Anthropologist* 70, 1075–95

Schegloff, E. A. (1973) Recycled turn beginnings: a precise repair mechanism in conversations turn-taking organizations. Mimeo, University of California Los Angeles, Department of Sociology

Schegloff, E. A. (1979) The relevance of repair to syntax-for-conversation. In T. Givon (ed.) *Syntax and semantics. Volume 12: Discourse and syntax* New York: Academic Press

Schegloff, E. A., Jefferson, G. and Sacks, H. (1977) The preference for self-correction in the organization of repair in conversation *Language* 53, 361–82

Schegloff, E. A. and Sacks, H. (1973) Opening and closings *Semiotica* 8, 289–327

Schwartz, J. (1980) The negotiation for meaning: repair in conversations between second language learners of English. In D. Larsen-Freeman (ed.) *Discourse analysis in second language research* Rowley: Newbury House

Scollon, R. (1979) A real early stage: an unzippered condensation of a dissertation on child language. In E. Ochs and B. Schieffelin (eds.) *Developmental pragmatics* New York: Academic Press

Scott, C. M. (1983) Adverbial connectivity in conversations of children 6 to 12 *Journal of Child Language* 11

Searle, J. (1969) *Speech acts* Cambridge: Cambridge University Press

Seibert, J. M. and Oller, D. K. (1981) Linguistic pragmatics and language intervention strategies *Journal of Autism and Developmental Disorders* 11(1), 75–88

Shatz, M. (1975) How young children respond to language: procedures for answering *Papers and Reports on Child Language Development* no. 10, Stanford University

Shatz, M. (1978a) The relationship between cognitive processes and the development of communication skills. In B. Keasey (ed.) *Nebraska symposium on motivation* Lincoln: University of Nebraska Press

Shatz, M. (1978b) Children's comprehension of their mothers' question-directives *Journal of Child Language* 5, 39–46

Shatz, M. and Gelman, R. (1973) The development of communication skills: modifications in the speech of young children as a function of listener. *Monographs of the Society for Research in Child Development*, volume 38, no. 5

Shugar, G. W. (1978) Text-constructing with an adult: a form of child activity during early language acquisition. In G. Drachman (ed.) *Salzburger Beiträge zur Linguistik: Akten des 1. Salzburger Kolloquiums über Kindersprache* Tübingen: Gunter Narr

Sinclair, H. and Bronckart, J. P. (1972) SVO: a linguistic universal? A study in developmental psycholinguistics *Journal of Experimental Child Psychology* 14, 329–48

Sinclair, J. M. and Coulthard, R. M. (1975) *Towards an analysis of discourse: the English used by teachers and pupils* Oxford: Oxford University Press

Slobin, D. (1978) A case study of early language awareness. In A. Sinclair, R. J. Jarvella and W. J. M. Levelt (eds) *The child's conception of language* New York: Springer

Snow, C. E. (1977) The development of conversation between mothers and babies *Journal of Child Language* 4, 1–22

Snow, C. E. and Ferguson, C. (eds) (1977) *Talking to children: language input and acquisition* Cambridge: Cambridge University Press

Söderbergh, R. (1974) The fruitful dialogue: the child's acquisition of his first language: implications for education at all stages *Project child language syntax* reprint no. 2, Stockholms Universitet: Institutionen för nordiska språk

Spradlin, J. E. and Siegel, G. M. (1982) Language training in natural and clinical environments *Journal of Speech and Hearing Disorders* 47(1), 2–6

Steffenson, M. S. (1978) Satisfying inquisitive adults: some simple methods of answering yes/no questions *Journal of Child language* 5, 221–36

Stern, D. (1977) *The first relationship: infant and mother* London: Fontana

Stern, D., Jaffe, J., Beebe, B. and Bennett, S. K. (1975) Vocalising in unison and in alternation: two modes of communication within the mother-infant dyad. In D. Aaronson and R. W. Rieber (eds) *Developmental psycholinguistics and communication disorders* New York: New York Academy of Sciences

Stern, H. H. (1978) The formal–function distinction in language pedagogy: a conceptual clarification. Paper read at *5th AILA congress* Montreal, August

Stokes, W. T. (1977) Motivation and language development: the struggle towards communication. Paper presented at *Biennial meeting of the Society for Research in Child Development* New Orleans, March

Stubbs, M. (1976) *Language, schools and classrooms* London: Methuen
Stubbs, M. (1981) Motivating analyses of exchange structure. In M. Coulthard and
M. Montgomery (eds) *Studies in discourse analysis* London: Routledge and Kegan
Paul
Stubbs, M. (1983) *Discourse analysis* Oxford: Basil Blackwell
Tollefson, J. W. (1976) A functional analysis of defective and non-defective requests
in the speech of mothers to children *Papers and Reports on Child Language
Development* no. 11, Stanford University
Tough, J. (1981) *A place for talk* London: Ward Lock
Trevarthen, C. (1979) Communication and co-operation in early infancy: a descrip-
tion of primary intersubjectivity. In M. Bullowa (ed.) *Before speech: the beginning
of interpersonal communications* Cambridge: Cambridge University Press
Trevarthen, C. and Hubley, P. (1978) Secondary intersubjectivity: confidence,
confiding and acts of meaning in the first year. In A. Lock (ed.) *Action, gesture and
symbol: the emergence of language* New York: Academic Press
Trower, P. (1983) Social skills and applied linguistics: radical implications for
training. In R. Ellis and D. Whittington (eds) *New direction in social skill training*
London: Croom Helm
Trower, P., Bryant, B. and Argyle, M. (1978) *Social skills and mental health*
London: Methuen
Trudgill, P. (1974) *Sociolinguistics* Harmondsworth: Penguin
Trudgill, P. (1975) *Accent, dialect and the school* London: Edward Arnold
Tyack, D. and Ingram, D. (1977) Children's production and comprehension of
questions *Journal of Child Language* 4, 211–24
Umiker-Sebeok, D. J. (1976) *The conversational skills of preschool children* Un-
published doctoral dissertation, Indiana University
Van Ek, J. (1976) *Systems development in adult language teaching: the threshold
level* Strasbourg: Council of Europe
Van Kleeck, A. and Frankel, T. (1981) Discourse devices used by language dis-
ordered children: a preliminary investigation *Journal of Speech and Hearing
Disorders* 46, 250–7
Volz, H. B., Klevans, D. R., Norton, S. J. and Putens, D. L. (1978) Interpersonal
communication skills of speech-language pathology undergraduates: the effects of
training *Journal of Speech and Hearing Disorders* 43(4), 524–42
Warden, D. (1976) The influence of context on children's use of identifying
expressions and references *British Journal of Psychology* 67(1), 101–12
Watson, O. M. and Graves, T. D. (1966) Quantitative research in proxemic
behaviour *American Anthropologist* 68, 971–85
Weir, R. (1962) *Language in the crib* The Hague: Mouton
Weitz, S. E. (1982) A code for assessing teaching skills of parents of developmentally
disabled children *Journal of Autism and Developmental Disorders* 12(1), 13–24
Wellman, H. M. and Lempers, J. D. (1977) The naturalistic communicative abilities
of two-year-olds *Child Development* 48 1052–7
Wells, G. (1977) Language use and educational success: an empirical response to
Joan Tough's 'The development of meaning' (1977) *Research in Education* 18,
9–34
Wells, G. (1978) Talking with children: the complementary roles of parents and
teachers *English in Edducation* 12(2), 15–38
Wells, G. (1979) Variation in child language. In P. Fletcher and M. Garman (eds)
Language acquisition Cambridge: Cambridge University Press
Wells, G. (1980) Apprenticeship in meaning. In K. E. Nelson (ed) *Children's
language volume 2*, New York: Gardner Press

Wells, G. (1981a) *Learning through interaction* Cambridge: Cambridge University Press

Wells, G. (1981b) Describing children's linguistic development at home and at school. In C. Adelman (ed.) *Uttering, muttering* London: Grant McIntyre

Wells, G., MacLure, M. and Montgomery, M. (1981) Some strategies for sustaining conversation. In P. Werth (ed.) *Conversation and discourse* London: Croom Helm

Wells, G. and Montgomery, M. (1981) Adult–child interaction at home and at school. In P. French and M. MacLure (eds) *Adult–child conversation* London: Croom Helm

Wells, G., Montgomery, M. and MacLure, M. (1979) Adult–child discourse: outline of a model of analysis *Journal of Pragmatics* 3, 337–80

Wells, G. and Raban, E. B. (1978) *Children learning to read* Final report to SSRC

Whiten, A. (1977) Assessing the effects of perinatal events on the success of the mother–infant relationship. In H. R. Schaffer (ed.) *Studies in mother–child interaction* New York: Academic Press

Widdowson, H. G. (1978) *Teaching language as communication* Oxford: Oxford University Press

Wilkins, D. A. (1976) *Notional syllabuses* Oxford: Oxford University Press

Willes, M. (1981) Learning to take part in classroom interaction. In P. French and M. MacLure (eds) *Adult–child conversation* London: Croom Helm

Wilson, J. (1980) Why answers to questions are not enough in social discourse *Belfast Working Papers in Language and Linguistics* 4, 60–84

Wootton, A. (1981) Children's use of address terms. In P. French and M. MacLure (eds) *Adults–child conversation* London: Croom Helm

Wulbert, M., Inglis, S., Kriegsman, E. and Mills, B. (1975) Language delay and associated mother–child interactions *Developmental Psychology* 11, 61–70

Yule, G. and Smith, H. (1981) Assessing spoken English: an attempt to be objective *Work in Progress* no. 14, Department of Linguistics, University of Edinburgh

Zakharova, A. V. (1973) Acquisition of forms of grammatical case by preschool children. In C. A. Ferguson and D. Slobin (eds) *Studies of child language development* New York: Holt, Rinehart and Winston

Author index

Subject index

adjacency pairs, 28, 32–3, 85
aphasic adults, conversational strategies, 261; functional communication of, 259–61
appropriacy, 30; and conversational disability, 233–6; and establishing reference, 205–6; in requests for action, 45–6, 57; and social skills training, 267
articles, 192; and conversational development, 10, 31, 239; *see also* definite article
artificial intelligence, 273
attention-directing, 40–3, 55–6, 75–84 *passim*, 131, 133, 138; and conversational disability, 233; and second-language learning, 218
attention-getting, 40–3, 55–6, 75–81 *passim*; and conversational disability, 232–3; and second-language learning, 218
autism, and appropriacy, 236; communicative intent, 233–4; and conversational disability, 231–2, 273; dialogue construction, 239–40; echolalia, 238–9; initiations, 233–4

background knowledge, 29, 202, 247

clarification requests, 15, 30, 50–2, 82–3, 164–79; of asphasic adults, 260; and conversational disability, 240–1; functions of, 167–9; of mentally retarded adults, 265; responses to, 166–8, 170–4; and self-repair, 178–9; in teacher–pupil interaction, 211; *see also* corrections; repairs, self
coherence, 29–30, 128–9, 141
cohesion, 29, 127–36, 158; and older children, 205–7
communicative competence, 7; and grammatical competence, 100, 163–9 *passim*, 176–7, 194–6; and second-language learning, 22
communicative intent, in autism, 233–4; in infancy, 60–3, 77, 79, 103
communicative language teaching, 22

communicative norms, 222–3
comprehension, of clarification requests, 166–7; and echolalia, 238; of questions, 136; of requests for action, 104–5, 235; strategies for, 250–2
contextual constraints, on language usage, 254–9
conversation, adult competence in, 202–3; cultural variation, 222–6; definition of, 3–6; and language development, 7–13, 89, 100, 168–9, 176–7; naturalistic studies of, 15–17; and older children, 201–8; and second-language learning, 21–3, 218–22; and speech therapy, 17–20, 254–9; and teacher–pupil interaction, 20–3, 208–18; *see also* prelinguistic communication
conversation analysis, 27–8, 85–6, 271
conversational breakdown, 50–2, 159, 180, 200, 246–7; in interethnic interaction, 222–6
conversational disability, 17–19, 26, 129, 149, 227–49, 272–3; case studies, 231–2, 241–8; interactional problems, 244–5; and language disability, 228–40 *passim*; transactional problems, 245–7
conversational moves, types; challenges, 36–7; follow-up, 34–5, 137–8; prospective, 33, 35, 39, 85; retrospective, 33–4, 35; retrospective–prospective, 35, 138–49, 158
conversational principles, 28, 52–3, 70
conversational processes, 28, 48–52, 159–200
conversational structure, 26–29, *passim*, 31–9, 54–5
corrections, 50–2, 57–8, 179–87; and conversational disability, 241; frequency in the data, 181–2; and second-language learning, 219; and self-repair, 179–80, 183–4; and teacher–pupil interaction, 211; *see also* clarification requests; repairs, self

definite article, anaphoric, 39, 78; and conversational disability, 233; for